DOCUMENTS
OF THE
THIRTY-FOURTH
GENERAL CONGREGATION
OF THE
SOCIETY OF JESUS

The Decrees of
General Congregation Thirty-Four
the Fifteenth of the Restored Society
and the Accompanying
Papal and Jesuit Documents

Rome
Curia of the Superior General

The Institute of Jesuit Sources
Saint Louis 1995

Number 14 in Series III: Original Studies Composed in English

This English text was prepared in Rome
by the Curia of the Superior General of the Society of Jesus
and edited in St. Louis at the Institute of Jesuit Sources
by John L. McCarthy, S.J.

© The Institute of Jesuit Sources
3700 West Pine Boulevard
St. Louis, MO 63108

Library of Congress Catalog Card Number: 95–81840
ISBN: 880810–19–0

DOCUMENTS
OF THE
THIRTY-FOURTH
GENERAL CONGREGATION
OF THE
SOCIETY OF JESUS

CONTENTS

INTRODUCTION

DECREE

OUR MISSION

ASPECTS OF JESUIT LIFE FOR MISSION

IN THE CHURCH

DIMENSIONS AND PARTICULAR SECTORS OF OUR MISSION

STRUCTURES OF GOVERNMENT

CONCLUSION

APPENDICES

List of Abbreviations

AAS: *Acta Apostolicæ Sedis*

AR: *Acta Romana Societatis Iesu*

CCEO: Code of Canon Law for the Eastern Churches

CIC: Code of Canon Law

Coll. d.:   *Collectio Decretorum*

Const.:   *Constitutions of the Society of Jesus*

EE: *Spiritual Exercises of St. Ignatius (=SpEx)*

FGC: Formula of a General Congregation

FPC: Formula of a Provincial Congregation

MHSI: Monumenta Historica Societatis Iesu

NC: *Normæ Complementariæ Constitutionum Societatis Iesu*

OC: *Obras Completas de S. Ignacio de Loyola*

PL: *Patrologia Latina*

SpEx: *Spiritual Exercises of St. Ignatius*

To the Whole Society

Dear Brothers,

The Peace of Christ

All of the responsibilities for action on its decrees entrusted to me by General Congregation 34—held at Rome from 5 January to 22 March 1995—have now been completed. Therefore, in the name of that same congregation, I hereby promulgate to the provinces and regions the decrees which it passed and all the legislative work it accomplished. This is being done so that they may be distributed to all the houses (*Coll. d.*, 3, §4) and be faithfully and everywhere observed by all (*Const.* [718]).

With the exception of Decrees 21, 22, and Decree 23, letters A, B, C, and D, the decrees of General Congregation 34 take effect as of today. Letter E of Decree 23, "Father General's Assistants and Counselors," actually took effect immediately after its approval in the congregation itself. In order that it be better known and understood before being put into practice, the remaining legislative work of the congregation—the *Constitutions* as annotated by the congregation and their "Complementary Norms"—will take effect as of 1 January 1996, the Solemnity of the Blessed Virgin Mary Mother of God and the Giving of the Name of Jesus, the titular feast of the Society. Decrees 21, 22, and Decree 23, letters A, B, C, and D, will take effect on that same day. Until then, the current law of the Society remains in force and is applicable in all circumstances.

On this occasion of the promulgation of the entire work of General Congregation 34, I invite the entire Society to give thanks to God

for his Spirit's gift of discernment, with which our gathering was especially marked

    for the gift of an inspiring diversity in the dele-
gates, which enriched our common path to
God

    for the gift of union in our apostolic body, which
was strongly expressed in the renewal of the
Constitutions

    for the gift of courage by which, through its de-
crees, the Society responded to all that was
ambiguous or erroneous in our way of praying,
working, and living in our Society

    for the gift of energy, with which on the threshold
of the third millennium the Society has
affirmed and renewed its vocation of serving
the mission of Christ

This act of giving thanks must include all those
who by their prayer or work, by their abilities or availability, proved to be the hand of God at work in the general
congregation. First among these is His Holiness John Paul
II, who followed the preparation for and work during the
congregation with great solicitude and goodwill. In the
letter included with this document, he gives new proof of
the trust he places in the Society of Jesus.

May the Lord, who has clearly blessed this beginning, bring to completion with his power and light the
implementation of this new and demanding mission.

Yours fraternally in Christ,
Peter-Hans Kolvenbach, S.J.
Superior General

Rome, 27 September 1995

On the 455th anniversary of the pontifical approbation of the
Society of Jesus

Enclosure: Letter of His Holiness John Paul II [See Appendix 5,
pp. 288–90.]

HISTORICAL PREFACE

1. ANTECEDENTS

On 12 February 1992 Father General Peter-Hans Kolvenbach wrote to all major superiors and moderators of provincial conferences "to inform you of a process I have set in motion for the preparation of our next general congregation." He was entrusting this preparation to three of his general counselors, Fathers Michael Amaladoss (themes), Urbano Valero (updating our law), and John J. O'Callaghan (general coordination). He wrote again on 8 September, describing "the progress made in the remote preparations for General Congregation 34, which could be convoked in the latter half of 1993 so as to begin its work in the first half of 1995." In the meantime the synod of bishops, on consecrated life, would take place and the Society itself would hold a symposium on the vocation and mission of the Jesuit brother.

A few days later, 27 September 1992, the anniversary of the confirmation of the Society, in a letter now addressed "To the Whole Society," Father General gave the exact dates for the official convocation and the beginning of the general congregation, as well as the deadline for holding the preceding province congregations.

At the Curia in Rome, the preparatory work progressed steadily. In January 1993 came the second edition of the two booklets dealing with the revision of our law, which had originally been presented at the congregation of provincials at Loyola in 1990. On 15 May 1993 the secretary of the Society sent out abundant literature relating to the "preparation of the province congregations." In May and August of that year, two "tabloids" were circulated, highlighting the problems that were regarded as most pressing; their content was spelled out in longer and more detailed essays. The whole Society now began to work in a great variety of ways, inspired by a further exhortation of Father General, dated Easter 1993, urging that the general congregation be "a moment of real discernment."

On 8 September 1993, as planned, Father General issued the official convocation of the general congregation, fixing its first plenary session for 5 January 1995. Together with the letter were some brief notes on who would participate, and seven "proposals of Father General for examination and discussion at General Congregation 34."

The province congregations were held within the prescribed time limit: they formulated their postulates, elected their delegates, and studied the proposals of Father General. When all had been completed, on 15 February 1994 Father General announced the setting up of the *Cœtus prævius officialis*, the commission charged with the immediate preparation of the general congregation (cf. FGC 12, §1), made up of Father General himself and "members of the congregation from each of the individual Assistancies": the three above mentioned general counselors and Fathers Carlos Cardó (ALM), Lisbert D'Souza (ASM), Jean Ilboudo (AFR), Gerwin Komma (ECE), Adolfo Nicolás (ASO), Vincent O'Keefe (USA), Salvatore Pandolfo (ITA), Valentin Pozaić (EOR), Gerardo Remolina (ALS), Guillermo Rodríguez-Izquierdo (HIS), and Mark Rotsaert (EOC).

On that same day Father General convoked the symposium that had been announced on the vocation and mission of the Jesuit brother: it was to be held at Loyola from 12 to 24 June, with the participation of thirty brothers, nineteen priests and one scholastic, representing the eleven assistancies of the Society.

The *Cœtus prœvius* held its first session in Rome, 13 to 21 April. The members "succeeded in familiarizing themselves with the postulates which had come thus far and identifying the major areas needing further preparation." Father General wrote again to the major superiors, with details about this meeting and other work being done. The letter bore the date 12 June, which he deliberately chose "to coincide with the opening session of the Symposium on the Vocation and Mission of the Jesuit Brother." The entire Society was asked to join in thanksgiving to the Lord for the "rich presence" among us of brothers. He also reported on the reply of the Holy See (28 March 1994) to his request for permission to discuss in the general congregation the possibility that in the future all formed Jesuits would be incorporated into the Society by the same solemn vows of poverty, chastity, and obedience: "His Holiness judges that the matter . . . should not be treated in the next general congregation."

The Symposium on the Vocation and Mission of the Jesuit Brother produced a total of twenty-seven propositions on "identity–mission–communion–formation," which Father General accepted both for his own governance and for transmission to the *Cœtus prœvius*. This he said in yet another letter, of 15 July 1994, where he also gave the names of the seven brothers being called to the general congregation as *procuratores ad negotia*, according to FGC 7: Brothers Bernard Coumau (EOC), Ian Cribb (ASO), Conrad Fonseca (ASM), Manuel Ibáñez Castillo (HIS), Charles J. Jackson (USA), Muwawa Ndolo (AFR), and Affonso Wobeto (ALM).

In the meantime the secretary of the Society, Father Hans Zwiefelhofer, undertook the task of putting together and systematically arranging the 637 postulates coming from the province congregations and the 142 sent so far by individuals. Each one was given a code name in Latin and placed in one of the fourteen categories that had previously been determined. The resulting "dossier" would facilitate the further work of the *Cœtus prœvius*.

This *Cœtus prœvius* was very busy from 4 to 25 July, handicapped by the heat of a Roman summer but assisted by a team of experts (Fathers José Javier Aizpún (GUJ), Michael Czerny (CSU), Vincent J. Duminuco (NYK), João Mac Dowell (BRC), Alois Riedlsperger (ASR), Elías Royón (TOL), and James W. Sauvé (WIS), with Isidro María Sans (LOY) assisting as secretary. The result was an updated list of postulates, which were now presented, first in order of arrival, and then in a new arrangement which indicated the provisional judgment about them: those to be put before the general congregation, others to be taken up by the ordinary (or extraordinary) administration of Father General, and finally some that were rejected. The vast majority obviously figured in the first group. The most important fruit of their efforts was the drafting of seventeen *relationes prœviœ*, corresponding to as many areas of concern. In each there was an account of the postulates involved and their overall content, with an assessment of the proposals they made and a suggested response. The last two of these *relationes*, dealing with the proposals of Father General and the way in which the revision of our law would be studied and voted on during the congregation, were prepared by a parallel commission meeting during those same days, chaired by Father Urbano Valero (CAS) and made up of experts in the Society's Institute: Fathers Norbert Brieskorn (GSU), Gianfranco Ghirlanda (ITA), Richard A. Hill (CFN), José Roque Junges (BRM), Geoffrey King (ASL), Zygmunt Perz (PMA), and Anthony Roberts (JAM), with secretarial assistance from Fathers José Antonio Artigas (TOL) and Estanislao Olivares (BET). The *relationes* developed by this second commission were expressly approved by the *Cœtus prœvius* itself.

These *relationes prœviœ* were translated into the three official languages of the congregation (English, French, and Spanish) and sent to all the delegates in September, as matter for reflection at the meetings that they would hold by assistancies during the following months. For all this material there is an authoritative, detailed, and grateful record in a letter sent by Father General on 30 August 1994 "To all the Delegates to the General Congregation."

In addition to the letter on the work of the *Cœtus prævius*, Father General informed "All Major Superiors" on 19 July 1994 of his decision to set a deadline for sending private postulates: "I would ask you to please notify the members of your province or region that all individual postulates must arrive in Rome on or before 1 October 1994."

A further communication of Father General, dated 20 October 1994, with information about the immediate preparations for GC 34, said: "Preparations for the congregation are moving ahead well. By now many of the assistancies have held meetings of all their delegates, finding them good occasions to begin to become familiar with each other as persons and to go over together the work of the *Cœtus prævius*. In Rome, the Interim Steering Committee is working to make concrete the process endorsed in principle by the *Cœtus*, to be proposed for the approval of the Congregation. As a way to introduce that process . . . I will ask you to start our work together with three days of prayer and reflection, individually and in small groups."

The time came, finally, to ensure that a support system was in place, with its innumerable practical details, prepared to function behind the scenes to facilitate the activity of the congregation, beginning with the arrival of the many delegates. A team was set up for this, charged with planning and executing all that concerned reception, accommodation in the Curia and the Domus Pacis, transport between the two, arrangements for printing, communicating, translating, informing, photocopying, obtaining documentation, celebrating the liturgy—even for taking care of the laundry.

2. INAUGURATION

Except for the few that came early, delegates arrived in Rome by various means on 3 and 4 January 1995; on the eve of the date fixed for the first session only three of the 223 members still had not arrived. The multiplicity of languages, facial features, and complexions left no doubt that the totality represented a truly universal Society. As for age, the range extended from the American Father Maurice Walsh (NEN) with a full seventy-eight years behind him to Father Simon P. Metena (ACE) from Zaire, who had just recently celebrated his thirty-seventh birthday.

At 8:30 on the morning of Thursday, 5 January 1995, in the Church of the Holy Spirit next to the Curia, the inaugural concelebration was presided over by Cardinal Martínez Somalo, prefect of the Congregation for Institutes of Consecrated Life and Societies of Apostolic Life. In his homily he commented on the Gospel of the day (John 1:25-43), which recounts the call of the first disciples of the Lord. This served as basis for his words of encouragement, before the final invocation to our Lady of the Way, "the support, guide and lodestar" of the Society in its evangelizing ventures:

> Christ himself will call to you once again: Follow me! He will grant you the abundant light of his Spirit that you might grasp what his call demands and what the Society must keep giving to the Church, in line with the service that St. Ignatius constantly urged, *ad majorem Dei gloriam*!

There was a brief session in the congregation aula, for instructions of a practical and technical nature, especially the use of the electronic equipment (which was subsequently employed nearly a thousand times, under the supervision of Father Sauvé). Then all moved to the *Sala Clementina* in the Vatican, where at 12 noon His Holiness Pope John Paul II received them in audience, with a warm message (cf. Appendix I) and "his blessing for the business which is to be handled in the congregation" (FGC 110).

At 5:30 P.M. of that same day the first official plenary session of GC 34 was held, chaired by Father General himself. After the recitation of the hymn *Veni Creator*, the name of each of the members was called (FGC 104). Father General explained the absence of three, as mentioned above, and the reason for the presence of some others. So too, he introduced the personnel that would help in the proper functioning of the activity of the congregation: translators, secretaries for minutes, press officers, technicians. Finally he put the two traditional questions required at the beginning of every congregation: "Num congregatio sit censenda plena et legitima [FGC 105]; num suppleri debeant omnes defectus, si qui forte acciderint, tam in congregationibus provincialibus quam alii quicumque" (FGC 107). The hearty "yes" to both questions was uttered in silence, thanks to the marvels of modern electronics that can begin the proceedings with just the touch of a button.

In the shade of a statue of St. Ignatius, donated by the Province of Upper Canada and placed beside the presidential table, the congregation was now launched on its course, committed to discern in the light of "the Supreme Wisdom" what must today "be determined for the greater glory of God."

There followed the announced triduum of "prayer and reflection," which occupied the weekend. Father General directed it himself, with three addresses which provided matter for personal meditation, to be followed by dialogue in small linguistic groups (Appendix II): "On the Call or Vocation of This Congregation" (in English); "On the Mission and Body of the Society" (in Spanish); "On Our Law and Our Life" (in French). The triduum reached its climax on Sunday the eighth, Feast of the Baptism of the Lord, with a solemn Eucharist at 6:00 P.M. in the auditorium of Domus Pacis, concelebrated by all the delegates and presided over by Father Nguyen Cong Doan, representing the Society in Vietnam.

In the course of the triduum, three general introductions were briefly presented: Father O'Callaghan recalled the purpose of the tabloids, the work of the *Cœtus prœvius*, the meetings by assistancies, and the activity of the preparatory committee; he also explained the alternatives envisaged by FGC 103, §1, for setting up the necessary commissions which would have to study the concrete themes, and suggested a possible timetable for this process. Father Czerny presented the booklet that had been distributed, "A Proposal for the Way of Proceeding of General Congregation 34." Father Valero introduced the "final scheme" (third edition, August 1994) for the revision of our law, and explained the plan proposed for discussing and voting on the material.

3. ORGANIZATION

Setting up the organizational structure of the congregation took some time; but it had to be done with quiet patience precisely to ensure that it would subsequently function with smooth efficiency. The initial steps were the simplest: to elect, first of all, the secretary of the congregation and his two assistants (FGC 109), the members of the *Deputatio de statu Societatis* (FGC 111), and of the *Deputatio ad negotia, sive de tractatione negotiorum* (FGC 112), which was thenceforth to be called the Coordinating Committee.

These elections were carefully prepared, in line with FGC 42, §5, in meetings by assistancies, chaired by the respective regional assistants: the first (on the evening of Sunday the eighth) was spent in reflection within the assistancy; the second (on Monday the ninth in the morning) in comparing one's conclusions with those of other assistancies—-thanks to the information that was collected and made available to the assistants between the two sessions.

Then came the successive elections, with secret balloting and with the following results. Secretary: the Provincial of Japan, Father Adolfo Nicolás; assistant secretaries: Fathers Pierre Belanger (GLC) and Jaime Oraá (LOY). *Deputatio de statu Societatis*: Fathers Jean Ilboudo (AFR), Carlos Cardó (ALM), Alvaro Restrepo (ALS), Varkey Perekkatt (ASM), Paul

Tan Chee Ing (ASO), Steven van der Grinten (ECE), Henri Made-lin (EOC), Lojze Bratina (EOR), Elías Royón (HIS), Gian Giaco-mo Rotelli (ITA), and Howard J. Gray (USA). Coordinating Committee *(ad negotia)*: Fathers Valerian Shirima (AFR), Fran-cisco Ivern (ALM), José Morales Orozco (ALS), Lisbert D'Souza (ASM), Joaquin G. Bernas (ASO), Franz Meures (ECE), Michael Czerny (EOC), Valentin Pozaić (EOR), José Fernández-Martos (HIS), Federico Lombardi (ITA), and Joseph P. Daoust (USA). This committee, at its first meeting that same Monday the ninth in the evening, chose three moderators who would chair the plenary sessions of the congregation in turns: Fathers Ivern, Rotsaert, and Shirima.

Once the basic organizational structure was in place, the procedure had to be determined as definitely as possible. The congregation would have to accept and approve, with whatever improvements were deemed desirable, the scheme presented on Friday the sixth. It was studied in assistancy meetings, which produced suggestions and amendments. The main ones were voted on in the plenary session of Wednesday the eleventh. Worthy of note are the restriction of speaking time, so that discussions might not be unduly prolonged, and provision for a periodic evaluation of the procedure now adopted, to allow for changes if experience should call for them. In this way the delegates had at their service an arrangement that was fairly clear and precise, and geared to the specific needs of this particu-lar general congregation.

On Thursday the twelfth came the time to set up the commissions envisaged in FGC 113 (cf. 103). First of all it was decided to adopt the second alternative proposed in FGC 103, §1: to entrust the task to "the General together with the *Deputa-tio de tractatione negotiorum.*" This group proposed three successive steps: (1) the whole congregation chooses the themes to be discussed, (2) the Coordinating Committee as-signs the chosen themes to the commissions that may be judged opportune, (3) the same committee appoints every delegate to a commission, taking account of the preferences expressed by the assistancies.

For the first step, a preliminary list was prepared, with forty-six themes: sixteen had been selected by the *Cœtus prœvius* in its original *Relationes prœviœ*, twenty-nine came from delegates gathered by assistancies, and one was proposed orally by an individual in his own name. A second list had twenty-nine topics relating to the revision of our law which the congregation might take up for particular study and discussion: thirteen had already been judged deserving of special attention by the preparatory technical commission in its seventeenth *Relatio prœvia*, and sixteen came from assistancies. The rest of the project for revision would be submitted to the congregation for a more global approval. The assistancies through their spokesmen could urge their preferences and proposals. On Friday the thirteenth an indicative vote was taken to determine the themes and questions to be given priority, at least at the beginning. The result was a total of twenty-two themes and twelve questions.

With this in hand as the fruit of the first step, the committee moved to the second and third. It decided to start with sixteen commissions and to postpone until later the study of the particular themes "Our Mission Today" and "The Identity of the Jesuit." It assigned to each commission some twelve to fifteen members, chosen in terms of competence, preference, and diversity, with a provisional coordinator named until each one could elect a president and secretary. It also circulated "a proposal for getting started." Likewise it undertook to screen the private postulates that had come in after the summer meeting of the *Cœtus prœvius,* or had been presented by delegates. Those accepted were transmitted to the relevant commissions. These were the topics allotted to the sixteen commissions:

1:    Formation; a strong appeal for excellence in studies
2:    Promoting vocations to the Society
3:    Cooperation with laity and others in mission

4: The revision of our law

5: The intellectual apostolate; theological reflection; the place and importance of theology; universities

6: Evangelization and interreligious dialogue

7: Evangelization and culture/cultures: inculturation

8: Means of communication

9: Our religious and community life

10: Proposals of Father General; interprovince cooperation; the international Roman institutions

11: *Sentire cum/in Ecclesia;* signs of the times; ecumenism

12: Leadership in the Society and in institutions; implementation of recent directives; planning

13: Characteristics of Jesuit ministry; our way of proceeding; discernment

14: The Jesuit brother

15: Promotion of justice; the position of women; the marginalizing of Africa

16: The priestly character of the Society: its meaning

4. DOCUMENTS

On Monday, 16 January, the commissions chose their presidents and secretaries and immediately began their work: prayer, reflection, discernment, drafting, comparing results. A week later each one presented a progress report to the congregation. In the meantime, thanks to suggestions from the assistancies, the Coordinating Committee revised the "way of proceeding," and the *Deputatio de statu* continued to refine its report.

Tuesday the twenty-fourth was graced with a brief visit from Cardinal Paolo Dezza, who was welcomed with affection and enthusiastic applause, and listened to with close attention and gratitude as he recalled memories of previous general congregations held in that very hall.

On 3 February the *Deputatio de statu* presented its revised report, which was received with applause and discussed for most of four subsequent plenary sessions. To reflect the content of these discussions, the *Deputatio* drew up a complementary report qualifying some elements of the original. In a subsequent note the Coordinating Committee called to mind the character and finality of this report: not being addressed to the whole Society, it does not require approbation, much less promulgation. The report is in fact confidential and has never been published by previous congregations. It is nevertheless a very useful document for the ordinary government and a point of reference for other documents drawn up by the congregation; moreover, it could provide material for the delegates, but only for statements made in their own name.

From 30 January on, the various commissions began to present their first drafts to the assembly, after obtaining the necessary clearance from the Coordinating Committee, which was always responsible for the progress of the proceedings. In this early phase, the whole congregation collaborated in the improvement of the first drafts for each of the commissions, while the assistancies and individuals also made comments and suggestions. With this in hand, each commission could redo its work in the next phase. The revised document was again presented at a plenary session, and subjected to debate, followed by an indicative vote to see if it was worth retaining. If it cleared this hurdle, it came to the final phase: further polishing in the light of the debate, one more presentation, precise amendments, and a final vote on these and then on the definitive text.

The first document to enter the second phase was on ecumenism. But the first to reach the finish line was on assistants and general counselors, in response to Proposal VI of Father General. This decree modified decrees of GCs 31 and 32, eliminating the distinction between "general assistants and counselors" and "regional assistants": all regional assistants would automatically be members of Father General's council.

In accordance with what had been determined, Father General proceeded on February the twenty-eighth to the naming of ten counselors (and regional assistants): Fathers Marcel Matungulu Otene (AFR), João Mac Dowell (ALM), Valentín Menéndez (ALS), Julian Fernandes (ASM), Paul Tan Chee Ing (ASO), Wendelin Köster (ECE), Elías Royón (EMR), Jacques Gellard (EOC), Bogusław Steczek (EOR), and Francis E. Case (USA). The congregation then elected four assistants *ad providentiam* (FGC 130-37) and an admonitor (FGC 138-41). In these elections, the four assistants *ad providentiam* were chosen from among the ten appointed counselors: Fathers Case, Fernandes, Gellard, and Menéndez; the same was true of the admonitor elected, Father Gellard.

Just about this time a general disquiet began to be noticed, a sort of crisis: time was running out, the documents seemed too many and not equally relevant, or were merely repeating what earlier congregations had said. So the Coordinating Committee decided to propose a "way out" to be followed in the third and last remaining month: to set up three teams that would trim the material produced, so as to arrive at briefer statements, though this might require a painful pruning of what was already in bloom.

One team was to work on an inspiring introduction to the whole body of decrees and juridical norms; another would put together all that referred to evangelization; and the last had to select from, and if necessary revise, the rest of the texts. The congregation approved this plan by a large majority.

The result is seen in the thematic index contained in the table of contents at the beginning of this volume: a comprehensive introduction, "United with Christ in Mission"; then a first unit on "Our Mission" with its own introduction and three specific documents on justice, culture, and interreligious dialogue; a second unit treating of some "Aspects of Jesuit Life for Mission": priests and brothers, chastity and poverty, vocations; a third concerned with the context of Jesuit mission "In the Church," beginning with our fundamental *sentire cum Ecclesia* and going on to speak of some of our companions on pilgrim-age: other Christian churches (ecumenism), the laity, and women; a fourth dealing in particular with the theme "Dimen-sions and Particular Sectors of Our Mission": communication media, intellectual work, educational institutions, parish minis-try, and ecology; yet a fifth on the topic "Structures of Govern-ment"; finally a conclusion stressing the authentic and basic "Characteristics of Our Way of Proceeding." The final voting was concluded on 20 March with the approval of the last eight of the proposed documents.

5. LAW

The revision of the law proper to the Society was from the beginning regarded as the central concern of GC 34; this had been already envisaged in GC 33. That could be why Father General devoted his third introductory talk to the topic "Our Law and Our Life." He recalled that St. Ignatius did not want to bequeath to us the constitutions as a finished product, and that his companion and successor, Father Laínez,

> saw in this unfinished work of Ignatius a summons to a creative fidelity, the Society's responsibility, when gathered in general congregation, to renew, enrich, and clarify with new apostolic experiences, demands, and urgencies, the way pointed out to us by the pilgrim Ignatius.

An extensive and meticulous work of preparation had been going on for several years. The congregation must now add the finishing touches, with the help of Commission 4, which had been entrusted with this topic, without forgetting that according to "the way of proceeding" that had been ap-proved, an effort had to be made to "integrate the study and treatment of the project for the revision of our law with the discussion of themes pertaining to our life and mission."

At the planning stage, the congregation reserved to itself the handling of twelve questions on law. Commission 4 now had to work on them in collaboration with other commissions which might be concerned with a particular question. In addition, it must further revise the project that had been presented to the congregation in its third edition (August 1994). This double task was attended to alongside the work of the other commissions, as reported in the previous section. The second presentation of each part of the Complementary Norms, as improved with some amendments, was begun on 23 February, with a general introduction by the president of Commission 4, Father King, and a special word about Parts I and II on the following day. At the opening prayer of the plenary session that morning, Father General contributed a reminder on the special importance of the subject, and a petition borrowed from St. Ignatius, that the Blessed Trinity deign to "confirm" the fruit of "our reflection and our voting" (Appendix III).

On Saturday, 18 March, with the approval of Part IX (Part X had been approved earlier together with Part V), the work of the congregation on this material having to do with our law was concluded. The event was celebrated with an enthusiastic burst of prolonged applause for Father Valero and his wholehearted and efficient dedication to this mission entrusted to him by the Society—clearly, with the assistance of many others. In token of gratitude he was given ten roses, one for each part of the Constitutions and their respective Complementary Norms. He placed the flowers at the feet of the statue of St. Ignatius, founder and first lawgiver of the Society.

6. CONCLUSION

On Wednesday the twenty-second came the approval of the faculties granted to Father General for the promulgation of the authorized text of the decrees passed by the general congregation, once such corrections as might be deemed necessary had been made and the revision of the law completed by taking account of what might have to be added to the Complementary Norms because of the decrees of this very congregation. Besides, the finishing touches had to be given to the authoritative

text of the Complementary Norms and the Notes to the Constitutions, in order to publish in a single volume the Constitutions,
the Notes, and the Complementary Norms. Father General and
four elected delegates (Fathers Johannes Günter Gerhartz,
Federico Lombardi, John O'Callaghan, and Mark Rotsaert) are
to ensure that any additions, corrections, editing, and translation
of the latter will be done according to the mind of the general
congregation.

During the time prescribed by FGC 128 for the presentation of, discussion of, and voting on possible "intercessions,"
the members engaged in a sincere and fruitful exchange of
their personal experiences in the course of the past three
months.

On 22 March at 2:55 P.M. the closure of the congregation
was decreed (FGC 143) and celebrated with a grateful *Te Deum
Laudamus* (FGC 145). Immediately, Father General dispatched
a telegram to His Holiness John Paul II, in his own name and
that of all the delegates, thanking him for his paternal regard,
reaffirming the unreserved loyalty of the Society to the Vicar of
Christ, and seeking his apostolic benediction on the results of
the general congregation. A cordial reply was received a few
days later, forwarded by Msgr. Giovanni Battista Re, *sostituto* in
the Secretariat of State (Appendix V).

That same evening, delegates and support staff gathered
at the Church of the Gesù for a final concelebrated Eucharist. In
a brief homily (Appendix IV) Father General expressed "in the
spirit of the Gospel of today" what all might expect as the
fruit of this GC 34.

• DECREE ONE •

INTRODUCTION:
UNITED WITH CHRIST ON MISSION

1 1. **The Work of General Congregation 34.** The major work of GC 34 has been the revision of our law and the orientation of our mission for today. The first project had two goals: to provide an annotated text of the *Constitutions* capable of influencing the present-day life of the Society and to make available a set of Complementary Norms to the Constitutions, derived for the most part from general congregations, to enable Jesuits to put the character and mission of the Society into daily practice. The orientation of our mission for today appears particularly in the decree "Servants of Christ's Mission" and its three companion decrees: "Our Mission and Justice," "Our Mission and Culture," and "Our Mission and Interreligious Dialogue."

2 2. While focusing on these two tasks, this general congregation also treated a number of important areas of Jesuit life and mission which are included as decrees or recommendations. Other important areas of Jesuit life—spiritual life, formation, obedience, community life, the local superior—which have been treated by recent general congregations and are incorporated into the Complementary Norms, are recommended to the ordinary government of the Society.

3   3. **Servants of Christ's Mission.** In its work, GC 34 stands in continuity with the spirit and emphases of GCs 31, 32, and 33. Like these congregations, GC 34 asks the Society to sustain both its spiritual and community renewal and its efforts to meet the challenges and opportunities of the modern world. In our review of the state of the Society, we faced our limitations and weaknesses, our lights and shadows, our sinfulness. But we also found much that was wise and good, especially the powerful and pervasive effort to pursue the service of faith and that struggle for justice which it includes. In the review of our graces over these years, we found again "the omnipotent hand of Christ, God and our Lord."[1] In gratitude for so much good accomplished and for so much forgiven, we follow this Christ, the Crucified and Risen Lord, in pilgrimage and labor. We see our renewal of the law and our review of our life and apostolic labor as one reality, the confirmation of our union as servants of Christ's mission.

4   4. **Pilgrimage and Labor.** The congregation invites the entire Society to read and pray over this updating of our law and orientation of our mission for today. One way of doing this would be in the light of the Ignatian images of pilgrimage and labor.

5   5. Just as the pilgrim Ignatius found that "God treated him . . . as a schoolmaster treats a child whom he is teaching,"[2] so Ignatius, as general and master of the spiritual life, continued his journey into the more profound discovery of God. The pilgrim search of Ignatius united him to Christ, led him to choose poverty with Christ poor, and to enter more deeply into the mystery of Christ's passion and resurrection. Out of his incessant search for God's presence and will, Ignatius developed a way of proceeding. This way of proceeding is found in

[1] *Const.* [812].

[2] *Autobiography* [27].

the pilgrimage of the Spiritual Exercises from sinner beloved and forgiven to disciple called to labor in the vineyard and to suffer with Christ; it is in the pilgrimage of the *Constitutions* from the first inquiry about the Society in the General Examen to the mature acceptance of responsibility for the Society in Parts V–X; it is in the personal examen of his own life where each Jesuit finds his own pathway to God, and in the communal narrative of these past thirty years of renewal and reorientation. Like that of Ignatius, our way of proceeding is both a pilgrimage and a labor in Christ: in his compassion, in his ceaseless desire to bring men and women to the Father's reconciliation and the Spirit's love, and in his committed care for the poor, the marginalized, and the abandoned.

6   6.   The *Autobiography* narrates the evolving power of grace which molded Ignatius into a man who opened himself to the needs of others. This simple reality, to help others, spurred Ignatius to study and training, to the gathering of companions, and, eventually, to the founding of the Society. That same simple reality, to help others, continues to inspire our Society today. The updating of our law and the decrees and recommendations of this congregation are animated by the desire to help people as Jesus Christ helped people. The documents of this congregation specify particular groups— the poor, lay men and women, persons of other religions—and focus on particular works from schools to parishes to research centers; the overarching motive is the simple Ignatian desire to help people in Christ. But the documents of this congregation also call us to learn how to be helped by people: how to be poor, how to see the Church as enriched by lay leadership, how to listen to the experience of women today, how to find God in the religious traditions of people from other beliefs, how to engage in respectful dialogue, how to become involved in the new cultural world of communi-

cation, and how to let the young give us hope and
dreams for the future.

7   7.   Ignatius presents a Christ who is on the move,
traveling through villages and visiting synagogues to
preach the Kingdom, going where people dwell and
work. This contemplative identification of Jesus on
mission is linked to the Election of the Exercises. In their
own communal apostolic discernment, which led to the
founding of the Society, Ignatius and his companions
saw this as their unique call, their charism: to choose to
be with Christ as servants of his mission, to be with
people where they dwell and work and struggle, to
bring the Gospel into their lives and labors.[3]

8   8.   As pilgrims on Christ's mission, we are ready to
be dispersed to any part of Christ's vineyard, to labor in
those parts of it and in those works which have been
entrusted to us.[4] This congregation is aware of the varied cultural and apostolic situations of the Society worldwide. In some parts of the Society we are becoming
fewer and older. In other parts of the Society we are
young, part of an emerging national consciousness, and
are beginning to have a new influence within the Society itself. Some of us live in countries only nominally
Christian and increasingly secular. Others of us live in
countries deeply religious but with few Christians. Others still work in countries where the Christian faith remains alive among the majority, especially among the
poor, but where it nevertheless faces the challenges of
injustice and secularism. Some of us are emerging from
years under totalitarian government and are redevelop-
ing Jesuit life and work. Yet all of us are called to be
servants of Christ's universal mission in the Church and
the world of today, to adapt the Society's apostolic prior-

---

[3] Deliberation of 1539, MHSI, Ignatiana s.III, pp. 1-7.

[4] *Const.* [603].

ities to our cultural situations and to our way of proceeding.

9   9.   In Jesus Christ, we can accept the magnitude of this challenge—to work at the integration of faith and justice, to strive to understand how the Gospel is to be inculturated, to embark with new zeal on the task of interreligious dialogue, to continue to join our professional and pastoral skills to the Ignatian way of proceeding. The Crucified Jesus reminds us that in weakness and vulnerability God's love can shine forth mightily. The Risen Jesus reminds us that our hope rests in his power over death and his continued identification with those who bear his name.

10   10. **Friends in the Lord.** A number of postulates asked for some further directions in the areas of spiritual and community life. Our efforts to meet these concerns brought us back repeatedly to Decree 11 of GC 32, "The Union of Minds and Hearts in the Society of Jesus." That decree is a classic statement. As such, it represents one more instance of the need for the Society to continue to implement the decrees we already possess.

11   11. Moreover, beneath the renewal of our law is a reverence for persons, an effort to make law serve the lived experience of Jesuits, to help the community of the Society become more united in its witness to the Gospel and in its labor. Other documents, on chastity, poverty, and vocations, underscore the opportunity we have in community life to bear witness that living in Christ can make men happy and wholesome, maturely capable of living and expressing their faith, willing to offer one another care, support, and challenge. Again, there is need for Jesuits themselves to be in dialogue with one another, to create an atmosphere of discerning listening and exchange. The decree on cooperation with laity summons us to an attitude of listening and exchange with those who are vital partners in our service

of Jesus Christ and his Church. While the term was rarely used, GC 34 was touching upon the Christian virtue of hospitality, of making the Society a symbol of welcome—to the poor, to lay people, to those searching for meaning, to those who want to talk seriously about religious issues. No community life is possible, however, and no renewal can be truly fruitful unless each Jesuit "keep before his eyes God, and the nature of this Institute which he has embraced and which is, so to speak, a pathway to God."[5] His vocation summons each Jesuit to find privileged time and space to pray with Christ, as friend to friend, learning from this encounter how to be a servant of his mission. This personal friendship in Christ, sustained by our Eucharistic fellowship, liberates us for the union of minds and hearts envisioned in Part VIII of our *Constitutions*.

12   12. **Conclusion.** In his address to the delegates, Pope John Paul II called the Society to discern its particular contribution "to the new evangelization on the brink of the third millennium."[6] As we present the renewal of our law and our orientation of the mission of the Society for today, this congregation is, first of all, filled with gratitude for all those Jesuits who have striven to make the Ignatian ideals of love and service their own in an eminent way. They include men who lived quietly and unknown; men who were renowned scholars, preachers, and teachers; men who laid down their lives for the Gospel, for the Church, and for the poor; men who lived simply and faithfully in a world that never understood their poverty, chastity, or obedience; men who brought our Society to this moment. We give thanks to God for them.

---

[5] *Formula* [3].

[6] John Paul II, Allocution to General Congregation 34, 5 January 1995, n. 2; cf. Appendix I.

13   13. Second, we are heartened by our younger brothers who will assume the leadership of our ministries in the years to come. For their dedication to Ignatian values, for their abilities in a variety of ministries, for their readiness for apostolic responsibility, we give thanks. We ask them to see their formation as guided radically by the updating of our law, so that they, along with the entire Society, can come to a re-cognition of—a renewed affection for—the Constitutions as the Society's privileged expression of its charism and spirituality: in a word, as the identity of the Jesuit.

14   14. Ultimately, the Society of Jesus is the mysterious work of God, calling us to live and labor in the vineyard of Christ our Lord. We can and should be good instruments revitalizing our lives and renewing our ministries.[7] But, finally, we must stand in surrender to the hope with which Ignatius ends the Constitutions, trusting that God will sustain this Society which bears the name of his Beloved Son.[8] We praise this God of our Lord Jesus Christ, asking his Spirit to be our guide as we live out what we have written here and journey with confidence and humility as servants of Christ's mission.

---

[7] Cf. *Const.* [813].

[8] Cf. ibid. [812].

• DECREE TWO •

SERVANTS OF CHRIST'S MISSION

15   1. As the Society of Jesus, we are servants of Christ's mission. In the thirty years since General Congregation 31, and particularly in the twenty years since GC 32, the Society has felt both the strength of the Crucified and Risen Christ and its own weakness: this has been a time of testing for us, but also a time of great grace. Our many faults we know and confess; our graces are more important because they come from Christ. Some have left us to serve the Lord in other ways of life; others, shaken by the events of this period, have a weakened confidence in the quality of our vocation. But we have also become, in a resilient way, a community of "friends in the Lord," supporting one another in the freedom which Christian love brings, deeply affected by the deaths of our Jesuit martyrs in this period. In these years, throughout the Society, we have been purified in the faith by which we live, and have grown in our understanding of our central mission. Our service, especially among the poor, has deepened our life of faith, both individually and as a body: our faith has become more paschal, more compassionate, more tender, more evangelical in its simplicity.

16   2. The Society has also become a body more diverse than ever before, engaged in a variety of ministries at the crossroads of cultural conflict, social and economic struggles, religious revivalism, and new opportunities for bringing the Good News to peoples all over the world.

17   •   Jesuits in Africa are engaged in the challenge of building up a young and vibrant African Church, rooted in the richness of different cultures, creating new bonds of solidarity among their peoples, and struggling to overcome the global forces that tend to marginalize the whole continent.

18   •   Jesuits in Asia and Oceania are engaged in the struggles of the poor and the indigenous peoples for justice; especially in Asian countries where Christians are a small minority, they dialogue with other cultural and religious traditions in an effort to put the Gospel in touch with Asian life and to bring the richness of Asian culture to the living of the Gospel.

19   •   Jesuits in Latin America, confronted by societies in which there are huge disparities between the lives of rich and poor, continue to stand with the poor as they work for the justice of the Kingdom. They also enable the voices of the poor to teach the Church about the Gospel, drawing upon the rich faith of the people and of indigenous cultures.

20   •   Jesuits in former Communist countries, after long years of harassment and imprisonment for their faith, are helping their people in their search for an authentic way of living in a regained freedom.

21   •   Jesuits in Western Europe, through a range of educational, spiritual, and pastoral ministries, are helping to maintain the vitality of faith and of Christian communities in the face of religious indifference. They also strive in a variety of ways to accompany and help those who are at the margins of society.

22   •   Jesuits in North America are dealing with the challenges of new forms of cultural and economic deprivation. They work in close cooperation with many others in trying to influence the complex structures of

society where decisions are made and values are shaped.

23   All of us are engaged in the Society's mission in ways appropriate to the varied contexts in which we work. For we have one mission, shared by priests and brothers, and many ministries which we undertake as a service of Jesus Christ and his work of reconciling the world to God.

24   3.   The Church, whose mission we share, exists not for itself but for humanity, bearing the proclamation of God's love and casting light on the inner gift of that love. Its aim is the realization of the Kingdom of God in the whole of human society, not only in the life to come but also in this life. We exercise our Jesuit mission within the total evangelizing mission of the Church.[1] This mission is "a single but complex reality which develops in a variety of ways": through the integral dimensions of life witness, proclamation, conversion, inculturation, the genesis of local churches, dialogue and the promotion of the justice willed by God.[2] Within this framework, in accordance with our charism, our tradition, and the approval and encouragement of popes through the years, the contemporary Jesuit mission is the service of faith and the promotion in society of "that justice of the Gospel which is the embodiment of God's love and saving mercy."[3]

25   4.   When Ignatius was confirmed in his mission at La Storta, the Eternal Father said to Christ, "I want you to take this man as your servant": it was at the will of the Father that Jesus Christ, carrying his Cross as a

---

[1] Cf. John Paul II, Allocution to General Congregation 34, 5 January 1995, nn. 2 and 9; cf. Appendix I.

[2] John Paul II, Encyclical letter *Redemptoris Missio*, n. 41.

[3] GC 33, D 1, n. 32. In other places in this present decree, this justice is also described as "the justice willed by God," "the justice of God's Kingdom," and God's "justice in the world."

standard of victory, took Ignatius as servant of his mission, to labor with him under that same Cross until his work is accomplished. It is a vision which confirms the call which Christ, the Eternal King, extends in the *Spiritual Exercises:*

> Whoever wishes to come with me has to be content with the same food I eat, and the drink, and the clothing which I wear, and so forth. So too each one must labor with me during the day, and keep watch in the night, and so on, so that later each one may have a part with me in the victory, just as each has shared in the toil.[4]

26   Ignatius, and all those called to this service, are taught to be companions in hardship with Christ in his ministry. In the Spiritual Exercises, we contemplate the mission of Christ as a response of the Blessed Trinity to the sins which afflict the world. We contemplate the Incarnate Son born in poverty, laboring to bring the Kingdom through word and deed, and finally suffering and dying out of love for all men and women. In the pedagogy of the Exercises, Jesus invites us to see in his earthly life the pattern of the mission of the Society: to preach in poverty, to be free from family ties, to be obedient to the will of God, to enter his struggle against sin with complete generosity of heart. As the Risen Lord, he is now present in all who suffer, all who are oppressed, all whose lives are broken by sin. As he is present, so we too want to be present, in solidarity and compassion, where the human family is most damaged. The Jesuit mission, as a service of the Crucified and Risen Lord, is always an entry into the saving work of the Cross in a world still marked by brutality and evil. Because we are companions of Jesus, our identity is inseparable from our mission. Nadal makes it clear that, for Ignatius, although the Risen Christ is now in glory,

---

[4] *SpEx* [93].

through the Cross he is present in the suffering which continues in the world for which he died: "Christ, having risen from the dead, and dying now no more (Rom. 6:9), still suffers in his members, and constantly carries his Cross so that he said to Paul, 'Why do you persecute me?'"[5]

27   5.   St. Ignatius was clear that, as the Society was not instituted by human means, so its ministries are preserved and fostered only by the all-powerful hand of Christ.[6] Thus, as we receive our mission from Christ, whatever fruitfulness it bears is entirely dependent on his grace. And it is the Risen Christ who calls and empowers us for his service under the banner of the Cross:

28   •   The Risen Christ, far from being absent from the world's history, has begun a new presence to the world in the Spirit. He is now present to all men and women and draws them into his Paschal Mystery. He continues to mediate God's work of bringing salvation, justice, and reconciliation to a world that is still broken by its sins.

29   •   The Risen Christ who calls us is the firstborn from the dead, the first of many brothers and sisters who, through his love, will enter God's embrace. He is the loving and healing presence among us, ensuring that the scars of brutality and death will not always disfigure our human history. His death on the tree of the Cross bears fruit that continues to be "for the healing of the nations" (Rev. 22:2).

30   •   The Risen Christ fulfills God's promises to the Jewish people and continues to bring all peoples together with them, to create one new humanity in the Spirit, uniting them in one living body (Eph. 2:15f.). In him, all human hostilities are healed.

---

5 MHSI, Ignatiana s. IV, p. 314.

6 *Const.* [812].

31   6. The mission of the Society derives from our continuing experience of the Crucified and Risen Christ who invites us to join him in preparing the world to become the completed Kingdom of God. The focus of Christ's mission is the prophetic proclamation of the Gospel that challenges people in the name of the Kingdom of his Father; we are to preach that Kingdom in poverty. He calls us to be at the very heart of the world's experience as it receives this promise of the Kingdom and is brought to receive God's gift in its fullness. It is still an experience of the Cross, in all its anguish and with all its power, because the enigmas of sin and death are still part of the reality of the world. He calls us "to help men and women disengage themselves from the tarnished and confused image that they have of themselves in order to discover that they are, in God's light, completely like Christ."[7] And so we undertake all our ministries with a confidence that the Lord takes us, as he did Ignatius, as his servants—not because we are strong, but because he says to us, as he said to St. Paul, "My grace is sufficient for you, for my power is made perfect in weakness" (2 Cor. 12:9).

The Graces Christ Gives

32   7. The Risen Christ's call to us to join him in laboring for the Kingdom is always accompanied by his power. A particular grace was given to the Society when GC 32 spoke of our mission today as "the service of faith, of which the promotion of justice is an absolute requirement."[8] This description of the main focus of our work and spirituality and its integrating principle is grounded in the Formula of the Institute, which, after speaking of the purpose of the Society—"to strive espe-

---

[7] Peter-Hans Kolvenbach, Discourse to General Congregation 34, 6 January 1995; cf. Appendix II, pt. 2.

[8] GC 32, D 4, n. 2.

cially for the defense and propagation of the faith and for the progress of souls in Christian life and doctrine"— identifies a range of activities which mediate this goal: ministries of the Word and ministries of interiority, ministries of sacramental service, teaching catechism to children and the unlettered. Finally, pointing to the centrality of the works of mercy in Christian life, it opens up a horizon of social ministries to be exercised by a Jesuit on behalf of those in need:

> Moreover, he should show himself no less useful in reconciling the estranged, in holily assisting and serving those who are found in prisons and hospitals, and indeed in performing other works of charity, according to what will seem expedient for the glory of God and the common good.[9]

33   8.   The commitment of the Society to a radical life of faith that finds expression in the promotion of justice for all derives its inspiration from this foundational declaration in the apostolic letter of Pope Julius III. We have recovered, for our contemporary mission, the centrality of working in solidarity with the poor in accord with our Ignatian charism. As though with new eyes, we read, as a prophetic text for our time, what Polanco under Ignatius's guidance wrote to the community at Padua in 1547:

> So great are the poor in the sight of God that it was especially for them that Jesus Christ was sent into the world: "By reason of the misery of the needy and the groans of the poor, now will I arise, says the Lord" (Ps. 11:6). And elsewhere, "He has anointed me to preach the Gospel to the poor" (Luke 4:18), a word which our Lord recalls when he tells them to give an answer to St. John, "The poor have the Gospel preached to them" (Matt. 11:5). Our Lord so preferred the poor to the rich that he chose the entire college

---

[9] *Formula* [3].

of his apostles from among the poor, to live and associate with them, to make them princes of his Church and set them up as judges of the twelve tribes of Israel—that is, of all the faithful—and the poor will be his counselors. To such a degree has he exalted the state of poverty! Friendship with the poor makes us friends of the eternal King.[10]

34   9. Being "friends of the Lord," then, means being "friends with the poor," and we cannot turn aside when our friends are in need. We are a community in solidarity with them because of Christ's preferential love for them. We understand more clearly that the sinfulness of the world, which Christ came to heal, reaches in our time a pitch of intensity through social structures which exclude the poor—the majority of the world's population—from participation in the blessings of God's creation. We see that oppressive poverty breeds a systemic violence against the dignity of men, women, children, and the unborn which cannot be tolerated in the Kingdom willed by God. These are the signs of the times which call us to realize that "God has always been the God of the poor because the poor are the visible proof of a failure in the work of creation."[11]

35   10. Pope John Paul II speaks of the pervading "structures of sin," particularly characterized by "the all-consuming desire for profit and the thirst for power" in all cultures. Because the life of the spirit is inseparable from social relations, he calls on people of all faiths and none to become aware of "the urgent need to change the spiritual attitudes which define each individual's relationship with self, with neighbor, with even the

---

[10] MHSI, I, 572-77, Letter 186, 7 August 1547. English translation in *Letters of St. Ignatius of Loyola*, ed. W. J. Young (Loyola University Press, 1959), p. 148.

[11] Peter-Hans Kolvenbach, "Our Mission Today and Tomorrow," *Faith Doing Justice: Promoting Solidarity in Jesuit Ministries* (1991), pp. 48f.

remotest human communities, and with nature itself."[12] It is a summons which we, as Jesuits committed to the action of the Holy Spirit both in the human heart and in the world, cannot refuse; consequently, in the conduct of our personal and community lives and in whatever ministries we undertake—whether works of pastoral service, academic scholarship, spiritual ministry, or education—we will live in ways which look to the fullness of the Kingdom in which justice, and not human sin, will hold sway. In the words of Pope John Paul II,

> Working for the Kingdom means acknowledging and promoting God's activity, which is present in human history and transforms it. Building the Kingdom means working for liberation from evil in all its forms. In a word, the Kingdom of God is the manifestation and realization of God's plan of salvation in all its fullness.[13]

36   11. Ours is a service of faith and of the radical implications of faith in a world where it is becoming easier to settle for something less than faith and less than justice. We recognize, along with many of our contemporaries, that without faith, without the eye of love, the human world seems too evil for God to be good, for a good God to exist. But faith recognizes that God is acting, through Christ's love and the power of the Holy Spirit, to destroy the structures of sin which afflict the bodies and hearts of his children. Our Jesuit mission touches something fundamental in the human heart: the desire to find God in a world scarred by sin, and then to live by his Gospel in all its implications. This, the instinct to live fully in God's love and thereby to promote a shared, lasting human good, is what we address by our vocation to serve faith and promote the justice of God's

---

[12] John Paul II, Encyclical letter *Sollicitudo Rei Socialis*, nn. 36-38.

[13] John Paul II, Encyclical letter *Redemptoris Missio*, n. 15.

Kingdom. Jesus Christ invites us, and through us the people we serve, to move, in conversion of heart, "from solidarity with sin to solidarity with him for humanity," and to promote the Kingdom in all its aspects.[14]

37   12. This faith in God is inescapably social in its implications, because it is directed towards how people relate to one another and how society should be ordered. In many parts of the world, we see social and moral disintegration. When a society has no moral and spiritual basis, the result is conflicting ideologies of hatreds which provoke nationalistic, racial, economic, and sexual violence. This in turn multiplies the abuses that breed resentment and conflict, and locks groups into an aggressive fundamentalism which can tear the fabric of society apart from within. Society then falls prey to the powerful and the manipulative, the demagogue and the liar; it becomes the center of social and moral corruption.

38   13. But a faith that looks to the Kingdom generates communities which counter social conflict and disintegration. From faith comes the justice willed by God, the entry of the human family into peace with God and with one another. It is not exploitative propaganda but religious faith, as the inspiration of the human and social good found in God's Kingdom, that alone can take the human family beyond decline and destructive conflict. If wrongs are to be acknowledged and resolved, then possessiveness, chauvinism, and the manipulation of power have to be challenged by communities grounded in religious charity, the charity of the Suffering Servant, the self-sacrificing love shown by the Savior. The community which Christ creates by his death challenges the world to believe, to act justly, to speak respectfully to one another of serious things, to transform its systems of

---

[14] Peter-Hans Kolvenbach, "Our Mission Today and Tomorrow," op. cit., p. 49.

relations, to take Christ's commandments as the basis of its life.

The Dimensions of Our Mission

39   14. We reaffirm what is said in Decree 4 of GC 32: "The service of faith and the promotion of justice cannot be for us simply one ministry among others. It must be the integrating factor of all our ministries; and not only of our ministries but also of our inner life as individuals, as communities, and as a worldwide brotherhood."[15] The aim of our mission received from Christ, as presented in the Formula of the Institute, is the service of faith.[16] The integrating principle of our mission is the inseparable link between faith and the promotion of the justice of the Kingdom. In this present congregation we want to deepen and extend, in a more explicit way, the Society's awareness of those integral dimensions of our mission to which Decree 4 drew attention and which are now reaching maturity in our experience and in our present ministries. We have found that whenever our ministries are conducted most fruitfully, these elements are present.

40   15. Decree 4, having made its central affirmation about the inseparability of the service of faith and the promotion of justice, then speaks of "our mission to evangelize," particularly through dialogue with members of other religious traditions and through the engagement with culture which is essential for an effective presentation of the Gospel.[17] Thus the aim of our mission (the service of faith) and its integrating principle (faith di-

---

[15] GC 32, D 2, n. 9.

[16] "[F]ounded chiefly for this purpose: to strive especially for the defense and propagation of the faith and for the progress of souls in Christian life and doctrine" (*Formula* [3]).

[17] GC 32, D 4, n. 24.

rected towards the justice of the Kingdom) are dynami-
cally related to the inculturated proclamation of the
Gospel and dialogue with other religious traditions as
integral dimensions of evangelization. The integrating
principle extends its influence into these dimensions
which, like branches growing from the one tree, form a
matrix of integral features within our one mission of the
service of faith and the promotion of justice.

41   16. In our experience since GC 32, we have come
to see that our service of faith, directed towards the
justice of God's Kingdom, cannot avoid these other
dimensions of dialogue and presence within cultures.
The proclamation of the Gospel in a particular context
ought always to address its cultural, religious, and structural features, not as a message that comes from outside, but as a principle that, from within, "animates,
directs and unifies the culture, transforming and remak-
ing it so as to bring about 'a new creation.'"[18]

42   17. In our positive approach to religions and cultures, we recognize that all of them—including the
"Christian West" throughout its history—have also found
ways of being closed to the true freedom offered by
God. Justice can truly flourish only when it involves the
transformation of culture, since the roots of injustice are
embedded in cultural attitudes as well as in economic
structures. The dialogue between the Gospel and culture
has to take place within the heart of the culture. It
should be conducted among people who regard each
other with respect, and who look together towards a
shared human and social freedom. In this way, too, the
Gospel comes to be seen in a new light; its meaning is
enriched, renewed, even transformed. Through dialogue
the Gospel itself, the Word ever ancient and ever new,
enters the minds and hearts of the human family.

---

[18] Pedro Arrupe, Letter to the Whole Society on Inculturation, *AR* 17 (1978): p. 257.

43   18. There cannot, in short, be an effective proclamation of the Kingdom unless the Gospel, having been brought to the very center of a society, touches its structural, cultural, and religious aspects with its light.

44   • There is effective dialogue with members of other traditions when there is a shared commitment to a transformation of the cultural and social life within which people live.

45   • The transformation of human cultures requires a dialogue with the religions that inspire them and a corresponding engagement with the social conditions that structure them.

46   • If our faith is directed towards God and his justice in the world, this justice cannot be achieved without, at the same time, attending to the cultural dimensions of social life and the way in which a particular culture defines itself with regard to religious transcendence.

47   19. Today we realize clearly:

> No service of faith without
>> promotion of justice
>> entry into cultures
>> openness to other religious experiences

> No promotion of justice without
>> communicating faith
>> transforming cultures
>> collaboration with other traditions

> No inculturation without
>> communicating faith with others
>> dialogue with other traditions
>> commitment to justice

> No dialogue without
>> sharing faith with others
>> evaluating cultures
>> concern for justice

48   20. In the light of Decree 4 and our present experience, we can now say explicitly that our mission of the service of faith and the promotion of justice must be broadened to include, as integral dimensions, proclamation of the Gospel, dialogue, and the evangelization of culture. They belong together within our service of faith—they are "without confusion, without separation"—because they arise out of an obedient attentiveness to what the Risen Christ is doing as he leads the world to the fullness of God's Kingdom. These dimensions within our unified mission develop the insights offered by our most recent congregations and the Society's apostolic experience in many parts of the world. Here, there is a profound, and Spirit-inspired, instance of *sentire cum ecclesia in missione*, appropriate to the ways in which our charism enriches the Church's evangelizing mission.

49   21. In the light of these reflections, we can now say of our contemporary mission that the faith that does justice is, inseparably, the faith that engages other traditions in dialogue, and the faith that evangelizes culture.

• *DECREE THREE* •

OUR MISSION AND JUSTICE

50   1.   In response to the Second Vatican Council, we, the Society of Jesus, set out on a journey of faith as we committed ourselves to the promotion of justice as an integral part of our mission. That commitment was a wonderful gift of God to us, for it put us into such good company—the Lord's surely, but also that of so many friends of his among the poor and those committed to justice. As fellow pilgrims with them towards the Kingdom, we have often been touched by their faith, renewed by their hope, transformed by their love. As servants of Christ's mission, we have been greatly enriched by opening our hearts and our very lives to "the joys and the hopes, the griefs and the anxieties of the men and women of this age, especially those who are poor or in any way afflicted."[1]

51   2.   And we have done so in many ways. The promotion of justice has been integrated into traditional ministries and new ones, in pastoral work and social centers, in educating "men and women for others," in direct ministry with the poor. We also acknowledge our failures on the journey. The promotion of justice has sometimes been separated from its wellspring of faith. Dogmatism or ideology sometimes led us to treat each

---

[1] Vatican Council II, *Gaudium et Spes*, n. 1. Cf. GC 33, D 1, n. 41.

other more as adversaries than as companions. We can be timid in challenging ourselves and our institutional apostolates with the fullness of our mission of faith seeking justice.

52   3.   Therefore we want to renew our commitment to the promotion of justice as an integral part of our mission, as this has been extensively developed in General Congregations 32 and 33. Our experience has shown us that our promotion of justice both flows from faith and brings us back to an ever deeper faith. So we intend to journey on towards ever fuller integration of the promotion of justice into our lives of faith, in the company of the poor and many others who live and work for the coming of God's Kingdom.

53   4.   For the vision of justice which guides us is intimately linked with our faith. It is deeply rooted in the Scriptures, Church tradition, and our Ignatian heritage. It transcends notions of justice derived from ideology, philosophy, or particular political movements, which can never be an adequate expression of the justice of the Kingdom for which we are called to struggle at the side of our Companion and King.[2]

New Dimensions of Justice

54   5.   The struggle for justice has a progressive and gradually unfolding historic character, as it confronts the changing needs of specific peoples, cultures, and times. Previous congregations have called attention to the need to work for structural changes in the socioeconomic and political orders as an important dimension of the promotion of justice.[3] They also urged working for peace and reconciliation through nonviolence; working to end discrimination against people based on race, religion,

---

[2] Cf. John Paul II, Encyclical letter *Centesimus Annus*, n. 25.

[3] Cf. GC 32, D 4, nn. 20, 40; GC 33, D 1, nn. 32, 46.

gender, ethnic background, or social class; working to counter growing poverty and hunger while material prosperity becomes ever more concentrated.[4] Each of us may focus our efforts in only one or other of these dimensions, but all of them are of continuing importance in the Society's overall mission of the promotion of justice.

55   6. More recently we have become increasingly aware of other dimensions of this struggle for justice.[5] Respect for the dignity of the human person created in the image of God underlies the growing international consciousness of the full range of *human rights*. These include economic and social rights to the basic necessities of life and well-being; personal rights such as freedom of conscience and expression and the right to practice and share one's faith; civil and political rights to participate fully and freely in the processes of society; and rights such as development, peace, and a healthy environment. Since persons and communities are intertwined, there are important analogies between the rights of persons and what are sometimes called the "rights of peoples," such as cultural integrity and preservation, and control of their own destiny and resources.[6] The Society, as an international apostolic body, must work with communities of solidarity in supporting these rights.[7]

56   7. In our times there is a growing consciousness of the *interdependence* of all peoples in one common heritage. The globalization of the world economy and society proceeds at a rapid pace, fed by developments in technology, communication, and business. While this phenomenon can produce many benefits, it can also

---

[4] Cf. GC 32, D 4, n. 20; GC 33, D 1, nn. 45f.

[5] Cf. John Paul II, Encyclical letter *Sollicitudo Rei Socialis*, n. 26.

[6] Cf. John Paul II, Encyclical letters *Redemptor Hominis*, n. 14; *Sollicitudo Rei Socialis*, n. 29.

[7] Cf. number 10, below.

result in injustices on a massive scale: economic adjustment programs and market forces unfettered by concern for their social impact, especially on the poor; the homogeneous "modernization" of cultures in ways that destroy traditional cultures and values; a growing inequality among nations and—within nations—between rich and poor, between the powerful and the marginalized. In justice, we must counter this by working to build up a world order of genuine solidarity, where all can have a rightful place at the banquet of the Kingdom.[8]

57   8. *Human life*, a gift of God, has to be respected from its beginning to its natural end. Yet we are increasingly being faced with a "culture of death" which encourages abortion, suicide, and euthanasia; war, terrorism, violence, and capital punishment as ways of resolving issues; the consumption of drugs; turning away from the human drama of hunger, AIDS, and poverty. We need to encourage a "culture of life." Measures to do this would include the promotion of realistic and morally acceptable alternatives to abortion and euthanasia; the careful development of the ethical context for medical experimentation and genetic engineering; working to divert resources from war and the international traffic in arms towards providing for the needs of the poor; creating possibilities for lives of meaning and commitment instead of anomie and despair.

58   9. Preserving the integrity of creation underlies growing concern for the *environment*.[9] Ecological equilibrium and a sustainable, equitable use of the world's resources are important elements of justice towards all the communities in our present "global village"; they are

---

[8] "But when you give a banquet, invite the poor, the crippled, the lame, and the blind" (Luke 14:13; cf. Luke 16:19-31). Cf. John Paul II, Encyclical letter *Sollicitudo Rei Socialis*, n. 33.

[9] Cf. John Paul II, Encyclical letter *Centesimus Annus*, n. 37.

also matters of justice towards future generations who will inherit whatever we leave them. Unscrupulous exploitation of natural resources and the environment degrades the quality of life; it destroys cultures and sinks the poor in misery. We need to promote attitudes and policies which will create responsible relationships to the environment of our shared world, of which we are only the stewards.

59   10. Our experience in recent decades has demonstrated that social change does not consist only in the transformation of economic and political structures, for these structures are themselves rooted in sociocultural values and attitudes. Full human liberation, for the poor and for us all, lies in the development of *communities of solidarity* at the grass-roots and nongovernmental as well as the political level, where we can all work together towards total human development.[10] And all of this must be done in the context of a sustainable, respectful interrelation between diverse peoples, cultures, the environment, and the living God in our midst.

Urgent Situations

60   11. As a congregation gathered from all over the world, we have become aware of critical situations affecting hundreds of millions of people which call for special concern in the Society. We do not mean to present an exhaustive list or to divert our efforts from unjust situations closer to each one of us. But the following are especially relevant to the Society as an international apostolic body and cry out for our urgent attention.

61   12. The *marginalization of Africa* in the "new world order" renders an entire continent paradigmatic of all

---

[10] Cf. John Paul II, Encyclical letters *Sollicitudo Rei Socialis*, nn. 27ff.; *Centesimus Annus*, n. 49.

the marginalized of the world. Thirty of the world's poorest countries are African. Two thirds of the world's refugees are African. Slavery, colonial and neocolonial subjugation, internal problems of ethnic rivalry and corruption have all created an "ocean of misfortunes" there. Yet there is also much life and great courage in the African people as they struggle together to build a future for those who will come after them. The general congregation asks the universal Society to do whatever it can to change international attitudes and behavior towards Africa.

62   13. The recent collapse of totalitarian systems in *Eastern Europe* has left behind devastation in all areas of human and social life. The people there are grappling with the difficult task of reconstructing a social order through which all can live in authentic community, working for the common good, responsible for their own destinies. In years past, many people, including Jesuits, gave magnificent witness to solidarity, fidelity, and resistance. Now they need the cooperation and familial assistance of the international community in their struggle for a secure and peaceful future. The Society must do everything possible to stand by them.

63   14. *Indigenous peoples* in many parts of the world, isolated and relegated to marginal social roles, see their identity, cultural legacy, and natural world threatened. Other social groups—an example would be the *Dalits*, considered "untouchables" in some parts of South Asia—suffer severe social discrimination in civil and even ecclesial society. The general congregation calls on the whole Society to renew its long-standing commitment to such peoples.

64   15. In many parts of the world, even in the most developed countries, economic and social forces are *excluding* millions of people from the benefits of society. The long-term unemployed, young people without any possibility of employment, exploited and abandoned

children of the streets, the aged who live alone without social protection, ex-convicts, victims of drug abuse and those afflicted with AIDS—all these are condemned to lives of dire poverty, social marginalization and precarious cultural existence. They require of us the attention which our biblical tradition demands for "the orphans, widows, and strangers in your midst."

65 16. There are over forty-five million *refugees and displaced persons* in today's world, 80 percent of whom are women and children. Often lodged in the poorest of countries, they face growing impoverishment, loss of a sense of life and culture, with consequent hopelessness and despair. The Jesuit Refugee Service accompanies many of these brothers and sisters of ours, serving them as companions, advocating their cause in an uncaring world. The general congregation appeals to all provinces to support the Jesuit Refugee Service in every way possible. And we call on the international Society to join efforts with other international institutions and organizations to combat the injustices which uproot peoples from their land and families.

Implementation

66 17. The promotion of justice requires, before all else, our own continuing personal conversion—finding Jesus Christ in the brokenness of our world, living in solidarity with the poor and outcast, so that we can take up their cause under the standard of the Cross. Our sensitivity for such a mission will be most affected by frequent direct contact with these "friends of the Lord," from whom we can often learn about faith. Some insertion into the world of the poor should therefore be part of the life of every Jesuit. And our communities should be located among ordinary people wherever possible.

67 18. During their formation, young Jesuits should be in contact with the poor, not just occasionally, but in a

more sustained manner. These experiences must be accompanied by careful reflection as part of the academic and spiritual formation and should be integrated into training in sociocultural analysis. Living contact with other cultures and a style of life in which "at times they feel some effects of poverty" will help them grow in solidarity with the poor and with the "other" in our richly diverse world.[11] Continuing formation of older Jesuits should also foster such experiences of different social and cultural realities.

68   19. In each of our different apostolates, we must create communities of solidarity in seeking justice. Working together with our colleagues, every Jesuit in his ministry can and should promote justice in one or more of the following ways: *(a)* direct service and accompaniment of the poor, *(b)* developing awareness of the demands of justice joined to the social responsibility to achieve it, *(c)* participating in social mobilization for the creation of a more just social order.

69   20. Forming "men and women for others" is appropriate not only in our educational institutions but in ministries of the Word and the Spiritual Exercises, in pastoral apostolates and communication. Social centers and direct social action for and with the poor will be more effective in promoting justice to the extent that they integrate faith into all dimensions of their work. Thus each Jesuit ministry should work to deepen its particular implementation of our full mission of faith and justice, which cannot but be enriched by efforts towards a more effective dialogue and inculturation.

70   21. Jesuit institutions can use the following means to help in implementing our mission: institutional evaluation of the role they play in society, examination of whether the institution's own internal structures and policies reflect our mission, collaboration and exchange

---

[11] *Const.* [287].

with similar institutions in diverse social and cultural contexts, continuing formation of personnel regarding mission.

71 22. Each province should evaluate its apostolic planning using the Ignatian criteria found in the Constitutions, read in the light of our mission today.[12] When understood in the light of the faith which seeks justice, the criterion of "greater need" points towards places or situations of serious injustice; the criterion of "more fruitful," towards ministry which can be more effective in creating communities of solidarity; the criterion of "more universal," towards action which contributes to structural change to create a society more based on shared responsibility. After decisions are made, it is of crucial importance to evaluate the process of implementation. Annual review of the accomplishment of objectives during the year can help determine objectives for the coming year. Serious and regular review of effectiveness in carrying out our mission will give credibility and realism to our province and institutional planning.

72 23. At the interprovincial and international levels, the Society must continue to find ways to collaborate with other national and international groups or organizations, both nongovernmental and official, for a part of our responsibility as an international apostolic body is to work with others at the regional and global level for a more just international order. The Society must therefore examine its resources and try to assist in the formation of an effective international network so that, also at this level, our mission can be carried out.

73 24. Above all, we need to continue with great hope on our journey towards the Kingdom. As "servants of Christ's Mission," we base our hope ultimately in Jesus Christ, crucified and risen, to preserve, direct, and carry us forward in our service of faith and promotion of

---

[12] Cf. *Const.* [622f.].

justice.[13] And we can thus keep seeking justice insistently.

> The Society continues to insist on the promotion of justice. Why? Because it corresponds to our very spirituality. . . . The promotion of justice signifies a call for the Society to insert ourselves even more profoundly in the concrete lives of peoples and nations—as they actually are and not as we think they ought to be.[14]

74   Thus our pilgrimage will lead us again to sharing more and more deeply in the joys and the hopes, the griefs and the anxieties of all God's people.

---

[13] *Const.* [134], [812].

[14] Peter-Hans Kolvenbach, "Our Mission Today and Tomorrow," op. cit., p. 49.

OUR MISSION AND CULTURE

75   1. General Congregation 34 has brought together Jesuits from the cultures of Asia, the former Communist countries of Eastern Europe, the European Community, Africa, North America, Australia, and Latin America; this composition has heightened our awareness of the diversity of cultures in both the world and the Society, and of the need to address the importance for our mission of the *Gospel and culture.*[1]

76   2. In recent years, the Church has made this theme one of its central points of reflection. Pope Paul VI wrote that "the split between the Gospel and culture is without a doubt *the tragedy of our time.*"[2] More recently, Pope John Paul II has presented inculturation as one of the fundamental aspects of the Church's total evangelizing mission, and points to the *mutuality* between the Gospel and the cultures it engages. The Christian message is to be open to all cultures, bound to no single culture and made accessible to every human person through a process of inculturation, by which the Gospel introduces something new into the culture and

---

[1] "Culture" means the way in which a group of people live, think, feel, organize themselves, celebrate, and share life. In every culture, there are underlying systems of values, meanings, and views of the world, which are expressed, visibly, in language, gestures, symbols, rituals, and styles.

[2] Paul VI, Apostolic exhortation *Evangelii Nuntiandi*, n. 20.

the culture brings something new to the richness of the Gospel:

> Through inculturation the Church makes the Gospel incarnate in different cultures and at the same time introduces people, together with their cultures, into her own community. She transmits to them her own values, at the same time taking the good elements that already exist in them and renewing them from within.[3]

77   3.   The process of inculturating the Gospel of Jesus Christ within human culture is a form of *incarnation* of the Word of God in all the diversity of human experience, in which the Word of God comes to take up a dwelling place in the human family (cf. John 1:14). When the Word of God becomes embedded in the heart of a culture, it is like a buried seed which draws its nourishment from the earth around it and grows to maturity. Inculturation can also be related to the *Paschal Mystery*: cultures, under the impact of the liberating power of the Gospel, rid themselves of their negative features and enter the freedom of God's Kingdom. The Gospel brings a prophetic challenge to every culture to remove all those things which inhibit the justice of the Kingdom. Inculturating the Gospel means allowing the Word of God to exercise a power within the lives of the people, without at the same time imposing alien cultural factors which would make it difficult for them truly to receive that Word. "Evangelization is not possible without inculturation. Inculturation is the existential dialogue between a living people and the living Gospel."[4]

78   4.   This process has always been a part of the life of the Church: in the early Christian centuries, the

---

[3] John Paul II, Encyclical letter *Redemptoris Missio*, n. 52.

[4] Peter-Hans Kolvenbach, "Living People, Living Gospel," Address to the International Workshop on Native Ministry, Anishinabe, Canada, 12 October 1993.

Church, while proclaiming its faith in ways that a Hellenistic culture could receive, was at the same time shaped by that culture. Insights which first originated outside the Jewish and Christian context came to find a place within the very heart of Christianity. A similar process is going on today in many parts of the world, as representatives of indigenous cultures, the great religious traditions, and critical modernity bring insights which the Church must consider as part of the dialogue between Christian experience and the diversity of other experiences. In this way, the Church is recovering, in our times, the creativity shown in the early centuries and in the best of its evangelizing work.

79   5.   Particular challenges must be faced today in order to enable an existential dialogue of this kind to take place amid the wide variety of cultures in which the Church is present:

80   5, 1.   Contemporary secular culture, which has developed partly in opposition to the Church, often excludes religious faith from among its accepted values. Consequently, some cultures which were once shaped by Christian faith have, in differing degrees, turned away from Christianity towards a form of life in which the values of the Gospel are marginal. Religious belief is often dismissed as a disruptive source of social divisions which the human family has outgrown; in the eyes of many of our contemporaries, the Church has no credibility as a commentator on human affairs.

81   5, 2.   The great cultures of Asia, in spite of centuries of missionary activity, still do not regard Christian faith as a living presence at the heart of the Asian experience. In general, it is inseparably linked with a Western culture which they distrust. Many committed Christians in Asia feel a split between their Asian cultural experience and the still-Western character of what they experience in the Church.

82   5, 3. All over the world, the increasing pace of urbanization leads to impoverished millions in the great cities. These people are struggling with an agonizing cultural transition as they emigrate from rural areas and are forced to leave behind their traditional cultures. At the same time, this transition is producing a new cultural synthesis in which elements of traditional wisdom are woven into new forms of popular organization and celebration.

83   5, 4. Among indigenous people there has been a resurgence of consciousness of their distinctive cultures, and they must be supported with the liberating power of the Gospel.

84   5, 5. In Africa, there is a great desire to create a truly African Christianity, in which the Church and African cultures form an inseparable union. There is also a desire to free the Gospel from a colonial legacy which undervalued the quality of indigenous African cultural values, and to bring it into a more profound contact with African life.

Jesuit Mission and Culture

85   6. As Jesuits we live a faith directed towards the Kingdom, through which justice becomes a shaping reality in the world; we therefore bring the particular quality of that faith into dialogue with members of the religions and cultures of our contemporary world. We have said in the decree "Servants of Christ's Mission" that "our mission of the service of faith and the promotion of justice must be broadened to include, as integral dimensions, proclamation of the Gospel, dialogue, and the evangelization of culture"; we have insisted on the inseparability of *justice, dialogue, and the evangelization of culture.*[5]

---

[5] GC 34, D 2, n. 20.

86 7. This is not just a pragmatic apostolic strategy; it is rooted in the mysticism flowing from the experience of Ignatius, which directs us simultaneously towards the mystery of God and the activity of God in his creation. Both in our personal lives of faith and in our ministries, it is never a question of choosing either God *or* the world; rather, it is always God *in* the world, laboring to bring it to perfection so that the world comes, finally, to be fully *in* God:[6]

> Ignatius proclaims that for human beings there is no authentic search for God without an insertion into the life of the creation, and that, on the other hand, all solidarity with human beings and every engagement with the created world cannot be authentic without a discovery of God.[7]

87 8. The mission of the Society, in service to the Crucified and Risen Christ, is directed to the ways in which he makes his presence felt in the diversity of human cultural experiences, in order that we may present the Gospel as Christ's explicitly liberating presence. Ours must be a dialogue, born of respect for people, especially the poor, in which we share their cultural and spiritual values and offer our own cultural and spiritual treasures, in order to build up a communion of peoples instructed by God's Word and enlivened by the Spirit as at Pentecost. Our service of the Christian faith must never disrupt the best impulses of the culture in which we work, nor can it be an alien imposition from outside. It is directed towards working in such a way that the line of development springing from the heart of a culture leads it to the Kingdom.

88 9. In the exercise of our mission, we bring a simple criterion from our Ignatian tradition: in our personal

---

[6] *SpEx* [235-37].

[7] Peter-Hans Kolvenbach, Discourse to General Congregation 34, 6 January 1995; cf. Appendix II, pt. 2.

lives of faith, we learn that we are in *consolation* when we are fully in touch with what God is doing in our hearts, and we are in *desolation* when our lives are in conflict with his action. So, too, our ministry of evangelizing culture will be a ministry of consolation when it is guided by ways that bring to light the character of God's activity in those cultures and that strengthen our sense of the divine mystery. But our efforts will be misguided, and even destructive, when our activity runs contrary to the grain of his presence in the cultures which the Church addresses, or when we claim to exercise sole proprietorial rights over the affairs of God.

89   10. This intuition is what has led Jesuits to adopt such a positive approach to the religions and cultures in which they work. The early Jesuits, in their schools, linked Christian catechesis to an education in classical humanism, art, and theater, in order to make their students versed both in faith and in European culture. It is also what prompted Jesuits outside Europe to express a profound respect for indigenous cultures and to compose dictionaries and grammars of local languages, and pioneering studies of the people among whom they worked and whom they tried to understand.

90   11. Particularly at the present time, when the sensitive quality of so many indigenous cultures is threatened by powerful, but less benign, pressures, we want to recover a reverence for culture as exemplified by the best of our predecessors. Throughout the world, Jesuits are working with great numbers of ethnic groups, tribes, and countries with traditional cultures. Theirs is a wonderful patrimony of culture, religion, and ancient wisdom that has molded their peoples' identities. These peoples are now struggling to affirm their cultural identity by incorporating elements of modern and global culture. We must do what we can to keep this relation between traditional cultures and modernity from becoming an imposition and try to make it a genuine intercultural dialogue. This would be a sign of liberation for both sides. Our intuition is that the Gospel resonates with what is good in each culture.

91 12. At the same time, we acknowledge that we have not always followed this intuition. We have not always recognized that aggression and coercion have no place in the preaching of the Gospel of freedom, especially in cultures which are vulnerable to manipulation by more powerful forces. In particular, we recognize that

92 • we have often contributed to the alienation of the very people we wanted to serve;

93 • Jesuit evangelizers have often failed to insert themselves into the heart of a culture, but instead have remained a foreign presence;

94 • in our mission, we have failed to discover the treasures of humanity: the values, depth, and transcendence of other cultures, which manifest the action of the Spirit;

95 • we have sometimes sided with the "high culture" of the elite in a particular setting: disregarding the cultures of the poor and sometimes, by our passivity, allowing indigenous cultures or communities to be destroyed.

96 We acknowledge these mistakes and now seek to profit from the cultural diversity and complexity within the apostolic body of the Society today. We realize that the process of inculturation is difficult yet progressive.

97 13. As the greater part of our men work within their own cultures, they will, in the service of faith, enter into dialogue with their own cultural world, witness to the creative and prophetic Spirit, and thus enable the Gospel to enrich these various cultures—and, in turn, be enriched by its inculturated presence in different contexts. We try to understand the reality of people's experi-

ence, because only then can the proclamation of the
Gospel relate to their lives. We bring the Gospel into an
open dialogue with the positive and negative elements
that these cultures present. In this way, the Gospel
comes to be seen in a new light: its meaning is enriched, renewed, even transformed by what these cultures bring to it. Father Pedro Arrupe drew attention to
the importance of inculturation for the contemporary Jesuit
mission:

> Inculturation is the incarnation of Christian life and of
> the Christian message in a particular cultural context,
> in such a way that this experience not only finds
> expression through elements proper to the culture in
> question, but becomes a principle that animates,
> directs and unifies the culture, transforming it and
> remaking it so as to bring about a "new creation."[8]

God's Dialogue with the World

98   14. The Gospel, God's prophetic word, continues
the dialogue which God has begun with all men and
women, who already share in *the mystery of unity* begun in creation.[9] It brings them explicitly into contact
with his *mystery of salvation.* God opens their hearts to
the *mystery of fullness*, "through the invisible action of
the Spirit of Christ," which awaits the human family as
its destiny.[10]

99   15. As disciples of the Risen Lord, we believe that
his Paschal Mystery radiates throughout the whole of

---

[8] Pedro Arrupe, Letter to the Whole Society on Inculturation,
AR 17 (1978): p. 230.

[9] John Paul II, *Address on the Day of World Prayer at Assisi,*
27 October 1986, *AAS* 79 (1987): pp. 865-71.

[10] Pontifical Council for Interreligious Dialogue and Congregation for the Evangelization of Peoples, *Dialogue and Proclamation:
Reflections and Orientations on Interreligious Dialogue and the Proclamation of the Gospel of Jesus Christ* (1991), n. 29.

human history, touching every religion, every culture, and every person, including those who do not know him and those who, in conscience, cannot bring themselves to have faith in him. The centrality of the Paschal Mystery, *Gaudium et Spes* declares,

> applies not only to Christians but to all people of good will in whose hearts grace is secretly at work. Since Christ died for everyone, and since the ultimate calling of each of us comes from God and is therefore a universal one, we are obliged to hold that the Holy Spirit offers everyone the possibility of sharing in this Paschal Mystery in a manner known to God.[11]

100 16. How everyone shares in the Paschal Mystery is known to God; that they share in it is what the Church is led by God to believe. It is the Risen Christ who is constantly active in all dimensions of the world's growth, in its diversity of cultures and its varied spiritual experience. As there is a unified goodness in God's work of creation, so in Christ's redemptive work, the fragmentation caused by sin is being healed by a single thread of grace throughout the restored creation.

101 17. One way of serving God's mystery of salvation is through dialogue, a spiritual conversation of equal partners, that opens human beings to the core of their identity. In such a dialogue, we come into contact with the activity of God in the lives of other men and women, and deepen our sense of this divine action: "By dialogue, we let God be present in our midst; for as we open ourselves in dialogue to one another, we also open ourselves to God."[12] We try to enable people to become aware of God's presence in their culture and to help them evangelize others in their turn. The ministry of dialogue is conducted with a sense that God's action

---

[11] Vatican Council II, *Gaudium et Spes*, n. 22.

[12] John Paul II, "Address to the Leaders of Non-Christian Religions" (Madras, 5 February 1986), *AAS* 78 (1986): pp. 769ff.

is antecedent to ours. We do not plant the seed of his presence, for he has already done that in the culture; he is already bringing it to fruitfulness, embracing all the diversity of creation, and our role is to cooperate with this divine activity.

102   18. The work of God in the diversity of human history is seen in the long process of enlightened human growth—still incomplete!—as expressed in religious, social, moral, and cultural forms which bear the mark of the silent work of the Spirit. In the conceptions of the mind, in the habits of the heart, in the root metaphors and values of all cultures—even, we might say, in the very process by which our physical bodies become capable of intense spiritual experience—God is preparing the conditions in his creatures for the loving acknowledgement of his truth, making them ready for the transformation promised in Christ. "All are called to a common destiny, the fullness of life in God."[13]

Our Mission and Critical Postmodern Culture

103   19. This is true even of those cultures where there is a difficult dialogue with men and women who think they have gone beyond Christianity or any religious commitment. We need to pay particular attention to them because of their influence throughout the world. Some cultures today are inclined so to restrict religious faith to the realm of the private and the personal, even regarding it as a strange eccentricity, that it is difficult for the Gospel to "animate, direct, and unify" contemporary secular culture.[14] We recognize that many of our contemporaries judge that neither Christian faith nor any religious belief is good for humanity.

---

[13] Dialogue and Proclamation, op. cit., n. 27.

[14] Pedro Arrupe, Letter to the Whole Society on Inculturation, *AR* 17 (1978): 256-81.

104   20. The problems of working in these contexts need no elaboration here, because the boundary line between the Gospel and the modern and postmodern culture passes through the heart of each of us. Each Jesuit encounters the impulse to unbelief first of all in himself; it is only when we deal with that dimension in ourselves that we can speak to others of the reality of God. In addition, we cannot speak to others if the religious language we use is completely foreign to them: the theology we use in our ministry cannot ignore the vista of modern critical questions within which we too live. Only when we make sense of our own experience and understanding of God can we say things which make sense to contemporary agnosticism.

105   21. This is a ministry which should not ignore the Christian mystical tradition that repeatedly treats of the wordless and imageless experience of God which surpasses human concepts: "Si comprehendis, non est Deus," said Augustine.[15] The experience of a silence surrounding the nature of God may be the starting point for many of our contemporaries, but it is also found within the depths of Christian experience and faith. There is a fragmentation of Christian faith in God in postmodern culture, in which human spirituality becomes detached from an explicitly religious expression. People's spiritual lives have not died; they are simply taking place outside the Church. "Post-Christian culture" witnesses, strangely and implicitly, to a reverence for the God who cannot be imaged by human beings without destroying the divine mystery: this is related to what Christians mean by "the Father." It also tries to find meaning within the very structure of human, embodied experience: this is related to the Christian belief that the "meaning" of the world (the "Logos") is made known to us in the humanity of Jesus. And there is a deep desire,

---

[15] St. Augustine, *Sermo* 117, *PL* 38, 663.

expressed through a concern for the environment, to revere the natural order as a place where there is an immanent, but transcendent presence: this connects with what Christians call the "Spirit."

106 22. The aim of an inculturated evangelization in post-Christian contexts is not to secularize or dilute the Gospel by accommodating it to the horizon of modernity, but to introduce the possibility and reality of God through practical witness and dialogue. We have to recognize that today humanity can find many answers in science which earlier generations could derive only from religion. In a predominantly secular context, our faith and our understanding of faith are often freed from contingent cultural complications and, as a result, purified and deepened.

107 23. A genuine attempt to work from within the shared experience of Christians and unbelievers in a secular and critical culture, built upon respect and friendship, is the only successful starting point. Our ministry towards atheists and agnostics will either be a meeting of equal partners in dialogue, addressing common questions, or it will be hollow. This dialogue will be based upon a sharing of life, a shared commitment to action for human development and liberation, a sharing of values and a sharing of human experience.[16] Through dialogue, modern and postmodern cultures may be challenged to become more open to approaches and experiences which, though rooted in human history, are new to them. At the same time theology, when developed with an eye to contemporary critical culture, may help people discover the limits of immanence and the human necessity of transcendence.

108 24. We need to recognize that the Gospel of Christ will always provoke resistance; it challenges men and women and requires of them a conversion of mind,

---

[16] Dialogue and Proclamation, op. cit., n. 42.

heart, and behavior. It is not difficult to see that a modernist, scientific-technological culture, too often one-sidedly rationalistic and secular in tone, can be destructive of human and spiritual values. As Ignatius makes clear in the Meditation on Two Standards, the call of Christ is always radically opposed to values which refuse spiritual transcendence and promote a pattern of selfish life. Sin is social in its expression, as is the counterwitness offered by grace: unless a Christian life distinctly differs from the values of secular modernity, it will have nothing special to offer. One of the most important contributions we can make to critical contemporary culture is to show that the structural injustice in the world is rooted in value systems promoted by a powerful modern culture which is becoming global in its impact.

Change and Hope

109   25. It is part of our Jesuit tradition to be involved in the transformation of every human culture, as human beings begin to reshape their patterns of social relations, their cultural inheritance, their intellectual projects, their critical perspectives on religion, truth, and morality, their whole scientific and technological understanding of themselves and the world in which they live. We commit ourselves to accompany people, in different contexts, as they and their culture make difficult transitions. We commit ourselves to develop the dimension of an inculturated evangelization within our mission of the service of faith and the promotion of justice.

110   26. "Ignatius loved the great cities"; they were where this transformation of the human community was taking place, and he wanted Jesuits to be involved in the process. The "city" can be for us the symbol of our current efforts to bring fulfillment to human culture. That the project, in its present form, is seriously flawed no one doubts; that we are more skeptical now than we were even thirty years ago is true; that there have been massive dislocations and inequalities is clear to all; that the totalitarian experiments of this century have been brutal and almost demonic in intensity none will dispute; that it seems sometimes to resemble the Babel and Babylon of the Bible is all too evident. But our aim is the confused but inescapable attempt to cooperate in the creation of that community which, according to the Book of Revelation, God will bring about—and God *will* bring it about—in the form of the holy city, the radiant New Jerusalem: "By its light shall the nations walk; and the kings of the earth shall bring their glory into it, and its gates shall never be shut by day—and there shall be no night there. They shall bring into it the glory and the honor of the nations" (Rev. 21:24-26). Until that day arrives, our vocation is to work generously with the Risen Christ in the all-too-human city where there is poverty of body and spirit, domination and control, manipulation of mind and heart; and to serve the Lord there until he returns to bring to perfection the world in which he died.

Perspectives

111   27, 1.   We must recognize the complexities of achieving a fully inculturated evangelization within the life of a people; while all our ministries have to be conducted with an awareness of their cultural dimension, the inculturation of the Gospel may be slow simply because cultural changes are slow.

112   27, 2.   We must recognize that our world is increasingly aware of the rights as well as the diversity of cultures, and that each cultural group is properly asserting the qualities of its heritage. We need to respect these diverse cultures in their self-affirmation and to work along with them creatively.

113   27, 3. In every ministry, we must recognize that the salvific work of God's revelation is already present in every culture and that God will bring it to completion.

114   27, 4. We must remember that we do not directly "evangelize cultures"; we evangelize people in their culture. Whether we are working in our own culture or in another, as servants of the Gospel we must not impose our own cultural structures, but witness to the creativity of the Spirit which is also at work in others. Ultimately, the people of a culture are the ones who root the Church and the Gospel in their lives.

115   27, 5. All of us need to recognize that every large culture contains within it a range of ethnic cultures and new subcultures which are often ignored.

116   27, 6. The call to inculturated evangelization is not simply for those working in a land other than their own. All of our works take place in a particular cultural setting with positive and negative features which the Gospel must touch.

117   27, 7. We need to listen carefully when people say that the Gospel does not speak to them, and begin to understand the cultural experience behind this statement. Does what we say, and what we do, correspond to the real and urgent needs of the people around us in their relationship to God and to others? If the answer is negative, then perhaps we are not fully engaged in the lives of the people we serve.

Guidelines

118   28. To further the Society's ability to promote inculturation, we offer the following guidelines:

119   28, 1. Our option for the poor should reach out also to their cultures and values, often based on a rich and fruitful tradition. This will permit a creative and

mutual respect within societies, and the promotion of a more fertile cultural and religious atmosphere.

120   28, 2.   The lifestyle of Jesuit communities should bear credible witness to the countercultural values of the Gospel, so that our service of faith can effectively transform the patterns of local culture.

121   28, 3.   Our commitment to social justice and ongoing human development must focus on transforming the cultural values which sustain an unjust and oppressive social order.

122   28, 4.   Each stage of our formation programs should root us in the cultures of the people we serve. They should focus on sharing the life and experience of those people and on trying to understand the culture from within.

123   28, 5.   There must be an integration of the dynamic of inculturation and the apostolic renewal both of Jesuits and of those who work with us. This is essential for our own conversion of heart and for a rediscovery of the freshness of the Gospel through its dialogue with culture.

124   28, 6.   An experience of a culture other than our own will help us grow into a vision more open to what is universal and more objective about our own native cultures.

125   28, 7.   Our educational institutions, in particular, have a crucial role to play in linking Christian faith to the core elements in contemporary and traditional cultures.

126   28, 8.   We commit ourselves to the creation of genuinely "local churches" which can contribute to the richness of the universal communion of the Church of Christ. We will also look for ways of creating indigenous theology, liturgy, and spirituality, and of promoting the right and freedom of peoples to encounter the Gospel without being alienated from their culture.

127 28, 9. As an international apostolic body, the Society is uniquely able to draw upon a range of cultural experience in its ministries and to promote an intercultural dialogue, contributing in this way to the Church's mission, at the service of God's plan to bring together all peoples into the communion of his Kingdom (Eph. 1:10; 2 Cor. 5:19).

OUR MISSION AND
INTERRELIGIOUS DIALOGUE

Introduction

128   1. If we imagine ourselves with the Trinity, in the spirit of Ignatius, looking down on the earth as the third millennium of Christianity is about to unfold, what do we see? More than five billion human beings—some male, some female; some rich, many more poor; some yellow, some brown, some black, some white; some at peace, some at war; some Christian (1.95 billion), some Muslim (1 billion), some Hindu (777 million), some Buddhist (341 million), some of new religious movements (128 million), some of indigenous religions (99 million), some Jewish (14 million), some of no religion at all (1.1 billion).[1] What meaning and what opportunity does this rich ethnic, cultural, and religious pluralism that characterizes God's world today have for our lives and for our mission of evangelization? And how do we respond to the racism, cultural prejudice, religious fun-

---

[1] *International Bulletin of Missionary Research*, 19, No. 1 (January 1995): p. 25. According to the editor, these statistics are taken from the *World Christian Encyclopedia*, updated and projected using a new demographic analysis provided by researchers at the United Nations. As with all statistics, they must be used with care.

damentalism, and intolerance that mark so much of today's world?

129   2. General Congregation 34 encourages all Jesuits to move beyond prejudice and bias, be it historical, cultural, social, or theological, in order to cooperate wholeheartedly with all men and women of goodwill in promoting peace, justice, harmony, human rights, and respect for all of God's creation. This is to be done especially through dialogue with those who are inspired by religious commitment, or who share a sense of transcendence that opens them to universal values.

The Church and Interreligious Dialogue

130   3. Vatican II has exhorted all Catholics to a dialogue which will "acknowledge, preserve, and promote the spiritual and moral goods found in other religions, and the values in their society and culture" in order to "join hands with them to work towards a world of peace, liberty, social justice, and moral values."[2] The Holy Father has repeatedly asked Jesuits to make interreligious dialogue an apostolic priority for the third millennium.[3] In a world where Christians comprise less than 20 percent of the population, it is imperative that we collaborate with others to achieve common goals. In the context of the divisive, exploitative, and conflictual roles that religions, including Christianity, have played in history, dialogue seeks to develop the unifying and liberating potential of all religions, thus showing the relevance of religion for human well-being, justice, and world peace. Above all we need to relate positively to believers of other religions because they are our neigh-

---

[2] Vatican Council II, *Nostra Aetate* nn. 2, 3.

[3] John Paul II, "Ad quosdam Societatis Iesu Sodales," 27 February 1992, *AR* 18 (1982): p. 728; Homily at General Congregation 33, 2 September 1983, *AR* 18 (1983): p. 1093; Allocution to General Congregation 34, 5 January 1995, n. 6; cf. Appendix I.

bors; the common elements of our religious heritages and our human concerns force us to establish ever closer ties based on universally accepted ethical values. Dialogue is "an activity with its own guiding principles, requirements, and dignity"[4] and it should "never be made a strategy to elicit conversions."[5] To be religious today is to be interreligious in the sense that a positive relationship with believers of other faiths is a requirement in a world of religious pluralism.

131   4.   The Society must foster the *fourfold dialogue* recommended by the Church:

> a.   The *dialogue of life*, where people strive to live in an open and neighborly spirit, sharing their joys and sorrows, their human problems and preoccupations
>
> b.   The *dialogue of action*, in which Christians and others collaborate for the integral development and liberation of people
>
> c.   The *dialogue of religious experience*, where persons, rooted in their own religious traditions, share their spiritual riches, for instance, with regard to prayer and contemplation, faith and ways of searching for God or the Absolute
>
> d.   The *dialogue of theological exchange*, where specialists seek to deepen their understanding of their respective religious heritages, and to appreciate each other's spiritual values[6]

---

[4] John Paul II, Encyclical letter *Redemptoris Missio*, n. 56.

[5] Federation of Asian Bishops' Conferences (FABC), published in G. Rosales and C. G. Arévalo, eds., *For All the Peoples of Asia* (New York: Orbis, 1992), p. 167.

[6] Pontifical Council for Interreligious Dialogue and Congregation for the Evangelization of Peoples, *Dialogue and Proclamation: Reflections and Orientations on Interreligious Dialogue and the Proclamation of the Gospel of Jesus Christ* (1991), n. 42.

132   This dialogue of theological exchange can more easily be carried on with religions which have a written tradition. However, the dialogue with indigenous religions is equally important. These religions express a sense of the divine and the transcendent which must be "approached with great sensitivity, on account of the spiritual and human values enshrined in them."[7] They play an important role in creating ecological harmony and human equality and have developed a great variety of expression and ways of communicating religious experience through devotional practices, ritual, dance, and song, which are a true source of blessings.

The Society and Interreligious Dialogue

133   5. Our experience in the service of faith and promotion of justice over the last twenty years has brought many of us into closer contact with believers of other religions. They have helped us to respect the plurality of religions as the human response to God's salvific work in peoples and cultures. We realize that God, who wants all people to be saved, leads believers of all religions to the harmony of the Reign of God in ways known only to him.[8] God's Spirit is in continuous dialogue with them. "Interreligious dialogue at its deepest level is always a dialogue of salvation, because it seeks to discover, clarify, and understand better the signs of the age-long dialogue which God maintains with humanity."[9] An open and sincere interreligious dialogue is our cooperation with God's ongoing dialogue with hu-

---

[7] Ibid., n. 14.

[8] Cf. Federation of Asian Bishops' Conferences, Statement of 20 November 1979, in Rosales and Arévalo, op. cit., p. 115.

[9] John Paul II, "Address to the Pontifical Council for Interreligious Dialogue," 13 November 1992. Cf. *Bulletin* of the Council, n. 82 (1993), p. 6.

manity. "By dialogue we let God be present in our midst, for as we open ourselves to one another, we open ourselves to God."[10] Interreligious dialogue is therefore "a work desired by God," "an integral element of the Church's evangelizing mission," which finds expression in the service of faith and the promotion of justice.[11]

134   6.   Our *service of faith* takes place today in a world that is becoming increasingly conscious of the plurality of spiritual experiences in diverse religions. Dialogue helps us to recognize that these religions are graced with an authentic experience of the self-communication of the divine Word and of the saving presence of the divine Spirit.[12] In ecclesial communion we experience in Jesus Christ the uniquely concrete revelation of the divine Word and the universally significant outpouring of the divine Spirit. With love and conviction we share this experience with our sisters and brothers of other religions, for "we are all pilgrims setting out to find God in human hearts."[13]

135   7.   Interreligious dialogue and *proclamation* of the Gospel are not contrary ministries, as if one could replace the other. Both are aspects of the one evangelizing mission of the Church.[14] "These two elements must

---

[10] John Paul II, "Address to the Leaders of non-Christian Religions," Madras, 5 February 1986, *AAS* 78 (1986): p. 769f.

[11] John Paul II, "Address to the Pontifical Secretariat for Non-Christians," 28 April 1987. (Cf. *Bulletin* of the Secretariat no. 66 [1987], p. 224; Dialogue and Proclamation, op. cit., n. 38).

[12] Cf. FABC statement of November 1986, in Rosales and Arévalo, op. cit., p. 259.

[13] Paul VI, "Address at the Eucharistic Congress," Bombay, 12 March 1964, *AAS* 57 (1965): pp. 124-26.

[14] "*Evangelizing mission*, or more simply *evangelization*, refers to the mission of the Church in its totality. . . . Proclamation . . . occupies such an important place in evangelization that it has often become synonymous with it and yet it is only one aspect of evangeli-

maintain both their intimate connection and their distinctiveness; therefore they should not be confused,
manipulated, or regarded as identical, as though they
were interchangeable."[15] Dialogue reaches out to the
mystery of God active in others. Proclamation witnesses
to and makes known God's mystery as it has been
manifested to us in Christ. Our spiritual encounter with
believers of other religions helps us to discover deeper
dimensions of our Christian faith and wider horizons of
God's salvific presence in the world. "Dialogue is a new
way of being Church."[16] Through proclamation others
encounter the compassionate God in the life, death, and
resurrection of Jesus Christ, whose Spirit brings about a
new creation in all realms of life. Without in any way
relativizing our faith in Jesus Christ or dispensing with a
critical evaluation of religious experiences, we are called
upon to grasp the deeper truth and meaning of the
mystery of Christ in relation to the universal history of
God's self-revelation. "It is the same Spirit, who has
been active in the incarnation, life, death, and resurrection of Jesus and in the Church, who was active
amongst all peoples before the Incarnation and is active
amongst the nations, religions, and peoples today."[17]

136   8. Our involvement in the promotion of justice
takes place in a world in which the problems of injustice, exploitation, and destruction of the environment
have taken on global dimensions. Religions have also
been responsible for these sinful elements. Hence our

---

zation. . . . Dialogue means all positive and constructive interreligious
relations with individuals and communities of other faiths which are
directed at mutual understanding and enrichment" (*Dialogue and
Proclamation*, op. cit., nn. 8f.).

[15] John Paul II, Encyclical letter *Redemptoris Missio*, n. 55.

[16] Paul VI, Encyclical letter *Ecclesiam Suam*, n. 63.

[17] FABC statement of November 1986, in Rosales and Arévalo, op.
cit., p. 259.

commitment to justice and peace, human rights, and the protection of the environment has to be made in collaboration with believers of other religions. We believe that religions contain a liberating potential which, through interreligious collaboration, could create a more humane world.[18] Through this process the Holy Spirit overcomes the structures of sin and creates anew the face of the world until God will be all in all. Jesus always focused on the human person as the center of religious beliefs and practices. Hence commitment to integral human liberation, especially of the poor, becomes the meeting point of religions. "Christians will join hands with all men and women of goodwill and work together in order to bring about a more just and peaceful society in which the poor will be the first to be served."[19]

Guidelines

137   9.   Though interreligious dialogue is an integral element of Jesuit mission, the forms of its practice depend on the concrete situations of our life and work. Indigenous religions and the great world religions, the new religious movements and the fundamentalist groups invite us to a dialogue that is proper to the perspective and challenge of each. Hence no universally valid guidelines can be given for the dialogue itself. What is important is that we grow in openness to the divine Spirit to be able to walk with others on a "fraternal journey in which we accompany one another towards the goal which God sets for us."[20] The following

---

[18] John Paul II, "Address to the Leaders of non-Christian Religions," Madras, 5 February 1986, *AAS* 78 (1986): p. 768.

[19] John Paul II, Message to the People of Asia, Manila, 2 March 1981. See *Bulletin* of the Secretariat for Non-Christians 46 (1981), p. 14.

[20] John Paul II, Allocution at the Day of Prayer for World

guidelines offer an orientation for developing a culture of dialogue in our life and ministry.

138   9, 1. Our spirituality should be characterized by a "deep respect for everything that has been brought about in human beings by the Spirit who blows where he wills."[21] Consequently, we must be alert to the global quest for a contemplative experience of the Divine, and compassionate towards the poor who seek justice and freedom. We will seek to be enriched by the spiritual experiences and ethical values, theological perspectives, and symbolic expressions of other religions.

139   9, 2. Genuine dialogue with believers of other religions requires that we deepen our own Christian faith and commitment, since real dialogue takes place only between those rooted in their own identity. For this reason, we need a solid foundation in philosophy and theology, with a special focus on the person and mystery of Jesus Christ. GC 34 urges all Jesuits to study carefully the decrees of Vatican II, the papal documents, and the statements of episcopal conferences on the value and necessity of interreligious dialogue.

140   9, 3. In our formation a closer acquaintance with the beliefs and practices of other religions must be given through special courses and actual involvement in a pluralistic milieu. Since the core of all true religion consists in its capacity to lead people to an authentic and deeper spiritual experience, it is important that we strengthen in our formation the mystical dimension of Christian faith and Jesuit spirituality in encounter with the spiritual traditions of others.

141   9, 4. Our proclamation of the Gospel must be sensitive to the religious and cultural background of those to whom it is addressed, and "attentive to the

---

Peace, Assisi, 27 October 1986, *AAS* 79 (1987): p. 868.

[21] John Paul II, Encyclical letter *Redemptoris Missio*, n. 56.

signs of the times through which the Spirit of God is speaking, teaching, and guiding all men and women."[22]

142   9, 5. Theological reflection must dwell on "the significance in God's plan of the different religious traditions and the experiences of those who find in them their spiritual nourishment."[23] It has to explore the meaning of the Christ-event in the context of the spiritual evolution of humanity articulated in the history of religions.

143   9, 6. Our commitment to justice demands that we share in the life and the struggles of the poor and work with believers of other religions in creating basic human communities founded on truth and love.[24] In social action we willingly collaborate with them in the prophetic denunciation of the structures of injustice and in the creation of a world of justice, peace, and harmony.

144   9, 7. Our *social and cultural centers* will identify and promote the liberating dynamics of the local religions and cultures, and initiate common projects for the building of a just social order.

145   9, 8. Our educational institutions will conscientize their students on the value of interreligious collaboration and instill in them a basic understanding of and respect for the faith vision of the members of the diverse local religious communities, while deepening their own faith response to God.

146   9, 9. Pastoral service will prepare our Christian communities for dialogue. We must be concerned with people beyond the limits of the Christian community and help them experience God's compassionate love in

---

[22] *Dialogue and Proclamation*, op. cit., n. 78.

[23] Ibid.

[24] FABC statement of November 1985, in Rosales and Arévalo, op. cit., p. 254.

their lives. "We are all children of God and we must all work together in harmony for the mutual benefit of all."[25] The Church is a "community in pilgrimage journeying with peoples of other faiths towards the Kingdom that is to come."[26] In this process she is called to be the voice of the voiceless, in particular of the young, women, and the poor.

147   10. Some Jesuits have already been trained for the fourth aspect and are actively engaged in conversations among experts in religious traditions. Their experience has been rewarding and fruitful. Their own faith has been deepened and shared with others, and their respect for the spirituality of other religions has grown. But given the task ahead, their number is inadequate.

148   11. GC 34 encourages each assistancy to prepare Jesuits able to become experts in the fourth aspect of interreligious dialogue. Since this dialogue is becoming a global concern, such planning should include interprovincial and international exchange of persons and be done in collaboration with other groups. Jesuits involved in this aspect of interreligious dialogue have a two-directional responsibility: (1) to engage in honest, respectful dialogue with experts in the other religious traditions, and (2) to communicate the fruits of this dialogue to those of the Society engaged in the first three aspects of dialogue, in order to help them understand and appreciate its urgency. Since this is a new and uncharted frontier, there will certainly be misunderstandings and misconceptions. We are once again invited to make ours the presupposition of St. Ignatius: "to

---

[25] Paul VI, "Address to Non-Christians," Rome, 5 March 1967. See *Bulletin* of the Secretariat for Non-Christians 5 (1968): p. 65.

[26] FABC statement of August 1987, in Rosales and Arévalo, op. cit., p. 300.

be more eager to put a good interpretation on a neighbor's statement than to condemn it."[27]

Concrete Responses

149   12. Dialogue with the *Jewish* people holds a unique place. The first covenant, which is theirs and which Jesus the Messiah came to fulfill, "has never been revoked."[28] A shared history both unites us with and divides us from our elder brothers and sisters, the Jewish people, in whom and through whom God continues to act for the salvation of the world. Dialogue with the Jewish people enables us to become more fully aware of our identity as Christians. Since the publication of *Nostra Aetate* in 1965, the Catholic Church has radically renewed the Jewish-Christian dialogue after centuries of polemics and contempt in which our Society shared.[29] To enter into a sincere and respectful relationship with the Jewish people is one aspect of our efforts to "think with and in the Church."

150   13. The emergence of *Islam* as a religious, political, and economic force is a fact of our world even in Western Christian countries; it has truly become a global religion. Although rivalry, conflict, and even war in previous centuries have made dialogue in recent times more difficult, both the Church and the Society have striven to build bridges of mutual understanding between Christians and Muslims. In Vatican II the Church expressed her esteem for Muslims, recognizing the positive values in Islam and pointing to the close bond Muslims have with the Church.[30] The relations of the Society of Jesus

---

[27] *SpEx* [22].

[28] John Paul II, Allocution to the Jewish Community, Mainz, 17 November 1980, *AAS* 73 (1981): p. 80. (Cf. Rom. 11:29).

[29] Cf. Vatican Council II, *Nostra Aetate*, n. 4.

[30] Vatican Council II, *Nostra Aetate*, n. 3; *Lumen Gentium*. n. 16.

with Muslims go back to St. Ignatius himself, from the time he discerned his vocation at Manresa as the call to go to Jerusalem and remain there among Muslims. The experience of Jesuits who have approached Muslims with preparation, knowledge, and respect has often shown that a fruitful dialogue is indeed possible. However, in some places Jesuits have found it difficult to dialogue with Muslims, especially in states based on Islamic law. In such situations they feel apprehensive about possible violations of religious rights and even of basic human rights. To face such situations, Jesuits need great faith, courage, and the support of the rest of the Society.

151   14. *Hindus* in general welcome the Christian initiatives of dialogue. Their threefold way of spiritual growth through ardent devotion, profound meditation, and action for the welfare of all offers an integrated vision and way of life. Their profound philosophical enquiries and mystical perceptions, their noble ethical values, "ashram" heritage, and rich symbolism of popular religious practices—all open broad avenues for fruitful dialogue. In the context of social discrimination and revivalist movements, partly the result of religious ideologies, Jesuit involvement in dialogue between Hindus and Christians becomes a great imperative.

152   15. *Buddhism*, in its many forms, is a major religion influencing the lives of millions of people around the world. The Four Noble Truths and the Eightfold Path of the Buddha propose a view of this world based on its essential inadequacy and a way of life which, through the practice of ethical discipline, wisdom, and meditation, leads to a state of inner liberation and spiritual enlightenment. Buddhism calls its followers to a selfless universal compassion for all living creatures; it has a special appeal for contemporary men and women seeking a true, personal spiritual experience. Dialogue with Buddhists enables Christians to join hands with them to face the basic frustration so many feel today and to address together problems of justice, development, and peace; in addition, it invites Christians to rediscover the contemplative riches within their own tradition.

153 16. The phenomenon of religious *fundamentalism,* which is found in all religions, including Christianity, poses serious difficulties. A passionate concern to return to the foundations of each religion combined with a reaction to the onslaught of modern secular culture has given great impetus to the growth of revivalist movements. The history of oppression of one religion by a more dominant one has produced animosities and prejudices which add fuel to such movements. Often religious feelings and structures are manipulated by political, economic, cultural, or ethnic power groups in order to safeguard their vested interests. All this results in fundamentalist ideologies and movements within religious communities. Our Jesuit responsibility is "to understand why the members of a revivalist movement have taken their particular stance, and to discover in an unprejudiced manner their legitimate intentions and hurt feelings."[31] This can pave the way for dialogue and reconciliation, which would demand from us the willingness to acknowledge our past intolerant attitudes and injustices towards others.[32] Apostolic discernment should be used to determine what can be done in such situations.

Conclusion

154 17. As companions of Jesus sent into today's world, a world characterized by religious pluralism, we have a special responsibility to promote interreligious dialogue.

[31] FABC statement of 3 November 1988, in Rosales and Arévalo, op. cit., p. 309.

[32] Secretariat for Non-Christians, *Guidelines for a Dialogue between Muslims and Christians* (Ancora Press, 1971), pp. 74-77.

The Ignatian vision of reality provides the spiritual inspiration and ministerial grounding for this urgent task. It opens our eyes to the incomprehensible mystery of God's salvific presence *(Deus semper major)* in the world. It makes us sensitive to the sacred space of God's direct dealing with human persons in history. The contemplation of God laboring in all things helps us to discern the divine spirit in religions and cultures. The Kingdom meditation enables us to understand history as God's history with us. The Jesuit heritage of creative response to the call of the Spirit in concrete situations of life is an incentive to develop a culture of dialogue in our approach to believers of other religions. This culture of dialogue should become a distinctive characteristic of our Society, sent into the whole world to labor for the greater glory of God and the help of human persons.

Recommendations to Father General

155   18. GC 34 asks Father General to explore the feasibility of setting up a secretariat for interreligious dialogue to promote and coordinate Jesuit initiatives in this area. The secretary could help to ensure that training programs for Jesuits are organized in view of a wider involvement in dialogue. He could publish a bulletin for the exchange of Jesuit experiences and theological reflections in the area of dialogue.

156   19. The general congregation asks Father General to explore the possibility of establishing a department for the study of religions at the Gregorian University. This department could offer academic courses on Judaism, Islam, Hinduism, Buddhism, and other religions, as well as on the theology of religions. It could establish academic rapport with other universities and centers for religious studies in various parts of the world.

157   20. The general congregation asks Father General to explore the possibility of expanding the scope of the apostolate of the Jesuit community of the Pontifical Biblical Institute in Jerusalem, so that, in dialogue and in concert with other Christian centers in Jerusalem, the Jesuits there might explore programs in interreligious dialogue among Jews, Christians, and Muslims, along with their continuing work of biblical and spiritual renewal of Jesuits from various provinces.

• *DECREE SIX* •

THE JESUIT PRIEST: MINISTERIAL PRIESTHOOD AND JESUIT IDENTITY

Introduction

158   1. Dynamic movements in Church and society suggest that we undertake a specific consideration of the priestly dimension of Jesuit life more complete than the last three congregations were able to offer. We present, not an elaborated theology of priesthood, but only a way of considering the priestly dimension of Jesuit identity and mission in the light of our founding inspiration. We have in mind several concrete issues that affect the life of the Society in many parts of the world. Since Vatican II, the Church has undergone many changes which have also been felt within the Society. From different parts of the Society, Jesuits have requested a greater clarity and confidence about the nature of the priestly vocation as this is lived out in a Jesuit context. Younger Jesuits in particular, as they move towards priestly ordination, desire a deeper understanding of this aspect of our vocation.

159   2. In many countries, Vatican II has generated a powerful impulse among lay men and women to share more profoundly in the Church's ministries. But it remains important that Jesuits continue to have confi-

dence in the value of the apostolic service that they
offer precisely as priests.

160   3.   Since the council, priests in religious orders
have been called to a deeper relationship with diocesan
bishops. While recognizing our clear duty to cooperate
with bishops in and through the Church for the coming
of God's Kingdom, we see a need to express the particular quality of apostolic *religious* priesthood as part of
our Jesuit contribution to the Church's reflection and
mission.

161   4.   We are aware of the different experiences of
priesthood in our various cultural contexts. Because the
Society has never been more culturally diverse than it is
today and because a full engagement with human culture has been part of the Society's charism, we wish to
recognize these differences, while being at the same
time confident of the fundamental common features of
Jesuit ministerial priesthood.

162   5.   Finally, we are conscious that Jesuit priests
share a common apostolic calling with Jesuit brothers.
Within this foundational union, the qualities of both
vocations are an enrichment of the Society's total identity and mission, and we have tried to describe the
features of Jesuit ministerial priesthood with full respect
for the quality of the brothers' charism.

Our Common Mission

163   6.   The Epistle to the Hebrews says that Christ is "a
merciful and faithful high priest in the service of God"
who makes "a sacrifice of atonement for the sins of the
people" (2:17). Through their baptism, Christians participate in Christ's priestly work of reconciling the world to
God and are called to mediate this reconciliation in their
lives. As Jesuit religious, we give a particular expression
to this dignity through our consecration and our apostolic mission in the Society: ours is a "ministry of recon-

ciliation" (2 Cor. 5:18) in the service of Christ. We are deeply conscious that the Society of Jesus is made up of priests and brothers: we are a community of "friends in the Lord," sent in mission by Christ, and together we form "a complex apostolic body, wherein each companion shares in and contributes to a single apostolic vocation, respecting the personal call of the Spirit."[1] Each Jesuit enriches the Society's mission and contributes to what St. Paul calls "the priestly service of the Gospel of God" (Rom. 15:16).

Priesthood at the Service of the Church

164   7. By their ordination, Jesuit priests also share in the ministerial priesthood by which Christ, through the gifts of the Spirit, unceasingly builds up his Church, guides his people through the pastoral office, and leads them into the Kingdom of his Father.[2] The companions of Jesus who offer themselves to the Church for priestly ministry do so because they discern this as the will of the Lord, which the Church confirms by ordaining and commissioning them for ministerial service in its name. In this way, the Society relates its apostolic charism to the dynamic of the Church's ordained ministry; the Church, in turn, accepts this apostolic service offered by the Society and recognizes what Jesuits bring as an enrichment of the priestly office exercised in the Church.

165   8. At the time of its founding and throughout its history, the exercise of ministerial priesthood has been regarded as central to the Society's identity and apos-

---

[1] Peter-Hans Kolvenbach, Address to the First Congregation of Provincials (26 September 1990) 9, *AR* 20 (1990): p. 494.

[2] *Catechism of the Catholic Church*, n. 1547. "Only Christ is the true priest, the others being only his ministers" (Thomas Aquinas, *Heb.* 7.4).

tolic mission.³ For this reason, when he addressed General Congregation 32 Pope Paul VI declared ministerial priesthood to be an "essential character" of the Society:⁴ it is directed towards and necessary for the Society's apostolic mission to carry out whatever tasks the Church may ask of it. Jesuit priests receive ordination so that, by this commission, the Society can fully exercise the specifically Jesuit apostolic mission of "serving the Lord alone and the Church, his spouse, under the Roman Pontiff, the Vicar of Christ on earth."⁵

166   9.   Jesuit priesthood, therefore, is a gift from God for universal mission. By putting themselves directly at the service of the pope, the first Jesuits expressed their readiness to be sent wherever there was hope of the greater glory of God and the help of souls. Ignatius and his first companions, therefore, placed their priestly ministry, not at the service of a bishop's pastoral care for a particular diocese, but at the service of the Sovereign Pontiff for the service of the universal Church. Since the Society conducts its ministries with a constant readiness for new service, the scope of Jesuit priestly service is universal; its aim is apostolic and it is exercised under the pope's universal solicitude for the needs of the Church and the world.

Characteristic Activities

167   10. Inspired by Christ, "the first Evangelizer," and by the example of Ignatius and his first companions, Jesuit priestly service is exercised through a wide range of ministries.⁶ The apostolic letters of Paul III (1540) and

---

³ *Formula* [6].

⁴ Paul VI, Allocution to General Congregation 32, 3 December 1974, n. 2; cf. Documents of General Congregation 32, Appendix.

⁵ *Formula* [3].

⁶ John Paul II, Allocution to General Congregation 34, 5

Julius III (1550) approve a whole series of activities proper to Jesuit priests: ministries of the Word and ministries of interiority, ministries of reconciliation and teaching, ministries of sacramental service, teaching catechism to children and the unlettered, ministries of social concern. These characteristic activities of the first companions are the archetypes of Jesuit priestly service as exercised on behalf of the Church's mission, and they continue to inspire the Society today to undertake a program of "integral evangelization" concerned with the good of the whole human person. The Church asks the Society to engage in whatever "will seem expedient for the glory of God and the common good"; this is our "pathway to God."[7]

168   11. Since the foundation of the Society, Jesuits have exercised their ministry most particularly where the needs are greatest, where there are not others to minister to these needs, and where the more universal good may be found.[8] Jerome Nadal expressed this central aspect of our charism: "The Society cares for those persons who are either totally neglected or inadequately attended to. This is the basic reason for the founding of the Society, this is its power, this is what makes it distinctive in the Church."[9]

169   12. This spirit continues to shape what Jesuits do as priests: their ministry is particularly directed towards those who have not heard the Gospel, those who are at the margins of the Church or of society, those who have been denied their dignity, those who are voiceless and

---

January 1995, n. 7; cf. Appendix I.

[7] *Formula* [3].

[8] *Const.* [622].

[9] Nadal, MHSI, vol 90a, *Orationis Observationes*, "Societas curam habet earum animarum de quibus vel nullus est qui curet vel, si quis curet, is negligenter curat. Hæc est ratio institutionis Societatis, hæc virtus, hæc dignitas in Ecclesia" ([316] [p. 126]).

powerless, those weak in faith or alienated from it,
those whose values are undermined by contemporary
culture, those whose needs are greater than they can
bear.[10] For the Jesuit priest, the world is where he is to
be most active, in the name of Christ the healer and
reconciler. Pope Paul VI pointed to our presence at the
boundaries between human culture and the Gospel:

> Wherever in the Church, even in the most difficult
> and extreme fields, in the crossroads of ideologies, in
> the front line of social conflict, there has been and
> there is confrontation between the deepest desires of
> the human person and the perennial message of the
> Gospel, there also there have been, and there are,
> Jesuits.[11]

Present Tasks

170   13. Within the varied contexts in which the Society's
contemporary mission is conducted, common tasks are
to be found: how to find words that speak to the men
and women of our time who are no longer moved by
the Christian message, how to be faithful to the tradition
of the Church and at the same time interpret it in secu-
larized cultures, how to minister effectively to both the
poor and the rich, how to integrate our spiritual ministries with our social ministries, how best to serve in a
Church in which there are tensions, how to make evangelical poverty part of our contemporary witness, how to
mediate between different cultures and groups within
the same country, how to enable the Church to be truly
Catholic in the comprehensiveness and cultural variety
of its practice and faith; finally, how to enable the world
to become, in all aspects of its life, the Kingdom that
Christ proclaimed.

---

[10] GC 32, D 4, n. 42.

[11] Paul VI, Allocution to General Congregation 32, op. cit., n. 2.

171 14. A specific challenge today is to embody Christ's ministry of healing and reconciliation in a world increasingly divided by economic and social status, race and ethnicity, violence and war, cultural and religious pluralism. These divisions must be a focus of Jesuit priestly ministry because Christ's work of reconciliation breaks down the walls of division among peoples "in order to create in himself one new humanity" (cf. Eph. 2:14f.). We live in a broken world where men and women are in need of integral healing, the power for which comes ultimately from God. Therefore, Jesuit priestly mission is directed, inseparably, towards justice for the poor and the reconciliation of the world to God through the preaching of the Gospel.

172 15. In the light of our tradition, we can say that no ministry which prepares the way for the Kingdom or which helps to arouse faith in the Gospel is outside the scope of Jesuit priests. In recent years we have come to recognize that "it is for the priest, as sign and minister of the Lord's active presence, to be present in or to collaborate with all human efforts which help in establishing the Kingdom."[12] We have also described the Jesuit mission as engaging "under the standard of the Cross, in the crucial struggle of our time: the struggle for faith and that struggle for justice which it includes."[13] The ways in which this is implemented must always be appropriate to the milieus in which Jesuit ministry is conducted: this will take different forms in different contexts, according to circumstances. Many have asked if this is appropriate for Jesuit priests: do not some activities lie outside the range legitimate for priests? We answer that the Society's commitment to this mission is prompted, neither by a facile optimism about the progress of world history nor by a specific social program, but by a humble desire

---

[12] GC 31, D 23, n. 7.

[13] GC 32, D 2, n. 2.

to share in the work of Christ who reconciled the world to God through his priestly death. Our Jesuit martyrs, who have died for their faith and their people in many parts of the world, show that Jesuits live under the banner of the Cross. And the Cross is the sign that, as followers of Christ, we will be spared nothing: our Jesuit mission is conducted with faith in the Resurrection, since only God resolves the enigmas of suffering and death in this present age.

Drawing on Our Tradition

173   16. The way in which Jesuits exercise their ministerial priesthood takes its character from our apostolic mission to labor with Christ in proclaiming the Kingdom.[14] Our first companions envisaged a universal, itinerant ministry of evangelization, teaching, works of charity, and poverty of life: an evangelical *imitatio apostolorum*, a radical pattern of apostolic discipleship, was to be the wellspring for what they did as priests. "It is the primary vocation to be like the apostles which marks henceforth the way of being 'priest' in the Society of Jesus."[15] Under the inspiration of the Spiritual Exercises, they wanted to be like Christ in giving freely of themselves to anyone in need; they wanted to live like him who came not to be served but to serve; they wanted to act like him in preaching to the crowds; they wanted to share his concern for the needs of the poor and the sick. We recall that the Jesuit theologians at the Council of Trent were instructed by Ignatius to spend part of their time visiting hospitals and instructing small children; their public work of lecturing at the council

---

[14] *SpEx* [95].

[15] Peter-Hans Kolvenbach, op. cit., n. 7, *AR* 20 (1990): p. 493.

was to be balanced by acts of mercy which went unnoticed except by the poor who received them.[16]

174   17. In the conduct of their ministries, Ignatius wanted Jesuit priests to avoid ways of proceeding which the Spiritual Exercises present as contrary to the Gospel: riches and success, honors and recognition, power, pride, and prestige. He insisted that Jesuit priests should not accept appointment to bishoprics or to other ecclesiastical dignities, offices, and benefices, but should have the poverty and freedom necessary for mission. Ignatius wanted them to ask for the grace to be truly poor in companionship with Christ, to be obedient in their mission, to be held in low esteem if God would be thus served, and to live as "priests of Christ freely poor."[17] Jesuit priests today are to be like them in doing what they judge to be the most urgent and fruitful apostolic tasks, in an apostolic horizon unrestricted by divisions of class or culture, and with no regard for their personal gratification.

175   18. Wherever they are, Jesuit priests make their apostolic contribution to the life of the local church, while at the same time being faithful to their charism and keeping their freedom for mission. At any given moment, the Jesuit priest lives in a particular local church, and willingly cooperates with the local bishop in the Church's mission.[18] But he recognizes that, in every local Church, it is the particular charism of the *diocesan* clergy to be the primary agents of the bishop's pastoral care; because he is not a diocesan priest, he recognizes that he exercises his ministry in complementary ways. As such, a Jesuit tries to direct what he does as a priest

---

[16] "To the Fathers Sent to Trent" (1546), MHSI, vol. 22, MI, Series Prima (T. I., Madrid, 1903): pp. 386–89.

[17] Peter-Hans Kolvenbach, op. cit. n. 13, *AR* 20 (1990): p. 495.

[18] Vatican Council II, *Lumen Gentium*, n. 28.

towards those who are not easily reached by the Church's ordinary ministry.

176   19. Just as Jesuit priests form a common apostolic body with brothers, so it is also necessary that they promote and enhance the ecclesial service offered by religious in other communities and by lay men and women who want to share more profoundly in the Church's ministry. The recent growth of lay ministries in the Church, far from being a threat to what is offered by Jesuits in their priestly ministry, corresponds to one of the fundamental charisms of our Ignatian tradition. Through the Spiritual Exercises, Jesuits are particularly concerned with helping others enter more into their baptismal dignity as servants of Christ. Our Jesuit tradition recognizes that God deals with individuals, always to deepen in them the life of grace and always through them to strengthen the life of the Church; this is in perfect agreement with the perspective offered by the *Catechism of the Catholic Church* on the character of ministerial priesthood in the Church:

> While the common priesthood of the faithful is exercised by the unfolding of baptismal grace—a life of faith, hope, and charity, a life according to the Spirit—the ministerial priesthood is at the service of the common priesthood. It is directed at the unfolding of the baptismal grace of all Christians. The ministerial priesthood is a *means* by which Christ unceasingly builds up and leads his Church.[19]

177   20. From their Ignatian tradition, Jesuits bring to their ministerial priesthood a profound respect for the ways in which God is already at work in the lives of all men and women. God's action does not begin with what we do; already, in the blessings of creation, God has laid the foundation for what he will accomplish through the graces of redemption. Consequently, in the

---

[19] *Catechism of the Catholic Church*, n. 1547.

exercise of their ministerial priesthood, Jesuits try to see what God has already done in the lives of individuals, societies, and cultures, and to discern how God will continue that work. By drawing attention to the graced character of all human life, this insight influences the way in which Jesuit ministerial priesthood is exercised in different areas:

178 20, 1. It is always aimed at building up the human person in the individual character of each one's life of grace;

179 20, 2. It encourages us to become involved in disciplines which, although they may have no explicitly Christian perspective, are nevertheless central to the way in which human beings understand themselves and the world around them;

180 20, 3. It makes us take a positive attitude towards dialogue with the range of human cultures and the traditions of religious belief, morality, and spirituality found in our world;

181 20, 4. It opens the way to a positive ecumenical commitment, since it values the diversity and mutuality of charisms found in the different Christian traditions.

182 20, 5. It directs our attention towards those who, though they are excluded from power and wealth, are already rich in grace.

183 21. The ministries of the Word—the ministries named before all others in the Formula of our Institute—have always been of primary importance for Jesuit priestly ministry.[20] These ministries, which take as many forms as our mission demands, require for their effectiveness profound and dedicated study, especially a thorough knowledge of Scripture and tradition, skill in preaching, and a human maturity and cultural breadth.

---

[20] *Formula* [1]; cf. Vatican Council II, *Lumen Gentium*, n. 28; *Presbyterorum Ordinis*, n. 2.

The tradition of learned priestly ministry and intellectual excellence is deeply embedded in our way of proceeding. In the exercise of Jesuit ministerial priesthood, knowledge is not power but service of the Kingdom.

184 22. Christ's own ministry of words and deeds reached its consummation in the saving mystery of his death and resurrection: so Jesuit priests join the many forms of their ministry of the Word to the Church's celebration of the Eucharist, by which Christ draws people into his Paschal Mystery. The Word of God is proclaimed in different ways, so that all may find their place at the Eucharistic and Heavenly Banquet through the mercy of God. "God desires everyone to be saved and to come to the knowledge of the truth" (1 Tim. 2:4): this is the core of the Society's apostolic preaching and the reality which the Church proclaims at the Eucharist. Here the Risen Lord bestows life and enables the Church to become what it is, the body of Christ. Here, too, this least Society of Jesus is constantly re-created by our reception of the Word of Truth and the Bread of Life.

The Stages of Ministry

185 23. Each stage in the preparation for and exercise of priestly ministry introduces a new element which modifies and strengthens a man's identity as a Jesuit: he moves, first of all, from the life of a scholastic to accepting the Church's call to ordination. Then, working through the challenges of being a young priest, he will undertake active ministries, eventually passing to the priestly apostolic life exercised in old age. Each of these stages—linked to the natural life cycle—marks, not a diminution, but a deeper entry into the experience of Jesuit priestly life: what begins as a joyful act of trust in the call of the Lord and is then lived out with generous self-giving in ministry reaches its culmination when, in old age and perhaps great weakness, the Jesuit priest fully enters Christ's Paschal Mystery. The way in which this occurs will, of course, differ for each one according to the way God leads him, but usually there are significant moments in the process.

186   24. As he moves closer to priestly ordination, a scholastic may be anxious about his worthiness and suitability as a minister of Word and Sacrament: this may be the call of Christ, but has he the personal strength to accept it and live it? He may feel uneasy about the public role in the Church which ordination will bring: in some countries where public criticism of the Church is strong, there may even be external pressure on him not to identify himself with the hierarchical Church in this way. In other situations, a scholastic may be tempted to see priesthood as a way of entering a world of clerical privilege, rather than as a path of humble service. In a very personal way, he will face the fact that priestly ministry is always exercised in the context of ordinary human weakness and the complex historical development of the Church's life. Various factors can make a scholastic question the rightness of applying for ordination, and the Society must listen very carefully to his fears and help him choose priesthood freely as the way in which his Jesuit identity is to be placed at the service of God's Kingdom and Church. This is an important moment in a scholastic's discernment of the Ignatian tradition of *sentire cum ecclesia,* which is always prompted by a deeper *sentire cum Christo*—a desire to work with Christ in preparing the way for the Kingdom and, in this way, to serve the Church that is his Body. We should remember that Ignatius made a bold act of trust in Christ's Lordship of the Church when he placed the Society at the service of the sixteenth-century papacy: it was a dramatic gesture showing that, in the Ignatian tradition, humble service of Christ is inseparable from a loving service of the Church.

187   25. The first few years after ordination present a new set of challenges: priestly ministry is itself something new; only time, pastoral experience, reflection, and help from others—both from fellow Jesuits and from the people he is called to serve—will allow the full development of confidence, wisdom, and compassion in this vocation. He is simultaneously engaged in the task of integrating himself on a permanent basis into the apostolic body of the Society; it is a time when he is particularly in need of the support of superiors and the friendship of his fellow Jesuits. There is a certain ordinariness to his life: he no longer finds himself moving through the various stages of formation and receiving, at each juncture, formal approval from superiors.

188   26. In his work as a priest, as well as in encountering the diverse and sometimes conflicting expectations of the people he seeks to serve, he will also receive the warmth of their appreciation as someone who is compassionate and is trying hard to be of service. Lay people have an important role in building up his confidence in his ministry. The young priest will surely recognize that ordination has not taken away his human weakness. Sometimes these first few years can be a time when things go wrong, and the young priest may be confronted by an unexpected lack of coherence in his life: he may realize that the peace he is ordained to give to others is not completely filling his own heart. If he comes through this—and every Jesuit, in some cases dramatically, has a strong experience of his sinfulness—it can be a profound moment of grace as he confronts the frailty within which his ministry is exercised. In the words of St. Paul, who himself had to come to this understanding, "We have this treasure in earthen vessels to show that the transcendent power belongs to God and not to us" (2 Cor. 4:7).

189   27. In the years after final vows, the ordained Jesuit experiences all the pressures and complexities of priestly ministry in the Society: he will probably be engaged in a ministry which makes constant and exhausting demands on him; in addition he may be asked to undertake other responsibilities in the Society. He may find that much of his time is taken up with work that is directly neither pastoral nor sacramental, but is a response to the demands of our corporate mission and the broad range of activities proper to our Jesuit vocation. These are not peripheral to Jesuit priesthood, but are the acts of service by which we address the apostolic needs of our world.

190   28. Like every Jesuit, he holds himself in readiness to move at the request of superiors in the service of the Gospel—a readiness that does not become easier as he gets older. These are the years when only deepening love of Christ can balance the pressures of work. The task for the Jesuit priest, in the midst of these multiple demands, is to continue a life of faith and a generous and humble service of Christ. Even if he is not primarily involved in direct pastoral service of others, it will help him to keep his priestly identity alive if he is able to minister regularly to a sacramental community; lay people, especially the poor, build the personal faith of those who serve them.

191   29. Although the typical Jesuit priest continues to be engaged in apostolic work well beyond "retirement age," there generally comes a time when such external work must cease. When this happens, he can be tempted to think that his life has lost its primary purpose; he needs to learn from the Lord that, on the contrary, he is being offered a new way of carrying out his Jesuit apostolic mission. Old age in no way diminishes his priesthood and true apostolic vitality. Even if he can only attend the Eucharist and pray privately for the Lord's blessing on the work of the Church and his fellow Jesuits, it is precisely in this that he continues to be a valued apostle and worker. Here, perhaps most of all, he is called to live a life of priestly prayer for others, in union with Christ the High Priest who has gone before us as the pioneer of our faith (Heb. 12:2). In his address to the Society towards the end of his life, when he was very frail, Father Arrupe depicted the experience of many older Jesuits:

> More than ever, I now find myself in the hands of God. This is what I wanted all my life from my youth. And this is still the one thing I want. But now there is a difference: the initiative is entirely with God. It is indeed a profound spiritual experience to know and feel myself so totally in his hands.[21]

192   30. Finally, we ask all Jesuit priests to have confidence in the charisms of their ministry, and we also ask all brothers and scholastics to have confidence in the charisms which they receive: these are complementary gifts of the Spirit by which the Society is able to serve in the name of Christ. We ask for God's blessing on all that we do.

Recommendation to Father General

193   31. GC 34, while in full accord with the Society's charism and its desire to be available for mission, nevertheless firmly restates the Society's tradition to resist, insofar as is compatible with obedience, nominations to the episcopacy. For St. Ignatius this principle was vital for the mission and well-being of "this least Society" and was not contradictory to his desire to be available for mission. Jesuits were to serve the Church and the Supreme Pontiff, but not as bishops.[22] To clarify this issue, the general congregation urges Father General to continue in

---

[21] Pedro Arrupe, Message to the Society, 3 September 1983, *AR* 18 (1983): p. 987.

[22] *Const.* [817f.].

dialogue with the Holy See on this matter and, if it would be useful, to issue as a result further clear norms to be followed by any Jesuit informed that he is being considered as a candidate for the episcopacy.

DECREE SEVEN

THE JESUIT BROTHER

Introduction

194   1. The "Proposals" of the Loyola Symposium[1] together with a substantial number of postulates from provinces have manifested the Society's desire to probe more deeply into the meaning and import of statements of recent general congregations which describe the vocation and mission of the brother within the body of the Society.[2]

195   Responding to this desire, General Congregation 34 wishes to depict the role of the brother in a way that is more in accord with present reality, but always consistent with the description of the identity of a Jesuit given by Decree 2 of GC 32. In this way we intend to join fidelity to our origins with a renewal appropriate to the present moment.[3]

Identity

196   2. The Jesuit brother is a man who has accepted the call of the Father to be a "companion of Jesus." By

---

[1] 12–24 June 1994; cf. *AR* 21 (1994): pp. 54–59.

[2] GC 32, D 7; GC 32, D 8; GC 33, D 1, nn. 72–76.

[3] Cf. Vatican Council II, *Perfectæ Caritatis*, n. 2; Congregation for Religious and Secular Institutes and Congregation for Bishops, *Mutuæ Relationes*, n. 11, *AAS* 70 (1978): p. 480.

his vows he consecrates his life freely to help the mission common to the apostolic, religious, and priestly body of the Society: "the service of the faith of which the promotion of justice is an absolute requirement."[4]

197   3.   From the very beginning of his conversion, Ignatius felt called to "help others," to give himself entirely to the service of "the Eternal King and Lord of all."[5] The group of companions, "friends in the Lord," were to find in their discernment how they were to live their apostolic vocation in the Church: by founding a religious order.

198   At that decisive moment, the apostolic experience of Ignatius and his companions was already linked to the exercise of priestly ministry. Their experience was articulated in the Formula of the Institute, which enumerates the ministries they would perform to fulfill the specific purpose of the new order: "to serve the Lord alone and the Church, his Spouse, under the Roman Pontiff, the Vicar of Christ on earth."[6]

199   But the mobility which apostolic universality demanded, the multiplicity of pastoral ministries, and especially the need for help in carrying out the mission led Ignatius to accept into the body of the Society a diversity of members, priests and brothers, all of whom would share the same vocation and contribute to the one mission.

200   4.   From its beginnings the Society has conceived of itself as a universal "body." This Pauline metaphor (cf. 1 Cor. 12, 12ff.), much loved by St. Ignatius and used frequently in the Constitutions to refer to the entire Society, expresses his idea of our vocation as both one and diverse.

---

[4] GC 32, D 4, n. 2.

[5] Cf. *SpEx* [95].

[6] *Formula* [3].

201   All members of the Society, in a variety of social and cultural situations, have been graced with the same call to follow Jesus poor and humble. We have all heard the same invitation to serve him in his Church; we have all been sent on the same mission.

202   At the same time, Ignatius, "rejecting all egalitarianism and all uniformity . . . believed deeply in the diversity of vocations, which is based on the fact that God calls each one by name. It is only in this spirit of openness and acceptance that the various gifts which together make up the Society can blossom."[7] For this reason Ignatius considered grades in the Society as different ways of being incorporated into the one body and fulfilling one and the same mission, without implying in any way differences of perfection or merit in the divine service.[8] So "the apostolic body of the Society is modeled, like that of the apostles, on union in diversity . . . a *diversity united by the bond of charity*."[9]

203   5.   Recent general congregations, in affirming the unity of vocation in the Society, have reminded us of the need to examine our attitudes so that diversity is not an obstacle to being truly "united, heart and soul" (Acts 4:32). This congregation repeats that call to make the integration of all Jesuits into the one body of the Society more complete and more effective everywhere. We must exert ourselves to discover the ways in which our communities and our apostolic activities, the places we live and work as priests and brothers, can express simply and transparently the oneness of vocation and mission in the Society.

---

[7] Peter-Hans Kolvenbach, Address to the First Congregation of Provincials, *AR* 20 [1990]: p. 486.

[8] Cf. *Examen* [13].

[9] Peter-Hans Kolvenbach, S.J., "The Vocation and Mission of the Jesuit Brother," Loyola Symposium, *CIS*, n. 78 (1995), p. 12, citing *Const.* [624].

204   6.   Brothers, in the same way as priests, are integrated into the Society by reason of the one common call of the Lord to follow him in living out the evangelical radicality of religious life. But a vocation to religious life is distinct from a vocation to priesthood. "In some ways the religious brother embodies religious life in its essence, and so is able to illustrate that life with particular clarity."[10]

205   Therefore, the first and most important contribution of a brother is the gift of his own self, offered freely in service to the Lord.[11] As a consequence, through a life that is manifestly religious, he offers a prophetic witness, in the Church and in the Society, to the world of today.

Mission

206   7.   The brother lives his religious vocation as one "sent." He is essentially a man with a mission which he receives ultimately from Christ himself, through his superiors.[12] He carries out this mission as a member of an apostolic body completely dedicated "with God's grace not only to the salvation and perfection of the members' own souls, but also with that same grace to labor strenuously in giving aid towards the salvation and perfection of the souls of others."[13]

207   As members of the same body, brothers share in and contribute to the one apostolic vocation through the personal call of the Spirit, and enrich the mission of the Society by their participation in what St. Paul called "the priestly service of the Gospel of God" (Rom. 15:16).

---

[10] Ibid., Preface, p. 3.

[11] Cf. Pedro Arrupe, "Contribution of Jesuit Brothers to the Apostolic Community of the Society," *AR* 27 (1978): p. 381.

[12] Cf. GC 32, D 2, n. 14.

[13] *Examen* [3].

208   The specific missions which brothers can be given include many of the functions and ministries which the Formula of the Institute enumerates as proper to the Society.

209   These activities carried out by the first companions continue to inspire the Society today as well. GC 31 already affirmed that the apostolic activity of brothers is defined by those same principles which define the apostolate of the whole Society: attention to the greater service of God and the universal good.[14]

210   Today the Society describes our Jesuit identity in terms of the need "to engage, under the standard of the Cross, in the crucial struggle of our time: the struggle for faith and that struggle for justice which it includes."[15] Brothers, then, are intimately involved in every apostolic task of the Society through which this mission is carried out; they contribute to every kind of material and technical work at the service of the apostolate and of the body of the Society, and to the explicit proclamation of Jesus through spiritual help and conversation, the Spiritual Exercises, catechesis and teaching. They make themselves available to be sent to those who experience discrimination, to those deprived of dignity, to those without voice or power, to those searching for the meaning of their existence, to those whose faith is failing, to those who want to be told the Good News of Jesus, as well as to the communities and works which need their help in order to carry out the mission of the Society.

211   8.   The rich history of brother saints and blessed and the multiplicity of tasks and ministries in which brothers have been and are engaged throughout the world clearly show the variety and complementarity which

---

[14] Cf. GC 31, D 7, n. 2.

[15] GC 32, D 2, n. 2.

characterize the apostolic mission of the brother in the Society.

212   It is appropriate that, along with the figure of brothers like Alphonsus Rodríguez and Francisco Gárate, who achieved sanctity in domestic tasks, we make known the lives of others like James Kisai, Dominic Collins, and Nicholas Owen, who labored with dedication and generosity in the external ministries of the Society even to the surrender of their very lives. This will contribute to a more comprehensive image of the brother's vocation and can attract new vocations.

Communion

213   9. There have been significant advances since GC 31 in the integration and participation of brothers in the life and apostolic mission of the Society. Their formation has improved, they have been given responsibilities in important works and apostolic activities, they have been appointed to positions such as community and province consultors. Based on the positive results of these experiences, GC 34 encourages the whole Society to continue to move in the same direction: it is the best way to express the unity of vocation and mission in the body of the Society.

214   10. In some places the full realization of this integration still meets with resistance. Attitudes persist among us which call for conversion, and there is need for a greater esteem and appreciation of the brother's vocation; attitudes and sociocultural prejudices alien to the Gospel must not color mutual relations within the Society.

215   11. If everyone—priests, brothers, and scholastics— shares in all aspects of community life, including faith, domestic tasks, relaxation, prayer, apostolic discernment, the Eucharist, and the Spiritual Exercises, we will truly become "friends in the Lord." This sharing of life will help to build up communities of shared responsibility in our common following of Jesus, and complementarity in the one mission. To make this sharing a reality among us, we need human and spiritual maturity and a better formation in interpersonal communication.

216   12. Since the term "temporal coadjutor" is no longer in common use among us, GC 34 directs that in the future, in our official or other texts, only the term "brother" or "Jesuit brother" should be used, and not the term "temporal coadjutor."

217   13. The congregation asks Father General, if he judges it helpful, to set up an office (secretariat) or appoint a priest or brother (counselor) to be in charge of all matters related to brothers, for a more effective implementation of what is prescribed in this decree and in those of previous general congregations.

Formation

218   14. A reduced number of vocations ought not to result in lowered standards for admission to the novitiate. Those admitted to be brothers must be men of faith, committed to service, sufficiently mature, suited to life in community, and capable of being integrated into the body and mission of the Society.

219   Where it is deemed necessary, prenovitiate programs are to be established which can help candidates achieve the level necessary to enter the novitiate.

220   15. GC 34 believes it may be helpful that provinces sometimes admit candidates to the grade of *Indifferent* so that, in the course of the novitiate, they can better discern their vocation to priesthood or brotherhood.

221   16. Those responsible for the formation of brothers should help them to focus their deepest desires, and to fix firmly in their hearts an appreciation of their vocation, a will to serve, and an enthusiasm for the mission of the Society.

222   17. Well-structured formation programs are to be established for Jesuit brothers, in order to prepare them adequately for life, service, and social integration within the Society. Such programs are to include the human, communitarian, spiritual, theological, pastoral, and professional dimensions. Some of those with the requisite qualities are to be prepared to work as province vocation promoters and *formatores*. When possible, for the sake of greater integration, brothers in formation are to live in the same communities as scholastics. Provincials are to follow the development of formation programs closely, applying these norms with suitable flexibility.

223   18. Where a single province cannot manage such a program either because of a lack of resources or a reduced number of brothers, interprovincial or even interassistancy collaboration is recommended.

224   19. Brothers must have the opportunity to learn a foreign language, in accord with the recommendations of this general congregation found in the decree "Interprovincial and Supraprovincial Cooperation."[16] This will enable better communication with companions from other regions and allow greater availability for certain international missions.

225   20. To be effective in mission, all Jesuits need to be well informed in all that pertains to their apostolic work; they also need to be supported in their faith life. Consequently, formed brothers are encouraged to attend programs of ongoing formation in spiritual and psychological renewal and in pastoral and professional development.

---

[16] GC 34, D 21, n. 10.

Conclusion

226   21. GC 34 has introduced important changes in our law to achieve more effectively the integration and participation of brothers in the common vocation and mission of the Society. Among these changes, we note the following:

- a normative formulation of one specific vocation and mission: NC 6, §1, 1°-3°;
- eliminating the title "temporal coadjutor" in everyday language and in future official documents: NC 326, §4;
- special preparation for entrance into the novitiate, when this is necessary: NC 25, §2a;
- ordinarily, novitiate in common with scholastics: NC 43, §1;
- common formation in the novitiate for those aspects of our vocation which are common; separate formation for those which are distinct: NC 48, §§2f.;
- abolishing the rule that forbids additional education after entrance into the Society, and new rules about studies: Examen [117]; NC 81, §3; 83, §3; 98; 243, §2f.;
- modification of those passages in the Examen and the *Constitutions* that refer to tertianship only for scholastics: Examen [119], *Const.* [514, 516];
- encouraging communities that include priests, brothers, and scholastics in order to promote fraternal union and union in the apostolic mission: NC 326, §§ 3, 4c;
- granting passive voice for election as electors in a general congregation: GC 34, Decree 23, A. n. 2; this will be included in the revision of the

Formulas for General and Province Congregations;

- abolishing the limitation on the number of brothers with final vows who can take part in a province congregation: implicitly in GC 34, D 23, D, n. 4; this will be included in the revision of the Formula for a Province Congregation.

227   22. At the same time we wish to recall that if true *communion* is to be fostered among all members of the Society, the first and most necessary requirement is an attitude of mind and heart which esteems and welcomes each Jesuit as a brother and friend in the Lord: "What helps most . . . towards this end must be, more than any exterior constitution, the interior law of love and charity which the Holy Spirit writes and engraves in our hearts."[17]

---

[17] *Const.* [134].

DECREE EIGHT

CHASTITY IN THE SOCIETY OF JESUS

Introduction

228   1. In the course of the present century, in many parts of the world, the meaning of sexuality within human relationships has undergone significant change. Increasingly, men and women experience their sexuality as a gift which enables them to express intimate love and commitment. For many of them, sexuality is understood as part of the "sacrament of marriage" by which the love of God is experienced within their marital love for one another. At the same time, these decades have brought awareness of structural injustices imposed on women, as well as some of the distortions, exploitations, and abuses that have accompanied changing gender roles and expressions of sexuality. Moreover, contemporary advertising and entertainment have given sexual expression an unprecedented centrality within various cultures. These last few decades have been labeled "the sexual revolution."

229   2. During this same time period, celibacy has come under heavy criticism from within as well as from outside the Church. Thousands have left religious life or active priestly ministry to enter into marriage. The media have carried sensational stories of infidelity and abuse.

From all over the world, questions and doubts are posed about the meaning and the value of priestly or religious chastity.

230 3. General Congregation 34 wishes to address these questions, to say something directly and honestly about the meaning of chastity in Jesuit life and our resolve to continue to support it. We do not publish this decree because we judge that infidelity in chastity is widespread within the Society of Jesus. On the contrary, we are convinced that, despite the challenges and testing of these years, fidelity in chastity characterizes the life of the Society today as it has characterized it in the past, by the gracious goodness of God. This conviction is grounded on the extensive knowledge of their companions possessed by members assembled here from each province of the Society, confirmed by the congregation's lengthy examination of the present state of the Society. It is this graced fidelity that we hope to strengthen and confirm in the face of so many cultural forces that contradict it.

231 4. The purpose of this decree, then, is to give an authoritative answer to the following question: What is the chastity that a Jesuit vows and how can the Society of Jesus continue to foster it in its integrity?

The Call to Chastity

232 5. Ignatius understood the Society of Jesus to be rooted in a fundamental detachment and a determination to serve God totally.[1] The Society was to be one realization of the apostolic life: "Lord, we have left all things and have followed you" (cf. Luke 18:28). This renunciation for the Jesuit comprises "home or wife or

---

[1] *Examen* [53]: "Those founders' mind was that those received into [this Society] should be persons already detached from the world and determined to serve God totally."

brothers or parents or children for the sake of the Kingdom of heaven" (Luke 18:29). A deeply personal love makes it possible to follow Christ in this way, a love that chooses him in place of all that is renounced.[2] When a Jesuit speaks of this, he is speaking of his vow of chastity—a chastity that grace has made possible and that has been chosen, as was that of Jesus, to serve in mission the Kingdom of heaven.

233   6.   To the ridicule of some and the puzzlement of many, Ignatius maintained that a Jesuit is to strive to imitate in his chastity the purity of the angels.[3] But this does not mean that he is to act as if he regretted his body. He is rather called to embody in his life that singleness of vision and readiness for mission which is the Ignatian understanding of the angels. They were for Ignatius "the ministering spirits sent to serve." They lived in immediate familiarity with God, and they served as God's ministers in drawing human beings to himself.[4] In

---

[2] The Ignatian commentary upon Matt. 19:29 and Luke 18:30 is very strong, describing the Jesuit as "one who is dead to the world and to self-love and who lives only for Christ our Lord, having Him in place of *[en lugar de]* fathers or   brothers or of all things" (*Examen*, [61]).

[3] *Const*. [547].

[4] *SpEx* [329, 331, 335]; cf. *SpEx* [60]; OC [681], [683f.]: *Const.* [813]. This interpretation of the Ignatian understanding of the imitation of "angelic purity" in a chastity that unites singleness of heart in prayer and ministry is confirmed by the remarkable statement of Peter Ribadeneira: "Oyle dezir que quería haverse con los próximos como los ángeles para con nosotros, en dos cosas: una, en no faltar de su parte, dando las ayudas possibles, por quitarles de todo mal, etiam espiritual; 2o, en no se pertubar de cosa alguna por lo que les acaesciesse (como los ángeles no dexan de ver y gozar a Dios), ni contristarse en manera que perdiesse nada de su devoción. Dezía también que, aunque Dios destruyese toda la Compañía, él no pensava contristarse se en modo que perdiesse nada de sudevoción para con Dios" (Peter Ribadeneira, "Dichos y Hechos de N. P. Ignacio," MHSI, vol. 73, MI, *FontNarr,* II, 476). For the tradition behind this interpretation of "angelic purity," see the Carthusian Ludolph of Saxony, *Vita Jesu Christi,*

his chastity a Jesuit endeavors to realize in his actions and in his thoughts an analogous, undeflected union with God in prayer and ministry.

234   7. By the vow of chastity, then, a Jesuit is consecrated and united to God precisely as God is "laboring in all things" for the salvation of human beings.[5] Chastity is first of all his gracious gift, calling the Jesuit to a discipleship and renunciation that can free his heart from the natural concern for an exclusive relationship and draw it into the universal charity of God towards all men and women.[6] It is a gift to be, in this way, configured to Christ.

The Apostolic Character of Chastity

235   8. This life of chastity consecrated to God offers a living witness that Christ can engage human beings in so comprehensive a love and a prophetic reminder that we were created finally for that future life with God in which the children of the resurrection "will neither marry nor give in marriage" (Luke 20:34-36). In this way, living unmarried for the sake of the Kingdom of heaven preaches the Gospel in deeds rather than words. It can

---

ed. Rigollot (Paris, 1878), Pars I, caput xxii, sectio 6, and II, vi. Cited and translated by Joseph F. Conwell, S.J., "Living and Dying in the Society of Jesus or Endeavoring to Imitate Angelic Purity," *Studies in the Spirituality of Jesuits* 12, n. 3 (May 1980): pp. 7f.

[5] *SpEx* [236].

[6] Cf. GC 31, D 16, n. 3; *SpEx* [236]. The vow of chastity as understood here corresponds to the way it was expressed in the *Quinque Capitula* of 1539 and the Formula of the Institute of 1540—as the total giving of oneself to God's call. Only in the later version of the Formula, that of 1550, were the other vows added to the initial sentence. See Antonio M. de Aldama, S.J., *The Formula of the Institute: Notes for a Commentary*, trans. Ignacio Echániz (Rome: CIS, 1990), pp. 2f., 41. The phrase "exclusive human relationships" denotes those relationships that are so centered in themselves that they exclude or impede a sharing of this love with others.

disclose that God and the Kingdom of God—both as the passion and the hope of a person's life—can be absolute, prevailing in attraction over all other human values. For this reason, such a life has been seen in the Church throughout its history as a most suitable means "for religious to spend themselves readily in God's service and in works of the apostolate."[7]

236   9.   Accordingly, in our Society not only poverty and obedience but also chastity is essentially apostolic. It is not understood by Jesuits as directed exclusively to their personal sanctification, but as calling them to be one with Christ in labor for the salvation of the human race.[8] According to the whole intent of our Institute, we embrace apostolic chastity as a special source of spiritual fruitfulness in the world, as a means for a more prompt love and a more total apostolic availability towards all men and women.[9] That is why the chastity of Jesuits does not compete with marriage, but rather reinforces its value. Both point to a love and a fidelity which is deeper than sexual expression and of which Christian marriage and religious chastity are divergent and sacred realizations. Few are called to the life of a Jesuit, but for the man who is called, chastity only makes sense as a means to a greater love, to a more authentic apostolic charity.

237   10.   This may be especially relevant today, when so many tend to put whole classes of human beings beyond the horizons of their concerns, while at the same time identifying love with eroticism and hedonism and exploiting such an identification to fuel financial gain

---

[7] Vatican Council II, *Perfectœ Caritatis*, n. 12. Cf. *Presbyterorum Ordinis*, n. 16 and GC 31, D 16, nn. 3, 4.

[8] For this conjunction between the commitment to the apostolic life and to personal sanctification in "the same [grace]," cf. *Examen* [3]. The vows are then introduced as means to that end [4].

[9] GC 31, D 16, n. 4.

and human degradation. A love that is warmly human yet freely offered to all, especially to the poor and the marginalized, can be a powerful sign leading people to Christ, who came to show us what love really is, that God is love.[10]

238   11. Because of his chastity, a Jesuit can live in radical apostolic availability. His assignments always have something of the provisional about them; he must remain open to the summons of obedience to another place, to another task. This detachment from *stabilitas,* from the definition of himself within a single family or extended set of relatives or even a particular church, culture, and place, characterizes a Jesuit. It is constitutive of his obedience, and it is his remaining celibate for the Kingdom of God that makes such obedience for mission possible. If this apostolic availability is not to cripple his affectivity, it is only because his chastity embodies a contemplative love that includes all human beings and makes the Jesuit open and able to find God everywhere.

239   12. To God, then, and to his world, Jesuits have chosen to offer in union with Christ the sincere, simple, and demanding life of consecrated chastity.[11]

The Matter and Meaning of the Vow of Chastity

240   13. Because of the confusion in current times, we must be as clear as possible about the meaning of this vow if we are to observe it as part of the shared meaning of our lives. It arises from and is based upon a conscious and free decision under grace.[12] By his vow of chastity, a Jesuit devotes himself to the Lord and to his service in such a unique love that it excludes marriage

---

[10] GC 32, D 2, n. 26.

[11] GC 31, D 16, n. 2.

[12] GC 31, D 16, n. 6.

and any other exclusive human relationship, as well as the genital expression and gratification of his sexuality. Thus the vow entails the obligation of complete continence in celibacy for the sake of the Kingdom of heaven.[13] Following the evangelical counsel of chastity, the Jesuit aspires to deepen his familiarity with God, his configuration to Christ, his companionship with his brother Jesuits, his service to others, and at the same time to grow in his personal maturity and capacity to love. The witness of many Jesuits confirms that there is a deep happiness in such a life of personal love and service.

The Cost of This Discipleship

241   14. A Jesuit should not deceive himself about the cost of such a decision. It involves renunciation of conjugal intimacy, denial of the very human desire for his own children, and turning away from a unique affective bonding that is one of life's richest experiences and a normal condition for human growth. He surrenders the joys of belonging to and living within his own family. If he did not sometimes feel the painful loss of some of humanity's most lovely and most tender joys, he would be less than human. Other joys, even deeper joys, will enter his life, but they cannot remove all sense of void.

242   15. Through his chastity, then, the Jesuit lives in some solitude—not loneliness, but solitude. There will be times when this solitude will become a desert, as he experiences little or no satisfaction or support in what is around him; at other times, it may even become the cross, the experience of futility, anguish and death.[14]

243   16. Throughout his life a Jesuit will give his time and his talents to others without thought of recompense.

---

[13] CIC 599.

[14] GC 31, D 16, n. 5.

He does not build his own business or his own career, because he does not build his own home and family. His chastity has made it possible for him to grow in his poverty. At the end of his life, through his vow of chastity, he will have become poor in a way that his previous talents and education and energies made impossible. Now all of these belong to yesterday; they have been spent for others. He has finally become poor as did Christ, who, "although he was rich, made himself poor for our sakes" (2 Cor. 8:9).[15] He has become a man who possesses neither family nor property, has built up nothing for himself, and looks to God for the definition of his life. This poverty that flows from his chastity is not the destruction of his Jesuit life; in many ways it is its completion and fulfillment.[16] But he should not disguise the cost of such a life.

Normative Principles and Guidelines

244   17. **Prenote:** While many of the constitutive elements of being a Jesuit have been treated elsewhere, they give indispensable support to a life of chastity and will be included here so that Jesuit life and its requirements can be seen as an organic unity.

---

[15] Ignatius alludes to this text in his letter to Peter Contarini (August 1537), OC [631f.].

[16] Jesuits have found an eloquent expression of this in the farewell message of Father Pedro Arrupe to the Society: "How I wish I were in a better condition for this meeting with you. As you see, I cannot even address you directly. But my general assistants have grasped what I want to say to each one. More than ever, I now find myself in the hands of God. This is what I have wanted all my life, from my youth. And this is still the one thing I want. But now there is a difference: the initiative is entirely with God. It is indeed a profound spiritual experience to know and feel myself so totally in his hands" (*AR* 18 [1983]: pp. 986f.)

245   18. I.   The *familiarity with God* and the friendship with Christ that lie at the origins of his vocation sustain a Jesuit in his fidelity. It was this love that first drew him to such a life; the commitments of chastity cannot continue or flourish without its continual growth. This conscious, loving union with God is prayer, whether at formal moments of explicit focus or as the atmosphere that permeates each day.

Guidelines

246   19.   [1] This should be a principal concern of all Jesuits: to seek the conscious presence of the Lord in such private prayer as meditation, contemplation, and the examination of conscience and in such community prayer as the liturgy of the hours, communal discernment, and group spontaneous prayer. In their manifold occupations, Jesuits can learn to reverence the divine presence as the horizon in which they live, to apprehend the immanent providence of God that draws them into its own working for the salvation of human beings, and to hold on to God as the purpose that energizes their work—learning thus to find God in all things. The celebration of the Eucharist—frequently together as a community—ought to be central to such a life, and the sacrament of reconciliation ought to exercise a significant influence over it. Annually, they are to commit themselves conscientiously to making the Spiritual Exercises. All of these components of Jesuit life flow from the fundamental directive of the Formula of the Institute: Let the one who wishes to live our life "take care, as long as he lives, first of all, to keep before his eyes God."[17]

247   20.   [2] From experience, the Society has learned that pivotal to its fidelity in chastity has been the strong though humble and simple devotion to the Bless-

---

[17] *Formula* [3].

ed Virgin that has flourished among us since the time of St. Ignatius.[18]

248   21. II. *Community life* figures importantly here. It is not that the community compensates for a wife and children, but rather that it can and does support a life that is lived in their denial. Through the many forms of their mutual presence to one another and their investment of themselves in one another's lives, Jesuits mediate to each other the presence of that Lord to whom they have offered themselves through their vow of chastity. It is this mediation, this interchange that makes their community religious. The continual and vital commitment of Jesuits to one another is a condition for a concomitant growth in chastity.[19]

249   Thus the apostolic chastity of a Jesuit cannot be lived in an aloof withdrawal from others. As a true "gift from above," apostolic chastity should lead to communion both with one's brother Jesuits and with the people we serve. It is sad if chastity is so corrupted that it leads only to a self-enclosed bachelorhood.[20] Community life, then, must be not only a support but also the privileged context for living a wholesome and humane chastity. When community life is strong in its support and truthful in its challenge, then Jesuits are inspired through their chastity to make visible the God who labors to help others. It is important both to appreciate and to develop the strong bond between apostolic chastity and apostolic community.

Guidelines

250   22.   [3] Our houses are to be communities where the life of prayer and the interchange with one

---

[18] For the radical foundation of this experience of the Society in the prior experience of Ignatius himself, see *Autobiography* [10].

[19] GC 32, D 16, n. 7b.

[20] *SpEx* [184].

another of religious values habitually characterize daily life. There should be periods of the day and of the week in which the members of the community meet for prayer, recreation, and meals. It is also important that there should be longer periods of recollection and prayer during the year in which Jesuits in the community share with one another the religious realities and mission by which they live. In a manner appropriate to the Society, liturgy ought to mark the rhythm of the Jesuit community, as it is to characterize any vital Christian community. Each of its members is called by the Society today to take the responsibility to foster such a community.[21]

251 23. [4] These communities should embody a deeply Christian hospitality "according to the custom of different places" so that we share what we have and what we are with men and women to whom we are related in friendship or committed in our apostolate. On the other hand, Jesuits need a certain privacy in special parts of the house. Since the customs of various cultures differ so radically, it is left to province government to determine what is appropriate in this matter. In general, it can be said that these arrangements are to be such as to obviate any ambiguity that could occasion misinterpretations.[22]

252 24. III. The *life of ministry* also strengthens that attachment to the Lord which is the source of chastity. There is a consciousness of Christ in ministry that is not available to the Jesuit outside this apostolic experience, the Christ to whom he is united as the instrument wielded by the divine hand.[23] It is also the same grace by which Jesuits move in fidelity and growth towards God

---

[21] For a full description of the Jesuit community as well as a description of the process by which one is built, cf. GC 32, D 11.

[22] CIC 667, 1.

[23] *Const.* [813].

as that by which "they labor in giving aid towards the
salvation and perfection of the souls of their fellow men
and women."[24] Furthermore, chastity belongs essentially
to our chosen way of relating to others. The sense of
meaning and the joy that come from apostolic experience in turn sustain the significance of the chastity that
made this apostolic life possible. This can be especially
true when ministry is realized within the world of the
oppressed and of the poor. But in every case, this mutual support between Jesuit chastity and ministerial
commitments is only possible if Jesuits minister gratu-
itously and without orienting this pastoral work to their
own enhancement.

Guidelines

253   25.   [5] The Society expects from every Jesuit
not only fidelity to his vows but the normal public signs
of this fidelity. Jesuits should embody in their ministry
and in their lives an unequivocal "professional" conduct
(modestia) that manifests their commitments as priests
and as religious.[25] Their manner of proceeding—both as
a community and as individuals—ought to preclude any
ambiguity about their lives, enabling those to whom they

---

[24] *Const.* [3].

[25] A "professional" relationship implies much more than a
merely contractual or even business relationship in that, unlike these
latter, it is conducted not between equals but between two unequal
parties, one of whom (the professional) has expertise and experience
in the relevant area, while the other (the client) is ignorant in this area
and requires access to professional skills and acumen. The professional to this degree is, quite legitimately, in a position of power and
authority. To act "professionally" involves not only making one's
expertise available but also not abusing the power relationship to
manipulate the client. It requires objectivity, impartiality, sensitivity,
and delicacy both in making the expertise available and in empower-
ing the client to pursue his or her interest, rather than inducing in the
client a dependence on the professional.

minister to rely instinctively upon their disinterestedness and fidelity.

254   26.   [6] It is especially important that those in ministries like spiritual direction, counseling, or therapy keep appropriate "professional" boundaries, aware of the possibility of affective transference and countertransference, and resistant to confusing such ministerial relationships with those of intimate friendship.[26]

255   27.   [7] The differences among particular cultures and attitudes require that Jesuits be especially sensitive in this area. Those traveling abroad are to attend carefully to the local feelings and attitudes concerning the relations between women and men. It would be unreasonable for traveling Jesuits to expect local people to view their conduct as it would be understood in their own native land. Failure to take this into account can result in a witness contrary to the very gospel values they have given their lives to proclaim.

256   28. IV. *Discernment and self-discipline* are imperative for fidelity in chastity. Contemporary popular culture is heavily influenced by commercial propaganda, advertising, and the lucrative exploitation of sexual sensibilities for financial gain. Excessive passive entertainment can become addictive and debilitating. In this area, a Jesuit must be critically aware. The directions of Ignatius and the experience of the Society over the past centuries emphasize that a certain sober realism, discernment, and abnegation are necessary to deal with the many influences that enter into a Jesuit's life. This need for discipline of the body and of the mind has for millennia been recognized in many spiritual traditions, and Jesuits can learn much from these spiritual masters to

---

[26] Cf. Pedro Arrupe, "Our Way of Proceeding," *AR* 17 (1979): pp. 718ff. Father Arrupe recalled that the first Jesuits seem to have showed in their ministry a special delicacy in the matter of chastity; their circumspection and their prudence in this area became proverbial.

discipline and integrate the body and the mind into a life of prayer and service.

Guidelines

257   29.   [8] Religious discretion is appropriately brought to bear on every element in Jesuit life, and this entails the practice of the examination of conscience, mortification, and custody of the senses. Concretely, a Jesuit ought to weigh the influences he admits into his life through entertainment, television, videos, reading, recreation, and travel as well as through personal relationships. To live an integral life, one must ask realistically whether this or that particular influence or practice strengthens or weakens a life of fidelity in chastity and its public witness.[27] Furthermore, a Jesuit should not be ashamed to honestly notice the temptations and desires that would prompt him to behavior incongruent with his commitments. Instead, he ought to seek help in dealing with these desires and inclinations.

258   30.   [9] Everyone should be aware that any failure in living faithfully the vow of chastity or any ambiguous relationships can afflict others cruelly, both spiritually and psychologically. Besides the issue of serious sin, such behavior can compromise the credibility of the Society within a culture that is skeptical about any fidelity in chastity and seriously injure its apostolic effectiveness.

259   31. V. *Affective Maturation:* Since grace presupposes nature, spiritual maturation goes hand in hand with an adequate affective maturation. Affective matura-

---

[27] Certain directions from the Spiritual Exercises could profitably be adapted and brought to bear to aid a decision to put order into the manifold cultural influences that surround a Jesuit if and when those influences become disordered. For example, the "Rules for Ordering Oneself in the Matter of Eating" [210-17], which Ignatius places within the Third Week, and "The First Method of Prayer" as this relates to the "five senses of the body" [238-48].

tion means the development and the integration of all the forces and emotions of the human personality; it embraces more than just the sexual, but it presents a special challenge to a life with the renunciations that our chastity involves. The process of affective maturation for the individual Jesuit takes place within the context of his human relationships. It occurs in and through all phases of life, but especially at moments of crisis.

Guidelines

260   32.   [10] The individual Jesuit must recognize, first of all, that under grace he bears the responsibility for his own human growth. It is he above all who must see that his life is characterized by that equilibrium which empowers him to remain conscious of his feelings and in contact with the deepest stirrings of his motivations and human powers. With discernment he must learn to differentiate among the "motions" within his life, to follow in the direction of those that move him towards God and to deny satisfaction to those that do not.[28] Second, he should not attempt to isolate himself from the challenges and crises of life, but to deal with these with such honesty that he finds his relationship with God and his own self-acceptance deepened.[29] Third, he ought to see to it that he can give both his feelings and his creativity appropriate expression, and he is to develop an educated sensibility for the humane achievements of life that are found in the arts, literature, music, and so forth. Fourth, he must avoid a style of life and of work that puts him under excessive affective stress or that necessitates a continual suppression of his

---

[28] *Const.* [260]; *SpEx* [331-36].

[29] See, for example, the petition for grace in the First Week of the Exercises, in which the exercitants pray for the understanding of their own internal disorder [63], and also the directions for the repetition, that one returns in prayer to those areas in which one has found the greatest desolation as well as the greatest consolation [62].

own feelings and leads eventually to affective regression, "burn-out," or some kind of psychic disturbance. Last and most important, friendships should be very much part of his life. The ability to form mature friendships with other Jesuits and with women and men who are not Jesuits, as well as the capacity to collaborate in equality with others, is a sign of affective maturity. Friendships can not only support a life of dedicated chastity but can also deepen the affective relationship with God that chastity embodies.

261   33.   [11] Spiritual direction is an indispensable aid towards spiritual and affective maturation. Spiritual directors can help those being directed to bring affective experiences into these conversations for an appreciation and discernment of their meaning. But a spiritual director must not confuse the ministry of spiritual direction with psychological counseling or therapy. If psychological problems emerge, the directee is to be recommended to a counselor, psychologist, or psychiatrist.

262   34.   [12] Superiors can contribute significantly to the affective growth of those whom they serve. They can further in their communities an atmosphere of understanding and of friendship among its members. On the other hand, they should not shrink from the more unpleasant responsibilities of their office: to set boundaries, to challenge their brothers to a more integral Jesuit life, and to insist that the community give unequivocal witness to its vowed life. As a matter of fact, maturation is often furthered more by this kind of challenge than by a permissiveness that looks for peace at all costs.

263   35. VI. The *Account of Conscience and Spiritual Direction* have been stressed in recent documents of the Society as critical for our religious life. They take on additional importance precisely in their contribution to the growth of Jesuits in chastity.

Guidelines

264 36. [13] Superiors should recognize as a principal task the fostering of mutual confidence and openness between their companions in the Society and themselves. This contributes wonderfully to the honesty and vitality of the account of conscience, the frankness of its interchange and the help that it can offer every Jesuit.

265 37. [14] It is very important that spiritual directors are given appropriate training, especially those that are *formatores*. This is additionally necessary today because of contemporary influences and issues regarding affective maturity and sexuality.

266 38. [15] Every Jesuit must realistically recognize that he will be as effective in helping others to lead a chaste life as he himself is faithful in leading such a life with integrity and is aware of his own inner inclinations, passions, anxieties, and emotions. Further, chastity is a shared responsibility of all Jesuits to safeguard seriously and to further through their mutual fraternal support and friendships as well as through the aid they offer superiors in their care for their companions and for the Society.

267 39. VII. *Admission and Dismissal.* Before admission into the novitiate—as later during the years of formation—the Society should attempt to examine realistically whether the candidate has the charism and character for this kind of life with its demands for celibate chastity. An affective maturation in the Society is only possible when a man possesses an adequate basic disposition, both spiritual and affective. While superiors carry grave responsibilities before God for the internal life of the Society and its public credibility, as well as for those who will be affected by the pastoral ministry of its members, their ability to carry out these responsibilities depends upon the willingness of both candidates and their fellow Jesuits to be open with them about whatever difficulties they have. While their responsibilities call them to accompany their fellow Jesuits in their spiritual journey with kindness blended with firmness, superiors can only make their best efforts, and these in the light of the knowledge they possess.

268   40. But superiors can find decisions about admission and dismissal deeply troubling, especially if they are unaware of the norms of the Society or if the rules given for their application are ambiguous and they feel alone in their difficult decision. To formulate such norms remains the office of the ordinary government of the Society, and their prudent application will "depend upon many particular circumstances of persons, times, and places," as Ignatius insisted.[30] In general, however, the long experience of the Society together with its fundamental documents indicates the following guidelines, while the norms for their application are to be set by the general.

Guidelines

269   41.   [16] Superiors—with compassion and understanding—should try to probe issues of emotional strain and inner distress that each candidate carries from his history, attempting to deal honestly with such questions as those of affective maturity, of genuine capacities for sexual abstinence, especially if the candidate has had a previous history of intimate sexual relations and other experiences of this nature. The Society and the candidate need to have as clear an appreciation of these factors as possible in order to make a sound judgment about the ability of the candidate to live our life.

270   42.   [17] When someone cannot live the vow of chastity with integrity, inner freedom, and joy, that is, when he cannot find God in his life of chastity, in

---

[30] *Const.* [211].

conscience he ought not to proceed to vows or to major orders but should leave the Society and find another way of life where he can serve God in peace and fidelity.[31]

271   43.   [18] With deep sorrow, it must be acknowledged that for the good of the Society and those affected by its pastoral mission, they should not remain in the Society, whatever their grade, whose repeated acts with another against chastity show them in all likelihood unable to live their public profession of chastity with integrity, even after appropriate therapeutic rehabilitation.[32]

272   44.   [19] According to his best knowledge and judgment, the superior should also challenge with fraternal concern and kindness those involved in inappropriate relationships or exclusive friendships that can compromise dedicated chastity, cause scandal, or wound the union of minds and hearts that is to characterize Jesuit life.

Recommendation to Father General

273   45. Since a general congregation has neither the time nor the resources to treat this entire matter in all of its dimensions, GC 34 asks Father General to establish a commission of experts who can examine thoroughly the issues attendant on the fidelity and credibility of chastity in the Society and on a sound affective formation of young Jesuits and those who are already formed. Further, we recommend that

---

[31] *Const.* [204f.], [819]. For the manner of "dismissal," cf. *Const.* [223–27].

[32] For the norms alluded to in this text and the discretion ["discrete zeal"] with which they are to be applied, cf. *Const.* [208], [210f.], [819]. Cf. also [212], [215]. For the usage in the early Society, see Jerome Nadal, MHSI, vol. 90, *Commentarii de Instituto Societatis Iesu,* bk. 5, "In Examen Annotationes," [75] (p. 160).

each conference of provincials work out the cultural adaptation of these guidelines, study the issues connected with affective formation, and outline the appropriate pedagogies for this development among Jesuits. The results of this study should be submitted to Father General for his approval.

DECREE NINE

POVERTY

Introduction

274   1. In response to the powerful calls of recent general congregations, Jesuits have made noticeable efforts to live a more authentic poverty, both personally and in communities.[1] Work with and for the poor has been promoted; the generosity and hospitality of our houses has increased; separation of community from work has brought greater clarity regarding expenses; there are more financial cooperation and a sharper sensitivity to justice. All in all, we have advanced in detachment, simplicity of life, solidarity, and fraternal sharing— attitudes which mark the evangelical poverty we promised.[2] For all of this, we must be grateful to God.

275   2. At the same time, despite this progress, we must admit that we have not yet reached the deeper renewal that General Congregation 32 in its Decree 12 asks of us in this regard. The postulates sent to this congregation

---

[1] GC 31, D 18; GC 32, D 12; D 2, nn. 20, 28; D 4, n. 49; GC 33, D 1, nn. 23-27; D 2.

[2] GC 32 already expressed the "analogic" character of the religious poverty (D 12, n. 7): "In a world of mass starvation, no one can lightly call himself poor. It is perhaps regrettable that we have no other word to designate this note of religious life, since poverty means very different things to different people. At the very least, religious poverty would try hard to limit rather than to expand consumption."

show dissatisfaction with our comfortable style of life; they call on us to consider whether our way of life bears credible witness to the vow of evangelical poverty.

276   3.   This is not a marginal concern. We know well that, for St. Ignatius, poverty is "a safeguard of religious life," whose lack "weakens, wears out, and ruins" our way of being.[3] Moved by the Spirit of Jesus, Ignatius and his first companions felt called to "preach in poverty."[4] The authenticity of our poverty is the test of our being or not being Jesuits manifestly following Christ "poor and humble," as we learned in the Spiritual Exercises.[5]

The Apostolic and Prophetic Dimension of Our Poverty

277   4.   Our poverty is apostolic because it witnesses to God as the one Lord of our lives and the only Absolute; it distances us from material goods and frees us from all attachment so that we can be fully available to serve the Gospel and dedicate ourselves to the most needy. In this way poverty is itself a mission and a proclamation of the Beatitudes of the Kingdom.

278   5.   Our poverty is also prophetic. In recent decades the cry of the poor has become more piercing. But the gap between rich and poor is being reinforced rather than diminishing. Unbridled capitalism produces disproportionate growth for some economic sectors, exclusion and marginalization for many others. Contemporary

---

[3] Cf. *Const.* [553], [816]. Cf. also Letter to the Fathers and Brothers at Padua, 7 August 1547, MHSI, *Epp.S.Ign.*, I, 572–77. Although written by Polanco at the request of St. Ignatius, it contains the attitude of the founder regarding poverty understood as a gift of God which draws Jesuits to the poor, "the friends of the [Eternal] King."

[4] To Jaime Cassador, 12 February 1536, S. Ign., *Epp. et instruct.*, MHSI I, 96. Cf. *Spiritual Diary* (MHSI, *Const.* I, 86–158, n. 15); *Deliberation on poverty* (MHSI, *Const.* I, 78–83).

[5] Cf. *SpEx* [116].

society is infected by consumerism, hedonism, and lack of responsibility. The values considered important today are personal fulfillment, competition, efficiency, and success at any cost. In view of this panorama of contrasts, our personal and community poverty becomes a sign and message of a different logic, that of evangelical solidarity.

279 6. Poverty is the unequivocal condition of our credibility.[6] In the face of the attitudes and values that dominate the mentality of the world today, the radical exercise of evangelical poverty becomes a countercultural witness to the value of gratuity which St. Ignatius praised so much.[7] By this gratuity we profess the boundless and freely bestowed love of God who gave his Son for us in the total emptying of the Incarnation and the Cross. By our poverty we also show that we as persons and as "body" consider ourselves the "least Company" which lives from God and for God rather than putting its trust in material goods, since the powerful love of the Lord acts through our littleness.

Guidelines and Helps

280 7. In order to renew our apostolic poverty, GC 34 wishes to insist again on some of the more pressing recommendations given us by recent general congregations.

281 8. 1. Our *manner of life* personally and in communities has to be simple, hospitable, and open. There are certainly Jesuits and communities which live an exemplary, austere life. However, we must admit that in some instances the style of our life is far from that lived by modest families of the locale. We must sincerely examine whether in certain spheres (travel, personal

---

[6] Cf. GC 33, D 1, n. 48.

[7] Cf. *Examen* [4]; *Formula* [4]; *Const.* [398], [565], [816].

cars, private use of television, meals in expensive restau-
rants, vacations, the number of domestic employees,
and so forth) we live according to the requirements of
our poverty; we must also ask whether we truly earn
our livelihood by our labor.[8] A community life of shared
poverty is a source of joy, and unity of hearts is strength-
ened by sharing of goods.[9] The testimony of simplicity
and sobriety of life can also be a means for awakening
in some who visit us the desire to become companions
of Jesus. We firmly believe that a separation of living
quarters from workplace, as recommended by GC 31,
helps to strengthen the simplicity and intimacy of our
community life.[10]

282   9. 2. *Economic openness* and dependence on the
community for income and expenses are indispensable
for a life of fraternal poverty. From the community we
receive what we need; to the community we give everything that comes to us—as remuneration for our work,
stipends, alms, gifts, or in any other way.[11] This desire to
share with one's brothers without holding back anything
as one's own must remain characteristic of a Jesuit who
desires radically to follow Jesus. Since the use of modern conveniences such as credit cards and personal
bank accounts may bring one to live financially on the
margins of the community, all should be fully honest
with the superior regarding the use of money. Those
who have influential and well-salaried positions must be
especially alert; even though the acceptance of these
positions must be discerned with the superior and the
gain coming from them can never be a determining
factor in choosing them, they carry within themselves

[8] Cf. GC 32, D 12, n. 7.

[9] Cf. GC 31, D 18, n. 13.

[10] Cf. GC 31, D 19, n.7.

[11] GC 32, D 12, n. 8.

the temptation to live a more comfortable lifestyle.[12] In the same way clarity and austerity of life are not helped by appropriating for personal use the economic or material means pertaining to one's apostolic work.

283 10. 3. *Spiritual discernment* will make us "vigilant servants" regarding the evangelical quality of our lives.

284 11. *a.* The *personal* discernment so recommended by St. Ignatius can be practiced in prayer and the examen. Only the intimate knowledge of the Lord who has given up all for our sake will enable us to love him more deeply and follow him more closely in his detachment. The examen will help us to notice God's footprints in our lives, the God who calls us daily to dedicate ourselves "more" freely, since he himself desires to give himself "more," "to give himself to us as much as possible."[13] An aid here is spiritual direction which can make our personal discernment more sound and safe from any self-deception. A frank and trusting relationship between the members of the community and the superior is also desirable, so that he is not limited to giving permissions, but can really help each one to observe poverty in its purity and to overcome its difficulties.

285 12. *b.* An important topic for *community* discernment should be our lifestyle. What is required is that the community make a common plan that reflects its desire to live simply and in solidarity, a plan which can be easily evaluated at regular intervals. It must include the concrete means to attain simplicity and the manner in which the spirit of gratuity is manifested by the community; furthermore, it must specify how goods will be shared among the companions and with the poor. The time prior to the annual visitation of the pro-

---

[12] Ibid.

[13] *SpEx* [234].

vincial can be a suitable occasion for evaluation. Drawing up an annual budget, with careful and complete presentation to the community and not merely as a routine, has been found helpful as a means to evaluate lifestyle to see if it is comparable to "modest families of the region." Effort is needed to keep within the budget, and the community must be informed about how well this is being accomplished.[14] When these helps are neglected, "private incomes" can easily appear in the life of Jesuits and money can easily be spent on superfluities.

286   13. 4.   The changes in our administrative structures introduced by GC 32 are intended to enable communities to live more modestly and with a greater sense of shared responsibility. For this reason the *sharing of goods* has been established, so that community surplus is annually distributed to the apostolic work dependent on it, to other communities or works that are needy whether within the province or outside it, and to the poor.[15] As far as possible, apostolic institutions are also subject to the same fraternal law regarding other apostolic works in need of help.[16] The reform which separates the economic structures of community from those of the work has generally resulted in positive steps towards a greater solidarity of sharing and the greater economic openness so necessary in our communities and institutions. However, the desired results have not been achieved everywhere; at times there is simply a separation of administration and accounting, without having any effect on the economic standards of community life.[17] GC 34 asks that these reforms be carried out with sincerity; when observed carefully, they can trans-

---

[14] Cf. GC 32, D 12, n. 24.

[15] Cf. GC 32, D 12, nn. 25–29; GC 31, D 19, n. 6b.

[16] Cf. GC 32, D 12, nn. 12, 34.

[17] Cf. GC 33, D 1, n. 25.

form both our personal and community life and our apostolic activity.

287   14. 5.   In order to "feel" *[sentir]* the anxieties and aspirations of the dispossessed in an Ignatian way, we need *direct personal experience*.[18] Profound experience is what changes us. We can break out of our habitual way of living and thinking only through physical and emotional proximity to the way of living and thinking of the poor and marginalized.

288   15.   *a.* The *lived experience* of poverty and marginalization should accompany each Jesuit during his life, even when his main occupation will not be work with the neediest. It is the desire "when occasions arise, [to] feel some effects of [poverty]" that has to motivate our finding time for such experiences.[19] They can be occasions for radical conversion. It was among the poor of the hospitals and slums of Venice and Rome that the first members of the Society "experienced privation and need," but they also came to know that "a life removed as far as possible from all infection of avarice and as like as possible to evangelical poverty is more gratifying, more undefiled, and more suitable for the edification of others."[20] Therefore their desire for each one who would come after them was that "his food, drink, clothing, shoes, and lodging will be what is characteristic of the poor," and that these followers would seek "to reach the same point as the [first members] or to go further in our Lord."[21] From the witness of many companions who live with the poor, we know that, along with the hard lessons of poverty, such experiences bring the evangelical values of celebration, simplicity, and hospitality which so often characterize the life of the poor. Superi-

---

[18] Cf. GC 32, D 12, n. 5.

[19] *Const.* [287].

[20] *Formula* [5].

[21] *Examen* [81].

ors should facilitate such experiences and allow the
required time to those who want them.

289   16.   *b.* Solidarity with the poor cannot be the
concern only of some Jesuits; it has to typify our life and
our ministry. So whatever the mission given us may be,
we have to work within it *for* the benefit of the poor and
for a more just and fraternal world. Moreover, the insertion of communities in areas of poverty and marginalization is a special witness to love for the poor and for
the poverty of Christ.[22] Fortunately the number of these
communities has grown; in them Jesuits serve selflessly,
working *with* the poor and living *as* they do. Provincials
must continue to promote such communities so that,
while maintaining a strong sense of belonging to the
body of the province, they are a visible application of
our preferential option for the poor and contribute by
means of fraternal exchange to increasing the social
sensibility of the province.

290   17. 6.   We frequently make use of means and
institutions in our apostolates which in themselves are
not poor (since they must in fact always be suitable to
their apostolic purpose). Here it is fitting to recall that
effectiveness and apostolic poverty are two values
which must be kept in ongoing tension; this should be
the rule for each individual as much as for communities
and works.[23] Maintaining this difficult equilibrium requires constant discernment and a readiness to abandon such institutions and means when they no longer
result in the "greater service" of God.

Poverty as Grace

291   18. For St. Ignatius the material poverty of a Jesuit
was a grace; he asked that "it be loved as a mother,"

---

[22] GC 32, D 12, n. 10; D 4, nn. 35f., 49f.

[23] Cf. GC 32, D 12, n. 9; GC 31, D 18, n. 4.

called it a "jewel" and "beloved of God."[24] Grace always brings joy and peace, and we must appreciate poverty and desire it as a grace. However, for many of us this has not always been the case; we live it incoherently and, often, as an imposition. Let us decide "with great spirit and freedom," putting aside our fears, so that we may come closer to him who "makes all things new," to ask him, personally and in community, for the grace of poverty and the wisdom to live it as a gift. Renewed poverty will have the simultaneous effect of evangelical renewal in the quality of life of the Society. To live poverty as a grace in an egotistic world lacking a sense of responsibility for others will place us joyfully with the Son and with those among whom the Son wants to be, the poor and neglected of the earth.

---

[24] *SpEx* [147]; *Const.* [287] "Letter to the Fathers and Brothers at Padua," op. cit., n. 2.

THE PROMOTION OF VOCATIONS

292   1. The Society of Jesus cannot fulfill its mission without further vocations. General Congregation 34 therefore calls on all our companions to work vigorously for vocations. Clearly, a vocation is a gift from God, and no human effort can replace the action of the Spirit. Nonetheless, God uses human instruments. Each Jesuit and each Jesuit community must take responsibility for ensuring that we can carry out our mission in the years to come.

293   2. Our mission and spiritual heritage make us all promoters of vocations; vocation promotion simply means helping young people hear and respond to the stirrings of the Spirit in their hearts. Naturally, vocation promotion does not necessarily produce a vocation to the Society of Jesus. It leads to various types of a Christian response, and we must carefully respect the particular way in which the Spirit calls each person. At the same time, young people can only choose what they know and love. Every Jesuit and every Jesuit community must do everything possible actively to present the Society of Jesus to others in such a way that those whom God calls will know and appreciate who and what we are.

294   3. The quality of our lives as Jesuits gives a human image to God's call. If we really expect vocations, we must examine whether our relationship with God, our communities, and our apostolates are what we profess them to be. Destructive criticism, bitterness, and even contempt for our way of life and the vows are devastating for those who might be considering a Jesuit vocation. Fortunately, most Jesuits are positive and lead lives of great fidelity. Even so, many of us are too hesitant and too timid in offering what we have to others.

295   Does our prayer remain a secret except to ourselves, or do we talk about our experience of God, including its difficulties, with others and with our brother Jesuits? Do our communities remain mysterious to all except Jesuits, or are they open and welcoming to those who seek us? Do young people see us working together, sometimes struggling but still supporting one another, praying together? Does our apostolic zeal communicate itself to others, so that they, too, will want to commit themselves to God's service?

296   4. We must promote vocations as widely as possible, so that we might reflect the culture and experience of those we seek to serve. With special sensitivity and encouragement, we need to seek possible vocations among minority cultures, immigrants, and indigenous people.

297   We recommend that Father General, after studying the experience of vocation promotion in the whole Society, write a letter on the practical aspects of promoting vocations to the Society.

•   *DECREE ELEVEN*   •

ON HAVING A PROPER ATTITUDE OF SERVICE IN THE CHURCH

Introduction

298   1. When General Congregation 33 spoke of our "Life in the Church,"[1] it committed the Society once again to "serving the Church in her teaching, life, and worship."[2] In his final address to the congregation of procurators,[3] Fr. General Peter-Hans Kolvenbach reiterated this commitment. GC 34 reaffirms this long and permanent tradition of service proper to the Society, one to which we dedicate ourselves not only as religious but also, and especially, in virtue of the fourth vow of obedience to the pope in regard to missions.

299   2. This service is exercised in myriad humble, sometimes hidden, ways by Jesuit priests and brothers missioned to the labors of parish and mission station, pulpit and confessional, workshop and printing press, classroom and laboratory.

300   3. Equally humble and hidden is the service exercised by Jesuit theologians, by consultors of the dicas-

---

[1] GC 33, D 1, nn. 6–8.

[2] *Ibid*, n. 6.

[3] Peter-Hans Kolvenbach, Final Address to the Congregation of Procurators 67, 8 September 1987, nn. 8f., *AR* 19 (1987): pp. 1081–84.

teries of the Holy See, by consultants and resource persons for episcopal conferences and individual diocesan bishops. Along with the more public service of scholarly research, teaching, speaking, and writing, these are intellectual tasks that require freedom, openness, and courage in the objective service of truth.

301   4. Our Jesuit service can also be the dangerous commitment of witness and struggle against the forces of injustice and persecution, both social and religious, a witness that has been once again sealed by the blood of martyrs. In recent decades, as throughout our history, the heroism of our many brothers who have suffered and died for their fidelity to the Church bears clear and irrefutable witness that the Society's foundational commitment is truly "to serve the Lord alone and the Church, his spouse, under the Roman Pontiff."[4]

Church and World: The New Context

302   5. Jesuits today exercise this service in a world gripped by strong sociopolitical and technological changes, often of a revolutionary character, fueled by the struggle for justice, modernization, and development. This dialectic of change produces multiple problems from which the Society cannot be immune.

303   6. Since the Second Vatican Council, the Church has been engaged in its own dialectic of *traditio et progressio*. New strains and conflicts have arisen as it seeks to respond to the call for an evangelization that is ever old yet ever new. These tensions affect several aspects of the Church's life: liturgy, doctrine, ethics, discipline, pastoral ministry, and the inculturation of each of these.

304   7. Vatican II was a prophetic event, producing a momentous renewal within Catholicism not witnessed

---

[4] *Formula* [3].

since the Council of Trent. This dynamic ecclesial creativity reveals a People of God on pilgrimage, striving, under the guidance of the Holy Spirit, to live a recovered ecclesiology of collegial (or "synodal" for the Eastern churches) coresponsibility. Those disoriented by the inevitable conflicts that result from such an invigorating new vision should recall that most major ecumenical councils have set in motion a very lengthy process of reform and renewal which did not reach a lived consensus for centuries.

305   8. The ecclesiological renewal of Vatican II has helped us rediscover the Universal Church as a *koinōnia* of local churches under the entire college of bishops, of which the bishop of Rome is the head. This, in turn, has renewed our consciousness of the distinctive and inalienable ecclesial role of the laity in the life of the Church. Can we be surprised that this deepened sense of the coresponsibility of all God's people for the whole life of the Church has led to more voices speaking, and that they are not all saying the same thing? This is a source of vitality—as well as of creative tensions.

Challenges of the Times

306   9. Attentive to this summons to work with the People of God in the spirit of Vatican II and GCs 32 and 33, and invited by the Pope to help in the implementation of the same council, the Society renews its fidelity to the teaching of the Church as it discerns and confronts the signs of the times. For among those signs are contemporary developments that can pose intellectual, cultural, and pastoral challenges to that fidelity.

307   10. Hunger, religious and racial persecution, disordered economic and cultural development, the lack of political freedom and social justice; widespread socioeconomic discrimination, exploitation, and sexual abuse, especially of women and children; callous disre-

gard for the precious gift of life; pastoral challenges of secularity; social anonymity and the alienation of modern urbanization; the dissolution of the family: all these confront, often massively, the Church—and therefore ourselves—and demand our response.

308   11. Even positive developments are not without their ambiguities: remarkable advances in the life sciences and the accompanying new problems of bioethics, the need to nuance cherished theological theories in the light of contemporary hermeneutics and historiography, the new culture created by the explosion of mass media, internal problems of liturgical discipline and sacramental life provoked by modernization and inculturation. These are among the "new situations being presented to the Society, demanding, in full fidelity to the Magisterium of the Church, valid responses to so many healthy questions from the People of God" to which Father General alludes in his final address to the congregation of procurators.[5] This fidelity will adhere to the accepted norms of assent and to Catholic teaching on the hierarchy of truths and the development of Church doctrine, as contained in the official documents of the Magisterium and in the common teaching of proven Catholic theologians.[6]

309   12. A Jesuit, especially the scholar or theologian engaged in research and the molding of informed public opinion, will see these challenges as occasions for service. His mission must ensure that the Christian tradition maintains its respectability as a coherent and valid worldview in dialogue with the realm of secular scholarship and science. Only through the exacting labor of the

---

[5] Peter-Hans Kolvenbach, op. cit., n. 7, *AR* 19 (1987): p. 1081.

[6] Cf. Vatican Council II, *Unitatis Redintegratio*, n. 11; Congregation for the Doctrine of the Faith, *Mysterium Ecclesiæ*, 24 June 1973, nn. 4f., CIC 750-54; CCEO 598-600; *Catechism of the Catholic Church*, nn. 85ff.

scholarly enterprise, carried out with faith and in an atmosphere of freedom and mutual trust, can the Church remain an active force for good in the contemporary world of intellectual and cultural discourse. GC 34 expresses its deep appreciation to, solidarity with, and support for the Jesuits engaged in this crucial service to the Church today.

310 13. Such service requires courage and integrity; it can also involve pain. As Father General said, aware of "strong tensions within the Church from which the Society may not stand aloof, and through their very apostolic responsibility, Jesuits are inevitably dragged into conflictual, even explosive ecclesiastical situations."[7] Our response to such situations can give rise to tensions with some Church authorities. Despite—indeed, because of—our sincere desire to live in fidelity to the Magisterium and the hierarchy, there may be times when we feel justified, even obliged, to speak out in a way that may not always win us general approval and could even lead to sanctions painful to the Society and constituting an impediment to our work.

311 14. To do so does not put the Jesuit in a stance of disobedience or revolt. Ignatian obedience, in accord with the tradition of Catholic theology, has always recognized that our first fidelity must be to God, to the truth, and to a well-formed conscience. Obedience, then, cannot exclude our prayerful discernment of the course of action to be followed, one that may in some circumstances differ from the one suggested by our religious and Church superiors. Such discernment, and its respectful representation to superiors, is an authentic element of our Ignatian tradition confirmed in GC 31[8] and clarified in GC 32.[9]

---

[7] Peter-Hans Kolvenbach, op. cit., n. 4, *AR* 19 (1987): p. 1079.

[8] GC 31, D 17, n. 10.

[9] GC 32, D 11, n. 55.

312   15. At the same time, Ignatian obedience is one of concrete fidelity to the real, visible, hierarchical Church, not to some abstract ideal. This Church is not something distinct from us: it is the community of believers to which we belong and whose virtues and defects, triumphs and tragedies, we share. Once the discernment is accomplished and the representations made, the Jesuit attitude will ultimately be one modeled on the "Rules in Order to Have the Proper Attitude of Mind in the Church Militant" of St. Ignatius.[10]

313   16. In saying this we are well aware that the context in which Ignatius wrote these rules is very different from that of today. But Ignatian service in the Church is not a history lesson. It is a profound mystical bond that transcends the particularities of its historical origins in the sixteenth-century Church. Rooted in faith that the Holy Spirit is guiding the Church, it drives us to seek the *magis,* serenely confident that "to them that love God, all things work together unto good" (Rom. 8:28).

314   17. Therefore, if there is a time for speaking out, there may also be a time for silence, chosen by discernment or even imposed by obedience. If there is a time for representation, there is also a time for the abnegation of our intellect and will, which becomes for us a new way of seeing through the clouds of suffering and uncertainty to a higher truth and wisdom, that of the Cross.

The Jesuit Response: A Contemporary Perspective

315   18. A contemporary Ignatian response to these problems is given in the address of Father General to the congregation of procurators to which we have already referred.[11] It is not meant to provide an updated

---

[10] *SpEx* [352–70].

[11] Peter-Hans Kolvenbach, op. cit. nn. 8f., *AR* (1987): pp.

version of the "Rules in Order to Have the Proper Attitude of Mind in the Church Militant";[12] still less does it pretend to give an exhaustive treatment of the theme or of its history and interpretation.[13] We find instead a profound reflection on the foundational inspiration that motivated the Society to integrate itself more fully into a living experience of the mystery of the Church, in the spirit of the fourth vow in regard to missions that so distinctively unites us with the Holy Father.

316 19. This congregation makes its own the teaching of Father General's address and recommends it to the whole Society for attentive study in an atmosphere of prayer, examen, and individual and communal reflection and discernment. In accord with GC 33, Father General affirms that the Society must "seek to incorporate itself more and more vigorously and creatively into the life of the Church,"[14] and "learn in the Church, with the Church, and for the Church how to live our faith as adults in the conditions, cultures, and languages of this end of the century."[15]

317 20. If our love of Christ, inseparable from our love for his spouse the Church, impels us to seek the will of God in each situation, it can also oblige us to engage in constructive criticism based on a prayerful discernment. But it cannot justify a lack of solidarity with the Church, from which we are never in any way distinct or apart. In the elaboration and expression of our theological views and in our choice of pastoral options, we must always actively seek to understand the mind of the hierarchical Church, having as our goal the end of the Society to

---

1081–84.

[12] Ibid., n. 8; the updating was mandated by GC 33, D 1, n. 8.

[13] Ibid., n. 9.

[14] GC 33, D 1, n. 4.

[15] Peter-Hans Kolvenbach, op. cit. n. 17, *AR* 19 (1987): p. 1089.

help souls. At the same time, we must try to articulate the *sensus fidelium* and help the Magisterium discern in it the movements of the Spirit in accord with the teaching of Vatican II.[16] Formed by the experience of the Spiritual Exercises and desirous of being faithful to this Ignatian vision, we pray God to instill in us the spirit that animates these Ignatian rules.

318   21. Even when it is not possible to refrain from all critical observations in the objective evaluation of certain situations in the life of the Church, or even of the comportment of persons holding responsible positions in its service, we will always seek to do so in this spirit. As men of integrity, we must of course be true to our consciences. But we will speak (or keep silent) in prudence and humility, and with a sense of genuine respect and affection for the pastors of the Church, both local and universal.[17] We will strive for the honesty to gratefully acknowledge the grace of their guidance as a needed corrective to whatever may be tainted by narrowness or the limitations of what is personal and subjective. We will be aware that as members of the Society we are bound to them in a special way, and that our prime concern is to cooperate with them in building up and, where necessary, healing both the universal and local churches.

319   22. We will be conscious, too, that the Church cannot be explained in purely sociopolitical terms, but is animated by a transcendent Spirit that guides and authenticates the Christian community through the collegial action of the Pope and bishops,[18] and is affirmed by the *sensus fidelium*.[19]

---

[16] Cf. Vatican Council II, *Lumen Gentium,* nn. 12, 35.

[17] Cf. *SpEx* [353].

[18] Cf. *SpEx* [365].

[19] Cf. Vatican Council II, *Lumen Gentium*, nn. 12, 35.

The Jesuit Response: Concrete Modalities

320 23. We will recognize that, particularly in sensitive doctrinal and moral questions, it is often difficult for magisterial statements to explicitate exhaustively all aspects of an issue. Rather than indulging in selective and superficial criticism, we will look for the central message and, through discerning theological reflection, attempt to understand it in depth and explain it positively, respectfully, and clearly.

321 24. We will keep difficulties in perspective and not isolate them from their context. We will not underestimate the possibility of giving scandal, nor forget that between the extremes of premature, ill-considered public criticism and servile silence there exists the alternative of moderate and respectful expression of our views.[20] We will avoid particular interests and bear in mind the greater good of the whole Church. When possible, we will seek recourse through official channels;[21] we will remain in active dialogue and discernment with our own superiors in the Society, and conduct consultation and dialogue with other competent Church authorities in a spirit of mutual respect and understanding. To this end, wherever possible we will show ourselves ready to foster informal personal contacts of cordial friendliness with the local bishops in areas where we exercise our mission, and seek to contain and defuse possible sources of conflict before they develop.

322 25. If the Church appears to be attacked or defamed in the media, we cannot limit ourselves to a dismissive condemnation of such abuses. We must enter the world of communication and defend the truth,

---

[20] Cf. John Paul II, Allocution to General Congregation 34, 5 January 1995, n. 6; cf. Appendix I.

[21] Cf. *SpEx* [362].

while at the same time honestly acknowledging conflicts and polarities within the Church. Though we will do so without sharpening tensions or weakening authority, we cannot avoid issues which, as news, the media will present in any event.

323   26. We must cooperate with the media so that the Church's true face can appear and the Gospel be inculturated in this new mass culture as well. We will strive to see that issues conducive to good receive effective media attention. Though we remain always loyal to the truth, our Ignatian sense of *sentire cum ecclesia* will lead us to present what is praiseworthy in the Church, revealing the bonds of affection that make us love the Church and cleave to it as a source of life, solace, and healing, as an internal authority for genuine religious experience, as a nurturing matrix of our deepest values.[22]

Conclusion: Fidelity to Our Jesuit Charism to Serve

324   27. If in today's world the Society is to be engaged "in the most difficult and extreme fields, in the crossroads of ideologies, in the front line of social conflict," as the Holy Father said in his address at the beginning of this congregation,[23] repeating the words of Pope Paul VI at the opening of GC 32,[24] we are there as "men whom Christ himself sends into the world to spread his holy doctrine among people of every state and condition."[25]

325   28. In that same spirit, on this eve of the third millennium we pledge ourselves once again to generous

---

[22] Cf. *SpEx* [353–63].

[23] John Paul II, Allocution to General Congregation 34, 5 January 1995, n. 8; cf. Appendix I.

[24] Paul VI, Allocution to General Congregation 32, 3 December 1974, n. 2; cf. Documents of General Congregation 32, Appendix.

[25] Ibid; cf. *SpEx* [145].

service of all our brothers and sisters. This service will be Christian only if anchored by fidelity to him who makes all things new. It will be Jesuit only if it is in union with the successor of Peter. For this union has always given us the assurance—indeed, it is the visible sign—"of our communion with Christ, the first and supreme head of the Society which by its very name is his: the Society of Jesus."[26]

---

[26] Ibid.

DECREE TWELVE

ECUMENISM

326   1. The signs of the times give stark proof of the fact that a faith doing justice must necessarily lead to ecumenical and interreligious dialogue and cooperation. In many parts of the world, it is precisely religious divisions that are a force contributing to injustice, violence, and even warfare. In situations of conflict, often fueled by historic confessional hostilities, ecumenism calls us to pardon and to love as essential components of a Gospel-inspired struggle for justice and reconciliation. As peoples move towards ever closer political, economic, social, and cultural unity, and as nations once divided by centuries of hatred and conflict form new supranational economic and political structures, the historic divisions of Christianity represent a flagrant counterwitness to the Gospel message "ut omnes unum sint" (John 17:21).

327   2. Therefore General Congregation 34 reaffirms the Society's commitment to ecumenism in the most vigorous and explicit terms; it is an apostolate not only in need of revitalization in its present moment of crisis but one for which the Society is suited by its global outreach and numerous institutions dedicated to formation in the Christian spirit.

328   3. Ecumenism is not only a specific work for which some Jesuits must be trained and missioned; it is a new way of being a Christian. It tries to be more than just honest and truthful and fair; it attempts to work disinterestedly in service of the truth. It seeks to see things from the other's point of view and to take seriously the other's critique of one's own communion and its historic errors and failings. Like Ignatius's preamble to the Spiritual Exercises,[1] it seeks to put the best interpretation on what the other says and does. In a word, ecumenism seeks what unites rather than what divides; seeks understanding rather than confrontation; seeks to know, understand, and love others as they wish to be known and understood, with full respect for their distinctiveness, through the dialogue of truth, justice, and love.[2]

329   4. In choosing the path of ecumenism, the Society is responding not only to its discernment of the signs of the times but to the repeated calls of the Church[3] and preceding general congregations.[4] It is also responding, with even greater urgency today, to the exigencies of the ministry of faith and justice. The need, therefore, is not for new legislation, but for a more effective implementation of existing legislation.

330   5. Consequently, the general congregation

a. recommends greater attention to initial and ongoing ecumenical formation in the Society, in accordance with the norms of GC 31, Decree 26, nn. 4-8, and

---

[1] Cf. *SpEx* [22].

[2] Cf. GC 32, D 4, n. 37.

[3] Cf. especially (1) Vatican Council II, *Unitatis Redintegratio, Lumen Gentium, Orientalium Ecclesiarum,* and *Dignitatis Humanæ.;* (2) John Paul II, Apostolic letter *Tertio Millennio Adveniente*, n. 16; also his allocutions at GC 33, 2 September 1983, n. 6, and at GC 34, 5 January 1995, n. 5; (3) *The 1993 Directory on Ecumenism* of the Pontifical Council for Promoting Christian Unity.

[4] GC 31, D 26; GC 33, D 1, n. 37; *Complementary Norms*, 253, 4° and 269, §§2f.

The 1993 Directory on Ecumenism, Section II, nn. 55-91, especially 79[5]

   b. draws attention to the recent norms of the Congregation for Catholic Education for courses in ecumenism and Eastern Christian studies[6]

   c. recommends an attentive fostering of ecumenical sensitivity in all our ministries

   d. reaffirms the concrete proposals of GC 31, Decree 26, nn. 9-14 concerning the practice of ecumenism

----

[5] One could also usefully consult the document of 20 May 1993, *Ecumenical Formation: Ecumenical Reflections and Suggestions: A Study Document of the Joint Working Groups between the Roman Catholic Church and the World Council of Churches* (Vatican Press, 1993).

[6] Congregation for Catholic Education, Letter of 6 January 1987, Prot. N. 340/86.

DECREE THIRTEEN

COOPERATION WITH THE LAITY IN MISSION

331   1. A reading of the signs of the times since the Second Vatican Council shows unmistakably that the Church of the next millennium will be called the "Church of the Laity." During the past thirty years increasing numbers of lay people have responded to the call to ministry flowing from the grace received in baptism.[1] The actualization of their vocation in so many and such varied situations has become the predominant way by which the People of God minister to the world in promotion of the Kingdom. This growth of lay ministry will surely continue to expand during the next millennium. The Society of Jesus acknowledges as a grace of our day and a hope for the future that laity "take an active, conscientious, and responsible part in the mission of the Church in this great moment of history."[2] We seek to respond to this grace by offering ourselves in service to the full realization of this mission of the laity, and we commit ourselves to that end by cooperating with them in their mission.[3]

---

[1] Vatican Council II, *Lumen Gentium*, n. 31.

[2] John Paul II, Apostolic Exhortation *Christifideles Laici*, n. 3.

[3] GC 31, D 33, n. 34; Peter-Hans Kolvenbach, Address to the Congregation of Provincials 1 *"De Statu Societatis,"* n. 19, *AR* 20 (1990):

332   2. We discover a similar grace if we read the signs of the times in the apostolic work of the Society of Jesus over the past thirty years. Spurred by the council, General Congregation 31 urged us to "foster the cooperation of the laity in our own apostolic works."[4] Since that time a growing cooperation with the laity has expanded our mission and transformed the ways in which we carry it out in partnership with others. It has enriched what we do and how we understand our role in that mission. Jesuit works in some areas of the world depend primarily upon lay persons for the carrying out of the mission of the Society. We foresee the expansion of lay apostolic leadership in Jesuit works in years to come and pledge ourselves to assist this development.

333   3. We also cooperate with many others: priests, men and women religious, with their distinct charisms, as well as people of all faiths and beliefs who seek to build a world of truth, justice, freedom, peace, and love. We are grateful for this cooperation and are enriched by it.

334   4. Jesuits are both "men *for* others"[5] and "men *with* others."[6] This basic characteristic of our way of proceeding calls for an attitude and readiness to cooperate, to listen and to learn from others, to share our spiritual and apostolic inheritance. To be "men

---

p. 451; Peter-Hans Kolvenbach, "To Friends and Colleagues of the Society of Jesus," *AR* 20 (1990): pp. 601–7.

[4] GC 31, D 33, n 6.

[5] Pedro Arrupe, "Men for Others," Address to the Tenth International Congress of Former Jesuit Students of Europe, 1973. English text printed by the Jesuit Secondary Education Association, U.S.A.

[6] Peter-Hans Kolvenbach, "To Friends and Colleagues of the Society of Jesus," *AR* 20 (1990): p. 602.

with others" is a central aspect of our charism and deepens our identity.

335 5. Because of the experiences of the recent past, many Jesuit provinces as well as many lay persons have urged this general congregation to take new steps forward in cooperation. In response to these requests we offer recommendations concerning *(a)* the Society's service to the laity in their ministry, *(b)* formation of both laity and Jesuits for this cooperation, *(c)* Jesuit cooperation with laity in works of the Society, other works, and associations, and *(d)* opportunities for the future.

a. Service to the Laity in Their Ministry

336 6. The expansion and variety of lay apostolic service in our day has remarkable dimensions. Many lay persons recognize their activity as Christian ministry and seek to be trained for and commissioned to this service. Others engage in apostolic service in a more informal and implicit manner. Still others participate in lay associations for varied apostolic purposes. In all these ways many lay men and women give witness to the Gospel. Where they live, worship, and work, laity are taking on greater responsibility for the ministry of the Church. Called to be holy and concerned for faith, justice, and the poor, they evangelize the structures of society.

337 7. The Society of Jesus places itself at the service of this mission of the laity by offering what we are and have received: our spiritual and apostolic inheritance, our educational resources, and our friendship. We offer Ignatian spirituality as a specific gift to animate the ministry of the laity. This apostolic spirituality respects the unique spirituality of the individual and adapts itself to present needs; it helps persons to discern their call and "in all things to love and serve the Divine Majesty."[7] We offer to laity the practical wisdom we have learned from more than four centuries of apostolic experience. Through our schools, universities, and other educational programs we make pastoral and theological training available. Perhaps most important, we join with them in companionship: serving together, learning from and responding to each other's concerns and initiatives, dialoguing with one other on apostolic objectives.

b. Formation of Laity and Jesuits

338 8. Putting ourselves at the service of the apostolate of the laity challenges us. We need to respond to their desire for formation so that they are able to minister as fully as possible according to their call and gifts. This formation should draw on the abundant resources and experiences of the Society. We should not hesitate to offer, when requested, the experience of the Spiritual Exercises and our spiritual direction. We can encourage them towards the apostolic priority of the service of faith and the promotion of justice with a preferential love of the poor. By responding in this way we offer who we are. As persons whose lives are centered on loving and serving God in all things, we should help others recognize and discern the apostolic possibilities of their lives and work. Laity who collaborate in Jesuit apostolates can expect from us a specific formation in Ignatian values, help in discernment of apostolic priorities and objectives, and practical strategies for their realization.

339 9. Cooperation with laity in mission requires the formation and renewal of all Jesuits. Initial formation must develop our capacity for collaboration with both laity and fellow Jesuits by means of education and

---

[7] *SpEx* [233].

experiences of ministerial cooperation with others. Ongoing formation in apostolic situations—if we listen to others, learn from their spirituality, and face together the difficulties of genuine cooperation—will deepen this capacity. Both in our initial and ongoing formation, lay people can help us understand and respect their distinct vocation as well as appreciate our own.

c. Jesuit Cooperation with Laity

340   10. Recent experience enables us to see three dimensions of our cooperation with others in mission: (i) lay collaboration in Jesuit apostolic works, (ii) the cooperation of Jesuits in the works of others, and (iii) our support of and contribution to lay apostolic associations related to the Society and its mission.

i. Collaboration in Works of the Society

341   11. We collaborate with the laity in works of the Society. A work of the Society substantially contributes to realizing the mission of the Society, manifests Ignatian values, and bears the name "Jesuit" with the Society's approval. The Society takes "ultimate responsibility" for this work.[8] Examples are Jesuit educational institutions, parishes, social centers, retreat houses, and the Jesuit Refugee Service.

342   12. Each such work must be guided by a clear mission statement which outlines the purposes of the work and forms the basis for collaboration in it. This mission statement should be presented and clearly explained to those with whom we cooperate. Programs are to be provided and supported (even financially) to enable lay people to acquire a greater knowledge of the

---

[8] GC 31, D 33, n 6. Civil laws, which vary from country to country, affect the way in which the Society exercises its responsibility and must be respected.

Ignatian tradition and spirituality and to grow in each one's personal vocation.

343   13. All those engaged in the work should exercise coresponsibility and be engaged in discernment and participative decision making where it is appropriate. Lay persons must have access to and be trained for positions of responsibility according to their qualifications and commitment. A lay person can be the director of a Jesuit work.[9] When this is the case, Jesuits receive from the provincial their mission to work in the institution, and they carry out this mission under the direction of the lay director.[10] In institutions where Jesuits are a small minority, special attention should be given both to the leadership role of lay colleagues and to appropriate means for the Society to assure the Jesuit identity of the work.

ii. Cooperation in Non-Jesuit Works

344   14. Our mission today also calls us to cooperate more closely with institutions, organizations, and activities which are not sponsored by the Society.[11] Among these are social development and welfare centers, educational and research institutions, seminaries and religious institutes, international organizations, labor unions, ecclesial base communities and grass-roots movements. This cooperation is a way of witnessing to the Gospel and to Ignatian spirituality. It allows us to enter into milieus where the Church wishes to be present. Our cooperation there can express solidarity with others

---

[9] Peter-Hans Kolvenbach, Final Address to the Congregation of Provincials 1, *AR* 20 (1990): pp. 508f.

[10] This direction is the authority over the institution and its mission rather than the religious authority which is the subject matter of our vows.

[11] GC 31, D 33, n. 3.

while learning from them in a way which enriches the Society and the Church.

345 15. Cooperation in these works should be in accord with the Society's criteria for the choice of ministries, especially service of the faith and promotion of justice. The Jesuit should be missioned with clear apostolic objectives and remain in continuous discernment with his superior and apostolic community.

iii. Cooperation with Associations

346 16. Many lay persons desire to be united with us through participation in apostolic associations of Ignatian inspiration.[12] The Society views positively this growth of lay associations. They give witness to the Ignatian charism in the world, enable us to undertake with them works of greater dimensions, and help their members to live the faith more fully. Jesuits are encouraged to study these various associations, to know them through personal contact, and to develop a genuine interest in them.

347 17. Among the privileged means both for the Christian formation of lay people in Ignatian spirituality and for partnership in a common mission, the Society actively promotes several different associations.[13]

348 • Christian Life Communities address people who, being formed in the Spiritual Exercises, hear a call to follow Jesus Christ more closely and to make a life commitment to work with others through apostolic witness and service. The community dimension supports this apostolic commitment. We pledge ourselves

---

[12] Peter-Hans Kolvenbach, "To Friends and Colleagues of the Society of Jesus," op. cit.

[13] This list does not in any way mean to exclude other communities or movements with which the Society has very privileged and fruitful links in various countries.

to share Ignatian spirituality with them and to accompany them in their mission.

349 • Jesuit Volunteer programs offer service marked especially by concern for the poor and work for justice, community living, simple lifestyle, and Ignatian spirituality. Provinces are encouraged to support these volunteer associations, to develop better national and international networks among them, and to recognize them as a work of the Society where desired and appropriate.

350 • Jesuit Past-student Associations enable those who once attended our schools to better carry out their responsibility to "make fruitful in their lives and in the world the formation they have received."[14] Qualified Jesuits should be assigned to help them in ongoing spiritual, ethical, and social formation, as well as in identifying apostolic needs.

351 • The Apostleship of Prayer seeks to form Christians shaped by the Eucharist, devoted to the Heart of Christ through the daily offering and prayer for the intentions of the Church, and committed to apostolic service. The Society supports and promotes this pastoral service entrusted to it by the Holy Father, as well as the Eucharistic Youth Movement.

d. Opportunities for the Future

352 18. The present moment is a moment of grace. As lay people continue to grow in their service to the world, the Society of Jesus will find opportunities for cooperation with them reaching far beyond our present experience. We will be stretched in our creativity and energy to serve them in their ministry. We will be called upon to take a supportive role as they become more

---

[14] Peter-Hans Kolvenbach, Address to the Third World Congress of Former Jesuit Students, Versailles 1986, *AR* 19 (1986): pp. 621–29.

responsible for our own apostolates. We will be challenged to live out more fully our identity as "men for and with others." As we look to this future, we suggest some possibilities for our response to this opportunity and grace.

i. Empowering the "Church of the Laity"

353 19. Lay men and women will assume more and more responsibility for the ministries of the Church in parishes, diocesan structures, schools, theological institutions, missions, and works of justice and charity. We can expect a flourishing of specialized ministries, ecclesial movements, and lay apostolic associations of more varied purpose and inspiration. With our charism and experience we will make a specific and needed contribution to these apostolic endeavors. For this we must increasingly shift the focus of our attention from the exercise of our own direct ministry to the strengthening of laity in their mission. To do so will require of us an ability to draw out their gifts and to animate and inspire them. Our willingness to accept this challenge will depend on the strength of our Jesuit companionship and on a renewal of our response to the call of Christ to serve his mission.

ii. Lay Leadership in Works of the Society

354 20. The emerging "Church of the Laity" will also have an impact on our own Jesuit apostolic works. This transformation can enrich these works and expand their Ignatian character if we know how to cooperate with the grace of the emergence of the laity. When we speak of "our apostolates," we will mean something different by "our." It will signify a genuine Ignatian partnership of laity and Jesuits, each of us acting according to our proper vocation. Lay persons will rightly take on a greater role of responsibility and leadership within these works. Jesuits will be called on to support them in their

initiative by Ignatian formation, the witness of our priestly and religious lives, and promotion of Jesuit apostolic
values. If our service will be more humble, it will also
be more challenging and creative, more in accord with
the graces we have received. This actualization of the
lay vocation can show more clearly the grace of our
vocation.

iii. Developing an Ignatian Apostolic Network

355   21. A challenge for future cooperation with the laity
in mission can be found in the number of individuals,
co-workers, former Jesuits, associations, and communities both lay and religious who find a common spirituality and apostolic motivation in the experience of the
Spiritual Exercises. The existence of so many Ignatian-
inspired persons testifies to the continuing vitality of the
Exercises and their power for apostolic animation. The
grace of the new era of the Church and the movement
to solidarity impel us to work more decisively to
strengthen the bonds among all these persons and
groups. Thus we can develop what might be called "an
Ignatian apostolic network."

356   22. Such a network will foster better communication and provide personal and spiritual support among
these persons and groups. It will maximize the mission
of Ignatian-inspired persons in their evangelization of the
world. In this way the Society of Jesus can make a
specific contribution to the new evangelization. The
shaping of this Ignatian apostolic network will require
wide consultation, careful discernment, and careful,
gradually developed planning. The general congregation
asks Father General, with the assistance of qualified
Jesuits and others, to study this possibility.

iv. Some Joined to the Society by Closer Personal Bond

357   23. The possibility of joining lay persons more closely to the Society was given official recognition in GC 31. It urged Father General "to study the ways by which such bonds and a more stable and intimate collaboration" could be achieved.[15] Some experience of closer bonding has occurred since then. GC 34 views this as one among several ways of future lay cooperation. It recommends ten years of experimentation of "juridical bonding" of individual lay persons to the Society of Jesus and offers directions for experimentation, asking the next general congregation to evaluate these experiments.

358   24. The purpose of these experiments with closer bonding is apostolic—to extend the missioning process of the Society to lay persons, who accompany and are accompanied by Jesuits in apostolic discernment and activity. The juridical bond will be some form of contractual agreement of the Society with individual lay persons; they may or may not form an association among themselves for companionship, mutual support, and apostolic strength, but they are not admitted into the body of the Society. The distinctiveness of their lay vocation is preserved; they do not become quasi religious.

359   25. Elements to be considered in experimental programs include

> *a.* procedures for selection of associates
>
> *b.* adequate and appropriate formation
>
> *c.* terms of agreement regarding rights, responsibilities, duration, and evaluation
>
> *d.* mutual discernment with the provincial or his delegate about mission

---

[15] GC 31, D 34.

e. norms for the possible communal life of associates

f. norms for informal relationships with Jesuit communities

g. preparation and assignment of Jesuits to accompany associates

h. financial and other practical arrangements

A Call to Renewal

360 26. Cooperation with the laity is both a constitutive element of our way of proceeding and a grace calling for individual, communal, and institutional renewal. It invites us to service of the ministry of lay people, partnership with them in mission, and openness to creative ways of future cooperation. The Spirit is calling us as "men for and with others" to share with lay men and women what we believe, who we are, and what we have, in creative companionship, for "the help of souls and the greater glory of God."

DECREE FOURTEEN

JESUITS AND THE SITUATION OF WOMEN IN CHURCH AND CIVIL SOCIETY

Introduction

361   1.   General Congregation 33 made a brief mention of the "unjust treatment and exploitation of women."[1] It was part of a list of injustices in a context of new needs and situations which Jesuits were called to address in the implementation of our mission. We wish to consider this question more specifically and substantially on this occasion. This is principally because, assisted by the general rise in consciousness concerning this issue, we are more aware than previously that it is indeed a central concern of any contemporary mission which seeks to integrate faith and justice. It has a universal dimension in that it involves men and women everywhere. To an increasing extent it cuts across barriers of class and culture. It is of personal concern to those who work with us in our mission, especially lay and religious women.

---

[1] GC 33, D 1, n. 48.

The Situation

362   2.   The dominance of men in their relationship with women has found expression in many ways. It has included discrimination against women in educational opportunities, the disproportionate burden they are called upon to bear in family life, paying them a lesser wage for the same work, limiting their access to positions of influence when admitted to public life, and, sadly but only too frequently, outright violence against women themselves. In some parts of the world, this violence still includes female circumcision, dowry deaths, and the murder of unwanted infant girls. Women are commonly treated as objects in advertising and in the media. In extreme cases, for example, in promoting international sex tourism, they are regarded as commodities to be trafficked in.

363   3.   This situation, however, has begun to change, chiefly because of the critical awakening and courageous protest of women themselves. But many men, too, have joined women in rejecting attitudes which offend against the dignity of men and women alike. Nonetheless, we still have with us the legacy of systematic discrimination against women. It is embedded within the economic, social, political, religious, and even linguistic structures of our societies. It is often part of an even deeper cultural prejudice and stereotype. Many women, indeed, feel that men have been slow to recognize the full humanity of women. They often experience a defensive reaction from men when they draw attention to this blindness.

364   4.   The prejudice against women, to be sure, assumes different forms in different cultures. Sensitivity is needed to avoid using any one simple measurement of what counts as discrimination. But it is nonetheless a universal reality. Further, in many parts of the world, women already cruelly disadvantaged because of war, poverty, migration, or race, often suffer a double disadvantage precisely because they are women. There is a "feminization of poverty" and a distinctive "feminine face of oppression."

The Church Addresses the Situation

365 5. Church social teaching, especially within the last ten years, has reacted strongly against this continuing discrimination and prejudice. Pope John Paul II in particular has called upon all men and women of goodwill, especially Catholics, to make the essential equality of women a lived reality. This is a genuine "sign of the times."[2] We need to join with interchurch and interreligious groups in order to advance this social transformation.

366 6. Church teaching certainly promotes the role of women within the family, but it also stresses the need for their contribution in the Church and in public life. It draws upon the text of Genesis which speaks of men and women created in the image of God (1:27) and the prophetic praxis of Jesus in his relationship with women. These sources call us to change our attitudes and work for a change of structures. The original plan of God was for a loving relationship of respect, mutuality, and equality between men and women, and we are called to fulfil this plan. The tone of this ecclesial reflection on Scripture makes it clear that there is an urgency in the challenge to translate theory into practice not only outside but also within the Church itself.

The Role and Responsibility of Jesuits

367 7. The Society of Jesus accepts this challenge and our responsibility for doing what we can as men and as

---

[2] John Paul II, Apostolic letter *Mulieris Dignitatem* and apostolic exhortation *Christifideles Laici*; Message for the World Day of Peace, 1 January 1995.

a male religious order. We do not pretend or claim to speak for women. However, we do speak out of what we have learned from women about ourselves and our relationship with them.

368 8. In making this response we are being faithful, in the changed consciousness of our times, to our mission: the service of faith, of which the promotion of justice is an absolute requirement. We respond, too, out of the acknowledgement of our own limited but significant influence as Jesuits and as male religious within the Church. We are conscious of the damage to the People of God brought about in some cultures by the alienation of women who no longer feel at home in the Church and who are not able with integrity to transmit Catholic values to their families, friends, and colleagues.

Conversion

369 9. In response, we Jesuits first ask God for the grace of conversion. We have been part of a civil and ecclesial tradition that has offended against women. And, like many men, we have a tendency to convince ourselves that there is no problem. However unwittingly, we have often contributed to a form of clericalism which has reinforced male domination with an ostensibly divine sanction. By making this declaration we wish to react personally and collectively, and do what we can to change this regrettable situation.

Appreciation

370 10. We know that the nurturing of our own faith and much of our own ministry would be greatly diminished without the dedication, generosity, and joy that women bring to the schools, parishes, and other fields in which we labor together. This is particularly true of the work of lay and religious women among the urban and rural poor, often in extremely difficult and challenging situations. In addition, many religious congregations of women have adopted the Spiritual Exercises and our Jesuit Constitutions as the basis for their own spirituality and governance, becoming an extended Ignatian family. Religious and lay women have in recent years become expert in giving the Spiritual Exercises. As retreat directors, especially of the Exercises in daily life, they have enriched the Ignatian tradition and our own understanding of ourselves and of our ministry. Many women have helped to reshape our theological tradition in a way that has liberated both men and women. We wish to express our appreciation for this generous contribution of women, and hope that this mutuality in ministry might continue and flourish.

Ways Forward

371 11. We wish to specify more concretely at least some ways in which Jesuits may better respond to this challenge to our lives and mission. We do not presume that there is any one model of male-female relationship to be recommended, much less imposed, throughout the world or even within a given culture. Rather we note the need for a real delicacy in our response. We must be careful not to interfere in a way that alienates the culture; rather we must endeavor to facilitate a more organic process of change. We should be particularly sensitive to adopt a pedagogy that does not drive a further wedge between men and women who in certain circumstances are already under great pressure from other divisive cultural or socioeconomic forces.

372 12. In the first place, we invite all Jesuits to listen carefully and courageously to the experience of women. Many women feel that men simply do not listen to them. There is no substitute for such listening. More than anything else it will bring about change. Unless we listen, any action we may take in this area, no matter how well intentioned, is likely to bypass the real concerns of women and to confirm male condescension and reinforce male dominance. Listening, in a spirit of partnership and equality, is the most practical response we can make and is the foundation for our mutual partnership to reform unjust structures.

373   13. Second, we invite all Jesuits, as individuals and through their institutions, to align themselves in solidarity with women. The practical ways of doing this will vary from place to place and from culture to culture, but many examples come readily to mind:

374   13, 1.   explicit teaching of the essential equality of women and men in Jesuit ministries, especially in schools, colleges and universities

375   13, 2.   support for liberation movements which oppose the exploitation of women and encourage their entry into political and social life

376   13, 3.   specific attention to the phenomenon of violence against women

377   13, 4.   appropriate presence of women in Jesuit ministries and institutions, not excluding the ministry of formation

378   13, 5.   genuine involvement of women in consultation and decision making in our Jesuit ministries

379   13, 6.   respectful cooperation with our female colleagues in shared projects

380   13, 7.   use of appropriately inclusive language in speech and official documents

381   13, 8.   promotion of the education of women and, in particular, the elimination of all forms of illegitimate discrimination between boys and girls in the educational process

Many of these, we are happy to say, are already being practiced in different parts of the world. We confirm their value, and recommend a more universal implementation as appropriate.

382   14. It would be idle to pretend that all the answers to the issues surrounding a new, more just relationship between women and men have been found or are satisfactory to all. In particular, it may be anticipated that some other questions about the role of women in civil and ecclesial society will undoubtedly mature over time. Through committed and persevering research, through exposure to different cultures, and through reflection on experience, Jesuits hope to participate in clarifying these questions and in advancing the underlying issues of justice. The change of sensibilities which this involves will inevitably have implications for Church teaching and practice. In this context we ask Jesuits to live, as always, with the tension involved in being faithful to the teachings of the Church while at the same time trying to read accurately the signs of the times.

Conclusion

383   15. The Society gives thanks for all that has already been achieved through the often costly struggle for a more just relationship between women and men. We thank women for the lead they have given and continue to give. In particular, we thank women religious, with whom we feel a special bond, and who have been pioneers in so many ways in their unique contribution to the mission of faith and justice. We are grateful, too, for what the Society and individual Jesuits have contributed to this new relationship, which is a source of great enrichment for both men and women.

384   16. Above all we want to commit the Society in a more formal and explicit way to regard this solidarity with women as integral to our mission. In this way we hope that the whole Society will regard this work for reconciliation between women and men in all its forms

as integral to its interpretation of Decree 4 of GC 32 for our times. We know that a reflective and sustained commitment to bring about this respectful reconciliation can flow only from our God of love and justice, who reconciles all and promises a world in which "there is neither Jew nor Greek, there is neither slave nor free, there is neither male nor female, for you are all one in Christ Jesus" (Gal. 3:28).

COMMUNICATION:
A NEW CULTURE

385   1. **A road and a call.** Our Father Ignatius identified the cultural shift of his time: the passage from the Middle Ages to the Renaissance. Recognizing the values of the emerging culture, with its concern for individuals and their spiritual growth, Ignatius oriented the Society of Jesus towards the future. He knew how to integrate gospel values and traditional cultural values with this new culture. Jesuits today are called to understand the changes that are occurring at the end of this twentieth century: the proliferation of electronic media and the so–called information revolution, as well as the new ways of learning and knowing that accompany them. This world of communication develops what is widely identified as a new culture, one that is nonlinear, image-oriented, intuitive, and affective in its understanding of the world.

386   2. **Ambiguity.** For all its marvels, this new world, characterized by an exponential development of the means of communication, is filled with ambiguities. Its media and language are often used in manipulative and undemocratic ways for negative and ephemeral ends. In addition, it often propagates a materialist or consumer-dominated mentality that fails to promote genuine human growth or make people receptive to the gospel message. Such false values sometimes threaten even our own Jesuit life. It is therefore necessary for us to become critical consumers and, even more, critical practitioners of social communication.

387   3. **Sector or dimension?** Communication in the Society has usually been considered a sector of apostolic activity, a field for some specialists who have often felt isolated or on the margin of the apostolic body. The Society must rather acknowledge that communication is not a domain restricted to a few Jesuit professionals, but a major apostolic dimension of all of our apostolates. Clearly, not all Jesuits need to be directly engaged in media. Nevertheless, every Jesuit, in order to be effective, must be aware of and well versed in the language and symbols, as well as the strengths and weaknesses, of modern communication culture. This is to create a shift in our awareness, making us realize that the new communication environment is a milieu in which large numbers of people can be reached and enriched, and where literacy, knowledge, and solidarity can be fostered.

388   4. **The service of faith.** The proposed cultural renewal will allow Jesuits more effectively to share the faith they are called to serve. Sometimes this will involve the direct proclamation of the Gospel and its values to large groups through mass media, or to smaller groups through group media. At other times a more indirect approach might be taken to awaken individuals to a better personal assimilation of the Christian message. In all cases this will require us to use language understood by both communication professionals and the inhabitants of the global village. Jesus, who himself communicated his Father's message through parables, miracles, and acts of compassion, must be our model.

389   5. **Justice in communication.** Communication is a powerful tool which must be used in the promotion of justice in our world. But we must also look critically at the authoritarian methods and unjust structures of communication and information organizations themselves. The promotion of justice within communication calls for the coordinated action of Christians and other people of goodwill in several areas. Freedom of the press and information must be promoted in countries where they are nonexistent or threatened by state control or ideological manipulation. An equitable flow of communication between industrialized and developing countries needs to be established. At present, the rich countries dominate the world with their information, films, and television programs. The voices and images of less powerful nations and cultures are largely absent from the global village. All Jesuits, especially philosophers, theologians, social scientists, those directly involved in the promotion of justice, as well as those involved in the production of creative works, should be conversant with communication ethics.

390   6. **Media education.** In the new media culture, it is important to educate media users to understand and make creative use of communication techniques and language, not only as individuals but also as participants in the social dialogue. Media education has as its goal a critical understanding which gives people the ability to sift out distortion, to identify hidden messages, and to make informed choices about media consumption. Such understanding returns power to the consumer and confers freedom from media manipulation and domination. Jesuit educators must be among the best "media-educated people" in order to participate in this broad educational task.

391   7. **People-oriented media.** The language of the new media culture can be spoken using simple and low-cost tools. Radio, especially used for popular education, is often an effective medium. More broadly, all Jesuits should learn to use alternative media such as posters, video and audio cassettes, and compact disks in their apostolic work. In some circumstances folk media, street plays, puppetry, or images in liturgy could be appropriate instruments for evangelization.

392   8. **A mission: Vatican Radio.** In response to the invitation from the Holy Father given at the beginning of this general congregation,[1] the Society commits itself to continue serving the universal Church through Vatican Radio. It is a concrete means for the Society to implement its mission to serve the faith and promote justice in the field of communication, within a framework of international collaboration.

393   9. **To understand and to speak the language.** We must provide well–organized communication curricula for all Jesuits in formation; we should also provide communication training as part of ongoing formation. In many places the Society has already begun to provide suitable training, integrated into the various stages of formation. These efforts must be sustained and, where lacking, adequate steps should be taken to ensure such training. Formation in communication will, among its important goals, ensure critical knowledge of the rhetoric of this new culture, foster an appreciation of its aesthetic dimension, develop the skills required for teamwork and for the effective use of media and information technology for the apostolate. Early in their formation, young Jesuits who show creative talent for communication work could be encouraged and enabled to pursue specialized training. Care should be taken to help Jesuits during their studies to integrate professional requirements and sound theological knowledge with the exigencies of religious life. The Society's Secretariat for Social Communication (JESCOM), among its other tasks, is to serve as a resource in developing communication programs for Jesuit formation.

---

[1] John Paul II, Allocution to General Congregation 34, 5 January 1995, n. 5; cf. Appendix I.

• *DECREE SIXTEEN* •

THE INTELLECTUAL DIMENSION OF JESUIT MINISTRIES

394 1. Since its foundation, the Society has held intellectual labor in high esteem, as a significant contribution to the discovery of the creative work of God and to the recognition of the legitimate autonomy of human inquiry. This tradition of the Society is particularly relevant today within the context of urgent issues confronting us in our mission. For this reason General Congregation 34 strongly reaffirms the distinctive importance of the intellectual quality of each of our apostolic works. The value of this aspect of our ministry is fundamental in contemporary circumstances, characterized as they are by changes which are as rapid as they are radical.

395 2. Where pietism and fundamentalism join forces to disparage human abilities, *human reason* will be ignored or held of little account. Contrariwise, especially in countries where secularism holds sway or which have recently emerged from Marxist atheism, some seem to regard *faith* as little more than a "superstition" which will gradually disappear in the face of ever more rapid human progress. But freedom and the ability to reason are attributes which characterize human beings as created in the likeness of God and are closely tied to genuine faith. Therefore, everywhere and in all circumstances, an intellectual tradition continues to be of critical importance for the Church's vitality as well as for the understanding of cultures which deeply affect each person's way of thinking and living. All of us experience the need to "explain" the hope that dwells in us (cf. 1 Pet. 3:15) and the concern to acknowledge "everything that is true, everything that is honorable, everything that is upright and pure, everything that we love and admire, whatever is good and praiseworthy" (Phil. 4:8).

396   3.   For this reason, GC 34 resolutely encourages a vigorous spiritual and intellectual formation for young Jesuits and ongoing spiritual and intellectual formation for every Jesuit. The Society, sensitive to present needs and challenges, must insist on the necessity not only for each one's ongoing acquisition of knowledge but also on the ongoing development of each one's personal capacity to analyze and evaluate, in our circumstances of rapid change, the mission which he has received. There can be no substitute for individual, painstaking, and, quite frequently, solitary work. Such capacity is indispensable if we wish to integrate the promotion of justice with the proclamation of faith, and if we hope to be effective in our work for peace, in our concern to protect life and the environment, in our defense of the rights of individual men and women and of entire peoples. Serious and active intellectual inquiry must also characterize our commitment to integral evangelization. This assumes a basic knowledge of the economic, social, and political structures in which our contemporaries find themselves immersed, and it cannot be ignorant of the development of traditional and modern cultures or of the effects of the emerging culture of communication. For evangelization to be effective, accuracy in knowledge, respect for the other in intercultural dialogue, and critical analysis are all imperative.

397   4.   In apostolic works which are more directly intellectual, professional formation and competence are to be accompanied by that legitimate responsible autonomy and freedom which are requisites for progress in scholarly teaching and research. Furthermore, today more than ever before, it is essential that we recognize the specific characteristics of each of the various scholarly disciplines, including science and technology. We must help our contemporaries to respect this autonomy and freedom and to recognize these specific characteristics. For those with faith, to deny "the rightful autonomy of science" can lead to tragedies well known in the history of recent centuries.[1] We who have learned to pray before the "Eternal Lord of all things" must, therefore, be especially careful to avoid the same mistakes under new forms.[2]

398 5. The intellectual dimension of every apostolic work also supposes that each Jesuit knows how to be active in companionship with others. Those engaged in an intellectual life experience periods of exaltation and of doubt, of recognition and of being ignored, of intense satisfaction and of bitter trial. More than is the case in other areas, an intellectual mission calls for a humble ability to accept praise and also to face rejection and controversy; this mission is constantly exposed to the judgment of others in conversations, in scholarly publications, and in the media. To accept this reality simply and directly is one way of being "servants of Christ's mission"—the Christ who continues his paschal mystery through us.

399 6. These characteristic challenges of the intellectual apostolate require that each of us acquire the ability to live the creative tension between profound insertion into all the details of our work and an open and critical attitude towards other points of view and other cultural or confessional positions. However, acceptance of such tension must not lessen our witness of personal com-

---

[1] Vatican Council II, *Gaudium et Spes*, n. 36.

[2] *SpEx* [98].

mitment to the service of the Church in its journey towards the Kingdom of God.

400   7.   Among the ways of being engaged in the intellectual apostolate in the service of the Kingdom of God, theological research and reflection has a special place and merits specific mention. Father Pedro Arrupe named theological reflection as one of the four priority apostolates of the Society of Jesus.[3] Among the urgent contemporary issues needing theological reflection, he listed humanism, freedom, mass culture, economic development, and violence. GC 32 cited and confirmed Father Arrupe's emphasis on theological reflection and also called for a social analysis of the structural causes of contemporary injustices and for Ignatian discernment regarding the appropriate apostolic response to these injustices.[4] GC 34 reconfirms the need for this theological reflection and, to the issues it must address, adds the contemporary understanding of the promotion of justice, including inculturation and interreligious dialogue.

401   Theological reflection, social analysis, and discernment are phases of a process which Pope John XXIII and Vatican II called "reading the signs of the times": the effort to discern the presence and activity of God in the events of contemporary history in order to decide what to do as servants of the Word.[5] This will bring the perennial sources of Catholic theology to bear upon the lived experiences, individual and communal, of the members of the faith community that is the Church, especially their experience of poverty and oppression; it relates Catholic theology to the secular disciplines, especially philosophy and the social and natural sciences, in

---

[3] Pedro Arrupe, Address to the Congregation of Procurators 65, 10 May 1970, *AR* 15 (1970): pp. 908f.

[4] GC 32, D 4, nn. 59f.; cf. nn. 44, 71–74.

[5] Cf. Vatican Council II, *Gaudium et Spes*, nn. 4, 11, 44.

order to discern, illuminate, and interpret the opportunities and problems of contemporary life.

402   8.   When theological reflection is undertaken with the seriousness of research and the creativity of imagination that it merits, within the broad spectrum of Catholic theology and in the midst of the varied circumstances in which Jesuits live and work, it can give rise to specific theologies which, in diverse times and places, incarnate the gospel message. Theological research and reflection in service of the Gospel can thus help to respond to the broadest questions of the human mind and the deepest yearnings of the human heart.

403   9.   Not only in our ministries, but also in our personal way of seeing and interpreting individual, social, cultural, and political situations, and even in our spiritual life, we can be guided by such reflection. It will be the more productive to the extent that it roots itself in a personal faith lived and expressed in the Christian community. It must be attentive to the questions which reality poses to believing men and women. And the Jesuit engaged in such reflection must know how to join awareness of contemporary circumstances with a careful listening to the voice of God in personal prayer.

• *DECREE SEVENTEEN* •

JESUITS AND UNIVERSITY LIFE

404   1.   Jesuits have been engaged in university teaching, research, and scholarly publication almost since the foundation of the Society. From astronomy to classical ballet, from the humanities to theology, Jesuits try to enter into the languages and discourses of their inherited or emerging cultures. They attempt to discover, shape, renew, or promote human wisdom, while at the same time respecting the integrity of disciplined scholarship. They also seek to accompany in faith the men and women molded by the potent cultural forces inherent in the university as an institution. St. Ignatius was aware of the wide cultural impact of universities and chose to send Jesuits there, as places where a more universal good might be achieved. Throughout our history we have continued to affirm this basic Ignatian intuition.

405   2.   Today, approximately three thousand Jesuits work in nearly two hundred of our own institutions of higher learning, touching the lives of more than half a million students; other Jesuits exercise this mission in other universities. This apostolic activity not only has an influence on the lives of students; it goes beyond the immediate university milieu. We recognize that universities remain crucial institutional settings in society. For the poor they serve as major channels for social advancement. In and through universities, important debates take place about ethics, future directions for economics and politics, and the very meaning of human existence, debates that shape our culture. Neither the university as an institution and as a value for humanity nor the still urgent imperative for an unflagging Jesuit commitment to our tradition of fostering university life stands in need of any fresh defense.

406   3. Moreover, many excellent documents already exist which treat the role and future of Jesuit universities.[1] General Congregation 34 wishes only to encourage Jesuits engaged in this important and traditional Jesuit work and to consider two relatively fresh challenges to Jesuit universities.

A Challenge from the Structure of Universities

407   4. During the past thirty years, Jesuit higher education has undergone very rapid development in size,

---

[1] Cf. •   GC 31, DD 28, 29, 30; GC 32, D 4; GC 33, D 1, n. 44

•   Pedro Arrupe, "Discourse at the Universidad de Deusto," Bilbao, May 1970 (Rome, C.I.S. 1971, pp. 102–16); "Apostolic Priorities," Address to the Congregation of Procurators, Rome, 5 October 1978 (*AR* 17 [1980]: pp. 518–81); "The Intellectual Apostolate as a Mission of the Society Today" (*AR* 16, [1976]: p. 76)

•   Peter-Hans Kolvenbach, "The Jesuit University Today," 5 November 1985, *AR* 19 (1985): pp. 394–403; "Address at the Centenary Celebration of the Universidad de Deusto," Bilbao, 5 June 1987, *Selección de escritos del Padre Peter-Hans Kolvenbach* (Provincia de España, 1992), pp. 377–84); "Address to the U. S. Jesuit Higher Education Assembly," 7 June 1989, S.J. Documentation 64 (August 1989): pp. 1–11; "La Universidad: Espacio para la unidad de las ciencias," Universidad Javeriana, Bogota, 26 February 1990; "Educación y valores: A la Universidad Iberoamericana sobre un nuevo modelo de Universidad," Mexico City, 23 August 1990; "Apostolado educativo, familia y sociedad nueva," Guadalajara, Mexico, 29 August 1990; "En el centenario de la Universidad Pontificia Comillas," October 1992

•   John Paul II, Apostolic constitution *Ex Corde Ecclesiæ* complexity, and more participative structures of government. During this same period, the number of Jesuits engaged in a university, or at least the proportion of Jesuits within the entire university community, has greatly diminished: lay and religious colleagues join with us in a common enterprise. In some places Jesuits no longer "own" our universities in any real sense. In others, government regulations create a situation in which we no longer fully "control" them. In places, some ecclesiastical superiors may be distrustful of the freedom necessary for a university truly to function in accord with its specific aims.

408   5.   In response to this challenge, Jesuits must continue to work hard, with imagination and faith and often under very difficult circumstances, to maintain and even to strengthen the specific character of each of our institutions both as *Jesuit* and as a *university*. As we look to the future, we need consciously to be on guard that both the noun "university" and the adjective "Jesuit" always remain fully honored.

409   6.   The noun guarantees a commitment to the fundamental autonomy, integrity, and honesty of a university precisely as a university: a place of serene and open search for and discussion of the truth. It also points to the mission proper to every university—its dedication to research, teaching, and the various forms of service that correspond to its cultural mission—as the indispensable horizon and context for a genuine preservation, renewal, and communication of knowledge and human values.[2] As Jesuits, we seek knowledge for its own sake and at the same time must regularly ask, "Knowledge for what?"

---

[2] John Paul II, Apostolic constitution *Ex Corde Ecclesiæ*, Art. 2.1.

A Challenge from Faith and Justice

410   7.   We affirm the adjective "Jesuit" no less strongly. This presupposes the authentic participation in our basic Jesuit identity and mission of any university calling itself Jesuit, or any university which operates ultimately under our responsibility. While we want to avoid any distortion of the nature of a university or any reduction of its mission to only one legitimate goal, the adjective "Jesuit" nevertheless requires that the university act in harmony with the demands of the service of faith and promotion of justice found in Decree 4 of GC 32. A Jesuit university can and must discover in its own proper institutional forms and authentic purposes a specific and appropriate arena for the encounter with the faith which does justice.

411   8.   We applaud the many ways in which Jesuit universities have tried to apply this decree, both in the lives of students through outreach programs of mutual contact and service with the poor, and in the central teaching, research, and publication aims of the university. If it remains true that most Jesuit universities must, in various ways, strive to do even more in order to embody this mission of service to the faith and its concomitant promotion of justice, this only reflects the challenge all Jesuits face to find concrete and effective ways in which large and complex institutions can be guided by and to that justice which God himself so insistently calls for and enables. The task is possible; it has produced martyrs who have testified that "an institution of higher learning and research can become an instrument of justice in the name of the Gospel."[3]

412   9.   The complexity of a Jesuit university can call for new structures of government and control on the part of the Society in order to preserve its identity and at the

---

[3] Peter-Hans Kolvenbach, Address to the Congregation of Provincials 1 (20 September 1990), *AR* 20 (1990): p. 452.

same time allow it to relate effectively to the academic world and the society of which it is part, including the Church and the Society of Jesus. More specifically, in order for an institution to call itself Jesuit, periodic evaluation and accountability to the Society are necessary in order to judge whether or not its dynamics are being developed in line with the Jesuit mission. The Jesuits who work in these universities, both as a community and as individuals, must actively commit themselves to the institution, assisting in its orientation, so that it can achieve the objectives desired for it by the Society.

413   10. Jesuit universities will promote interdisciplinary work; this implies a spirit of cooperation and dialogue among specialists within the university itself and with those of other universities. As a means toward serving the faith and promoting justice in accord with their proper nature as universities, they can discover new perspectives and new areas for research, teaching, and university extension services, by means of which they can contribute to the transformation of society towards more profound levels of justice and freedom. Thus our universities have a clear opportunity to promote interuniversity collaboration and, in particular, to undertake common projects between Jesuit universities of developed and developing countries.

414   11. A Jesuit university must be outstanding in its human, social, spiritual, and moral formation, as well as for its pastoral attention to its students and to the different groups of people who work in it or are related to it.

415   12. Finally, we recall how crucial it is for the whole Church to continue to have dedicated Jesuits engaged in university work. They are committed, in the most profound sense, to the search for the fullness of truth. We are assured that, despite occasional appearances to the contrary, the truth we seek will ultimately be one. That truth, rooted as it is in God, will make us free. GC 34 sends a warm word of greeting and encouragement to all those Jesuits dedicated to make authentic and currently fresh this long-standing but sometimes challenged Jesuit commitment to the university apostolate.

DECREE EIGHTEEN

SECONDARY, PRIMARY, AND NONFORMAL EDUCATION

416   1.   In the past twenty years, in response to General Congregations 32 and 33, significant apostolic renewal has been initiated and carried forward by the large number of Jesuits and lay people working in the apostolate of secondary education. In increasing numbers our educational institutions are accessible to students from economically disadvantaged groups. The quality of the education has improved in line with the principles enunciated in recent educational documents of the Society.[1] Jesuit-lay cooperation has developed significantly, with each party contributing in a distinctive way towards the total formation of the students. Our schools have become platforms, reaching out into the community, not only to the extended school community of parents, former students, and friends but also to the poor and the socially disadvantaged in the neighborhood. Furthermore, we have willingly shared our educational heritage with others when asked to do so.

417   2.   GC 34 gratefully acknowledges these developments and urges that they be continued. Allowing for diverse situations throughout the world, the ideas and practices drawn from the documents mentioned above

---

[1] *The Characteristics of Jesuit Education* (1987) and *Ignatian Pedagogy: A Practical Approach* (1993).

must inspire school mission statements, policies, programs and the entire school milieu. The Jesuit identity of our schools and Jesuit-lay cooperation can be ensured only by careful selection of administrators and teachers, both Jesuits and others, and—especially for those who will assume positions of major responsibility—adequate formation in the Ignatian charism and pedagogy. In some regions well-designed formation programs are already being offered to Jesuit and lay teachers and administrators; the Society's secretary for education should encourage such programs elsewhere; they can yield great dividends for the ends that we desire.[2]

418   3.   In response to different situations and for a variety of apostolic reasons, Jesuits in many areas are engaged in the apostolate of primary and preprimary education. We confirm that such schools "are very important and not contrary to our Institute" and also declare that because they can provide a solid academic and religious foundation during the formative early years, they can be one of the most effective services we offer to people, especially the poor.[3]

419   4.   The educational apostolate of the Society has been greatly enriched by the contributions made by centers of nonformal education, established in both rural and urban areas of developing countries. These centers provide education outside the traditional school system for both youth and adults among the poor. With the help of a participative pedagogy, they organize programs to eradicate illiteracy and supply training in technical and social skills, as well as offer a religious and ethical formation geared to the analysis and transformation of the society in which the students live. They educate their students as "men and women for others" who

---

[2] Cf. Pedro Arrupe, "Our Secondary Schools Today and Tomorrow," 13 September 1980, n. 21, *AR* 18 (1980): pp. 268–70.

[3] GC 31, D 28, n.16.

can assume leadership roles in their own communities and organizations. The number of persons whom we serve through these centers is very large; as a means towards the promotion of justice, this ministry of nonformal education is fully in accord with our Jesuit mission. Especially in the light of the decree "Servants of Christ's Mission," GC 34 encourages Jesuits, religious, and lay persons to continue their dedicated work in this important but difficult apostolate, and recommends cooperation between Jesuit centers for nonformal education and our Jesuit schools, universities, and social centers.

• *DECREE NINETEEN* •

PARISH MINISTRY

Parish Ministry Today

420   1.   Approximately 3,200 Jesuits labor in two thousand parishes throughout the world. In recognizing the important service to the Church represented by this investment of manpower, we affirm that "the parish apostolate is not contrary to our Constitutions" and add that, under certain circumstances, it is an appropriate apostolate for carrying out our mission of serving the faith and promoting justice.[1]

421   2.   The parish, moreover, offers a favorable context to live with the poor and to be in solidarity with them.

Goals and Characteristics of a Jesuit Parish

422   3.   A parish is Jesuit if, committed to the pastoral goals and policies of the local church, it also "participates in the apostolic priorities of the Society"[2] and in the mission plan of the province, according to "our way of proceeding."[3] As central to its life, the parish gathers

---

[1] GC 31, D 27, n. 10.

[2] Peter-Hans Kolvenbach, "Creativity in the Pastoral Ministry," to Jesuit pastors of South Asia (JEPASA), 1993.

[3] Pedro Arrupe, "Some Guidelines for the Parish Apostolate," *AR* 17 (1979): p. 893.

as a community to celebrate its joys, struggles, and hopes—in the Word, in the Eucharist, and the other sacraments—in well-planned, creative, and inculturated ways. A parish becomes an evangelized and evangelizing community committed to "justice and reconciliation" and makes its popular devotions relevant to contemporary needs.[4]

423   4. A Jesuit parish is energized by Ignatian spirituality, especially through the Spiritual Exercises, and by individual and communal discernment. It tries to provide well-developed programs in catechesis and formation for both individuals and families; it offers opportunities for spiritual direction and pastoral counseling. Following the model of the election in the Spiritual Exercises, it helps individuals to discern their vocation in life.

424   5. The parish opens itself progressively to ecumenical and interreligious dialogue and reaches out to alienated Christians as well as to nonbelievers. It grows into a participative church through such means as basic human and ecclesial communities and promotes opportunities for lay participation and leadership.

425   6. In its service of the faith, a Jesuit parish is called upon to develop strategies to promote local and global justice by means of both personal conversion and structural change. Networking with other Jesuit apostolic works as well as other ecclesial and civil organizations, it opposes all forms of discrimination and contributes to a genuine culture of solidarity which transcends parish boundaries.

The Jesuit in a Parish

426   7. A Jesuit is missioned to a parish, Jesuit or otherwise, in order to contribute meaningfully to its total life. He should be selected for his lived spirituality and pasto-

---

4 Cf. GC 32, D 4, nn. 17f.

ral competence. He must be able to interact positively with various age groups and should have the necessary skills for working collegially with laity and other members of the parish staff.

427   8.   Jesuits in parish ministry should have ongoing contact with other Jesuits, diocesan pastors, and other religious ministering in the region. They should spend time with them for collective reflection and common action.

428   9.   A Jesuit destined to become a pastor must have special training, especially in such skills as homiletics, liturgy, catechesis, sociocultural analysis, social communication, and conflict management. In addition, opportunities for contact with model parishes and appropriate pastoral training centers must be available to him for ongoing formation. It is also recommended that apostolic experiments in parishes be made available to Jesuits from the early stages of formation.

A Mandate to Father General

429   10.   We mandate Father General to evaluate and update our existing norms for accepting and withdrawing from parishes and to communicate the results to the whole Society.[5] Given the many different types of parishes in the world, provincials will need to adapt the norms to local situations.

---

[5] Cf. GC 31, D 27, n. 10.

• *DECREE TWENTY* •

ECOLOGY

(RECOMMENDATION TO FATHER GENERAL)

430   1.   The contemporary debate between development and ecology is often posed as an opposition between First World desires and Third World needs; in fact the terms refer to many interrelated problems throughout the world. The Society of Jesus can contribute to overcoming some elements of the dilemma by encouraging both international awareness and local action. The many postulates received offer rich suggestions on this subject.

431   2.   This congregation recommends to Father General that a study be made regarding the following issues:

2, 1.   How our Ignatian spirituality provides us with a foundation for a universal response

2, 2.   How our apostolates can contribute in their specific ways, and also can further effective collaboration, and

2, 3.   How this issue affects our lifestyle and the decisions that we make in our institutions

432   The results of this study should be communicated to the whole Society as an orientation for our way of proceeding.

DECREE TWENTY-ONE

INTERPROVINCIAL AND SUPRAPROVINCIAL COOPERATION

Our Vision

433   1. **Ignatian heritage.** The international character of our mission finds its genesis in the Trinitarian vision of Ignatius; its meaningful expression is found in our fourth vow of obedience to the Holy Father. Ignatius and his companions decided to form a single apostolic body to be placed at the disposal of the Vicar of Christ for universal mission. For Ignatius, the more universal was the service, the more was it divine. This has meant, throughout our history, that Jesuits are ready to go wherever in the world their service is most needed; availability is to be an attitude of the individual Jesuit and a characteristic of the whole Society: mobile, agile, responding to the needs of a fast-changing world.

434   2. **The world and the Church today.** Today, more than ever, the needs of the world constitute an urgent call to put our Ignatian universalism into practice. Growing consciousness of the world has given us a deeper realization that some problems are global in nature and therefore require global solutions: the division between rich and poor and the consequent need to seek an alternative socioeconomic world order, the struggle to overcome the international forces that tend to marginalize the entire continent of Africa, the need to rebuild entire societies after the collapse of totalitarian regimes, a better redistribution of the resources available for evangelization. The needs that call for common action are many; the difficult search for world unity requires the presence, witness, and involvement of the Society.

435   3. **Living our heritage.** Effective apostolic service also requires a lived awareness of the local church. We must promote inculturation in order to evangelize all peoples and all cultures. We must be apostolically rooted in a way that does not weaken the universal character of our call and service. We are to dedicate all our energies to the particular mission we have received, contributing to the dynamic life of the individual apostolic work, community, and province in which we serve, without losing our awareness of being sent into the Lord's universal vineyard. Together we form *unum corpus apostolicum*. To live this tension between the local and the universal is not easy; our universal consciousness needs to be nourished, expressed, and challenged.

What Have We Achieved?

436   4.   Recent general congregations have emphasized the universal dimension of our vocation and, in various ways, stressed the importance of international cooperation.[1] Provincials have been reminded that in addition to their responsibility for their own provinces, they share responsibility with Father General for the needs of the whole Society.[2] In response, many positive fruits have been produced. The awareness of being one universal body has grown. Ignatian universalism is being expressed in many distinct ways: mutual help and solidarity among different provinces and regions, sharing of information and experiences, interprovincial meetings

---

[1] GC 31, D 48, n. 8; GC 32, D 4, n. 81; GC 33, D 1, n. 46.

[2] GC 30, D 49; GC 32, D 4, n. 68; *Guidelines for Provincials*, n. 58.

and work groups, a variety of activities undertaken in common. In particular, conferences of major superiors have fostered better communication and attention to common problems; in some cases they have been able to establish common works.

437   5. However, we agree with Father General that "we do not exploit all the possibilities given to us by being an international apostolic body."[3] A certain kind of provincialism, the immediate demands of local needs, and a lack of appropriate interrelated structures have prevented us from realizing our global potential. If we are to respond to the calls of today's world in fidelity to our universal vocation, we must move beyond current accomplishments. We must deepen a worldwide spirit and strengthen formal structures and informal ties that will better enable global and regional cooperation. In the spirit of this general congregation, a spirit of implementation, we offer the following recommendations.

Recommendations

438   6. **Fostering an attitude of universalism.** In response to the grace of our Jesuit vocation, we must foster an attitude of universalism not only in the admission and formation of new members but as an interior attitude of all Jesuits, particularly those having responsibility for governance.

439   7. *Candidates:* The universality of the Society is to be presented to candidates; evaluation of their suitability is to take into account their openness to and capacity for this characteristic of our vocation.

440   8. *Formation:* The universality of the Society as a characteristic of our Ignatian charism is to be emphasized at each stage of formation. The appropriation of

[3] Peter-Hans Kolvenbach, Address to the Congregation of Provincials 1, Loyola, 1990.

this dimension of our charism can be reinforced by experiences of the universal Society such as international meetings of those in formation and opportunities to become familiar with another culture in another part of the world. As far as possible, Jesuits should receive a part of their formation in another culture.[4]

441   9. *Permanent formation:* One objective of ongoing formation is to foster an attitude of universalism through experiences of the universal character of the Society: every Jesuit should have such opportunities. This will not only develop a personal sense of Ignatian universalism but also enable provinces to develop a more global perspective.

442   10. *Facility in languages:* In order to facilitate communication with other cultures and throughout the universal Society, all are to learn languages other than their own, and the Society as a whole should try to have a common language. To that end, Jesuits in formation will learn English; those whose mother tongue is English will learn another modern language of global significance, to be determined by the cultural context in which they live. As far as possible, Jesuits who have completed initial formation are encouraged to follow the same principle.

443   11. *Being sent on mission to another culture:* The ideal of Jesuit universalism is that every Jesuit should be available for assignment anywhere in the world. In practice, since the transition from one culture to another may not be easy, screening and training procedures have to be established. In addition, we need to ensure that a man being sent to a different culture or on an international mission is psychologically mature enough to live what could be a less rooted style of life. To this end, some form of *informationes* should be used.

---

[4] General Norms for Jesuit Studies, n. 46.

444   12. *Governance:* For the effective living-out of our universality, it is essential that those responsible for governance in the Society, particularly provincials along with their consultors, have a strong sense of this charism and "possess the qualities and endowments so absolutely necessary for the establishment of true and productive cooperation among themselves. . . . Father General should, moreover, have these qualities in mind when naming provincials" and their consultors.[5] The meeting of new provincials with Father General is an appropriate time to emphasize their role in developing the universal character of the Society.

445   13. **Developing global and regional networking.** The official structure for the governance of the Society— Father General, his council, and major superiors throughout the world—constitutes a framework for the development of many different forms of global and regional cooperation and networking, with examples ranging from an interprovince novitiate to the Jesuit Refugee Service.

446   14. *Global networking:* Although numerous regional and international networks already exist, to exploit more fully the possibilities given us by being an international body, additional global and regional networks must be created. Such networks of persons and institutions should be capable of addressing global concerns through support, sharing of information, planning, and evaluation, or through implementation of projects that cannot easily be carried out within province structures. The potential exists for networks of specialists who differ in expertise and perspectives but who share a common concern, as well as for networks of university departments, research centers, scholarly journals, and regional advocacy groups. The potential also exists for cooperation in and through international agencies,

---

[5] GC 31, D 48, nn. 8, 1° b.

nongovernmental organizations, and other emerging associations of women and men of goodwill. Initiative and support for these various forms of networks should come from all levels of the Society, but the secretariats of the General Curia must continue to play an important role in establishing them.

447   In many respects, the future of international cooperation remains largely uncharted. With creative imagination, openness, and humility, we must be ready to cooperate with all those working for the integral development and liberation of people.

448   15. *Twinning:* Twinning, which has replaced the traditional concept of "mission regions," has become an increasingly effective instrument for mutually enriching exchanges between provinces around the globe. A thorough review of twinning is recommended in order to redefine its goals and functions, so that greater solidarity and a more effective matching of resources with needs can be achieved. Mission offices are invited to participate in this review, so that they may broaden their function to include a concern for greater cooperation and effectiveness.

449   16. **Conferences of Major Superiors.** General Congregation 34 reaffirms the establishment of conferences of major superiors, recommended by GC 31 as a structural means for interprovincial and supraprovincial cooperation; it strongly urges Father General to promote the development of these conferences.

450   17. *Variety:* It is recognized that for a number of reasons significant differences exist in the degree to which conferences have developed in the different regions of the Society. Rather than seeking uniformity, the design and the mode of operating of the various conferences of major superiors will reflect cultural and regional differences.

451   18. *Objectives:* In spite of their differences, for the sake of a necessary consistency among conferences it is recommended that the objectives of each include the following:

       a. to open the Society of a given region to the universal dimensions of the Society

       b. to help major superiors become more aware of their responsibility for the Society and the Church throughout the entire region

       c. to facilitate unity, communication, a common vision, and effective leadership among major superiors

       d. to set priorities, to plan for and coordinate common activities

452   19. *Composition:* The composition of a conference is determined by Father General after consultation and taking into account geographical and cultural factors, in order to ensure that cooperation among the provinces involved will be meaningful and fruitful. It may be necessary to restructure some existing conferences so as to increase the number of common interests among the member provinces.

453   20. *Conditions for effectiveness:* As conferences become more structured, true and productive interprovince and supraprovince cooperation will require the effective leadership of a moderator, along with statutes approved by Father General.

454   21. **Moderators of conferences of major superiors.** The moderator is to assist in the development of a common vision for the region and for the whole Society, and guide efforts towards the setting of priorities, planning, and decision making. As the executive of the conference, he carries out decisions, implements policies, and oversees common undertakings such as common works, projects, and services. He also promotes various forms of cooperation among the Jesuits in the provinces of the conference and their apostolic works.

455 22. *Authority of the moderator:* The moderator of a conference must have the authority needed to call its major superiors to research, planning, and setting of priorities, and then to call them to carry out the required actions both within provinces and regionally. The major superiors themselves remain jointly responsible for the implementation of actions decided upon and for the provision of the resources needed for common works. The respective authority and responsibilities of the moderator and of the major superiors of the conference, along with procedures for making decisions, are to be specified in the statutes approved by Father General.

456 23. *Common works:* When a common work is under the care of a conference, any division at the level of major superior between apostolic responsibility for the work and *cura personalis* of the Jesuits assigned to it on a permanent basis should be avoided as much as possible, so as to safeguard the normal conditions necessary for authentic Ignatian government.

457 24. *Personnel for common works:* Established rules and objective criteria will govern the assignment of personnel from the provinces and regions. When a major superior is asked to make a particular man available for a common work, he should normally give this request a priority at least equal to the needs of his own province or region.

458 25. *Meetings of moderators:* Moderators will be called together annually by Father General *(a)* to heighten their own sense of the universal character of the Society, *(b)* to gain a better understanding of the global priorities of the Society, and *(c)* to work with Father General in overseeing and encouraging the further development of regional and global cooperation. Stability rather than rapid turnover of membership within the group of moderators will enable these meetings to have the desired continuity that will make them more effective.

459   26. *Communication:* Communication among moderators, especially when called for by further development of regional and global priorities, is to be encouraged. In addition, regular communication between the moderators and their respective regional assistant(s) will enable everyone involved to serve the Society more effectively. Regional assistants for the provinces involved will be invited to meetings of the conference.

460   27. *Attendance at meetings:* All moderators, including those who are not also provincials, attend general congregations and meetings of provincials *ex officio*.

461   28. **Priorities.** Father General, with his staff and in his regular direct contacts with provincials and with the moderators of the conferences, will discern the greater needs of the universal Church and will establish global and regional priorities. These priorities are to be taken into consideration as conferences and provinces establish their own respective priorities. Annual letters should evaluate apostolic effectiveness based on these priorities.

•   *DECREE TWENTY-TWO*   •

INTERPROVINCIAL HOUSES AND WORKS IN ROME

462   1. Following a tradition that originated with St. Ignatius, and in the spirit of our fourth vow, General Congregation 34[1] confirms the commitment of the Society of Jesus to the interprovincial works entrusted to us by the Holy See[2] as reaffirmed by Pope John Paul II in his opening allocution to this congregation.[3] We recognize the valuable service which these institutions offer to the universal Church in the name of the whole Society; we are grateful to the Jesuits who have sustained them; at a time when their opportunities for service to the Church are increasing in importance, we wish to ensure, and even enhance, the effectiveness of these

---

[1] Three previous general congregations have recommended to Father General and the whole Society a special concern for the Pontifical Gregorian University and its associated institutes: GC 29, D 17, n. 2; GC 30, D 18, n. 1; GC 31, D 31.

[2] The interprovincial works in Rome entrusted to the Society by the Holy See include the Pontifical Gregorian University, the Pontifical Biblical Institute, the Pontifical Oriental Institute, the Pontifical Russicum College, Vatican Radio, and the Vatican Observatory. There are also interprovincial works of the Society itself: the Historical Institute, the College of St. Robert Bellarmine, and the International College of the Gesù.

[3] Cf. John Paul II, Allocution to General Congregation 34, 5 January 1995, n. 5; cf. Appendix I.

works. We therefore call upon the whole Society, especially major superiors, who share Father General's responsibility for these institutions, to unite in a common effort to further this important service to the universal Church.

463   2.   In order to address certain long-standing, complex, and potentially threatening concerns in an effective way, immediate and decisive action is needed. GC 34 therefore gives the following **mandates** to Father General:

464   3.   Father General shall commission a thorough evaluation of the Pontifical Gregorian University, the Pontifical Biblical Institute, and the Pontifical Oriental Institute, together with the support these institutions receive from the provinces. This evaluation, while respecting the specific academic character and autonomy of these institutions, is to include academic policies and programs, faculty recruitment and development, financial management and accountability, the structures of the Jesuit communities, and the governance structures of the works and of the Delegation for the International Roman Houses. We strongly recommend that the charge to conduct this evaluation be given to a group of persons with experience, expertise, and interest in these works, including representatives from these institutions and from outside them, and involving Father General's delegate. Based on the recommendations of this group, Father General shall take those measures necessary to strengthen these works significantly and ensure their future.

465   4.   The delegate of Father General shall, with the faculties of a major superior received from him, have religious and apostolic responsibility for the interprovincial houses and works in Rome and for the Jesuits assigned to them.

466   5. Father General shall establish a permanent interprovincial commission composed of representatives from the conferences of major superiors and including experienced educators and administrators, to assist him and his delegate with the ongoing governance of the interprovincial houses and works in Rome.

DECREE TWENTY-THREE

CONGREGATIONS AND GOVERNANCE

A. THE GENERAL CONGREGATION

467   1. General Congregation 34 has examined Decree 3 of GC 33 in the light of experience and the replies of the province congregations and has established the following:

468   1° The rules for the composition of a general congregation introduced by GC 33, D. 3, nn. 1 and 2, are to be maintained, but still *ad experimentum*.

469   2° Those elected in the province congregations should constitute a majority of the members of the general congregation.

470   2. In order to favor the participation of all members in the life of the Society, as recommended by Vatican Council II and prescribed in the revised Code of Canon Law,[1] GC 34 decrees that all formed coadjutors have the right to be electors in a general congregation and establishes the following with regard to their representation:

471   1° All formed members of the Society who do not already have the right to attend the general congregation *ex officio* have passive voice in the province congregation to be chosen as electors (and substitutes)

---

[1] CIC 631 n. 1; Vatican Council II, *Perfectæ Caritatis* n. 14.

to the general congregation.[2] During the latter, however, formed coadjutors will not have passive voice for election to an office for which the profession of four vows is required.

472   2° If the total number of formed coadjutors elected is more than 10 percent of the members (elected and *ex officio*) of the general congregation, the one most recently admitted to final vows will be replaced by a substitute elected from the same province who is professed of four vows.

473   3° In any case, Father General (or Vicar General) will provide for the participation of some brothers, at least as procurators *ad negotia*.

474   3.   The Formula of the Province Congregation and the Formula of the General Congregation are to be revised in conformity with what has been established in this present decree.

475   4.   GC 34 recommends that Father General establish a commission to study the possibilities and advantages of a new model for the general congregation which, while maintaining the Ignatian principles for such a congregation, would make it both more effective and more efficient. Among the areas to be studied would be a new examination of the significance and importance of the main criteria currently employed to determine the composition of a general congregation, which do not seem compatible with the goal of a notable reduction of its members. The results of these studies are to be discussed at the next general congregation.

476   5.   Moreover, GC 34 recommends to Father General that an evaluation be done of the preparation for and the way of proceeding in this general congregation. In the light of this evaluation and in order to prepare more effective methods and dynamics for treating business in

---

[2] FPC 59, §§ 2f.

GC 35, Father General may, with the authority delegated by this general congregation, modify those prescriptions of the Formula of a General Congregation that deal with preparation and the treating of business, if he judges it opportune, with the deliberative vote of all the Fathers of the General Curia who have a right *ex officio* to attend a general congregation.

B. Congregation to Elect a Temporary Vicar General

477   1.   Father General is to deposit in writing the name or names of the temporary vicar(s) general he wishes to appoint in case of his death[3] and in case of his incapacity.[4]

478   2.   The congregation to elect a temporary vicar general, if held, is to be composed of the following:

479   1° All the Fathers of the General Curia who have a right *ex officio* to be electors in a general congregation

480   2° All those Fathers who have an office in the place where the congregation is to be held which gives them a right *ex officio* to attend a province congregation, and who are professed of four vows, to be called by seniority of profession in such a way that the total number of members of the congregation shall not exceed forty

481   3.   The minimum number of members to begin the congregation is ten.

482   4.   The Formula of the Congregation to Elect a Temporary Vicar General is to be revised in conformity with what has been established in the Complementary Norms to the Constitutions and in the present decree.

---

[3] *Const.* [687].

[4] *Const.* [773, 786].

C. CONGREGATIONS OF PROCURATORS
AND PROVINCIALS

483   1.   GC 34 has examined Decree 39 of GC 31 in the light of experience and the replies of the province congregations and has established the following:

484   2.   The congregation of procurators will take place every four years, according to the modalities prescribed in the Formula for the Congregation of Procurators, n. 1, §1.

485   3.   The congregation of provincials is abolished.

486   4.   Approximately every six years beginning from the last general congregation, Father General shall convoke a meeting of all provincials, in order to consider the state, the problems, and the initiatives of the universal Society, as well as international and supraprovincial cooperation.

487   5.   Since province congregations will be convoked less frequently than in the past, it is recommended that provincials convoke other types of meetings which will promote the participation and coresponsibility of all its members in the discernment and life of the province.

488   6.   The Formula of the Congregation of Procurators is to be revised in conformity with what has been established in this present decree:

1°   Title: Formula of the Congregation of Procurators.

2°   N. 1, §1: "Every four years after the end of the last general congregation, counting from 26 September (unless another day of the same civil year seems more suitable to Father General), procurators from all the provinces are to convene who have been elected according to the prescriptions of the Formula of the Province Congregation."

3°   N. 1, §2: "It is not to be postponed for another four years but is to be held the following year."

4° Title I: the title itself is to be canceled (because there is no longer a Title II).

5° N. 2, §1, 2°: "Under the leadership of the Superior General, they are to confer on the state and more universal undertakings of the Society. For the better preparation of the members of the congregation of procurators, the Superior General should communicate to them in good time the points for consultation in the congregation."

6° N. 2, §2: "The congregation may put together and offer to the Society a report on the state of the Society": to be canceled.

7° N. 3: "The congregation is composed of the Superior General, the vicar or the coadjutor vicar, the assistants *ad providentiam*, the general counselors, the procurators elected by the provinces or their substitutes according to the Formula of the Province Congregation, nn. 3, § 1, 2°; 61; 96. The place of the assistants *ad providentiam* can be taken by their substitutes, named by the Superior General and approved by the majority of the provincials, provided the assistants whose substitutes they are, are not present."

8° N. 6: ". . . the Superior General with the assistants *ad providentiam* is to examine the acts of the province congregations."

9° Nn. 17, §§1 and 2: to be canceled.

10° N. 31, §1: ". . . are to be given to the Superior General with the assistants *ad providentiam* for approval."

11° Title II (nn. 36–40): all to be canceled.

D. THE PROVINCE CONGREGATION

489   1. GC 34, in accord with the provisions of GC 33, Decree 5, has reexamined the norms for the province congregation in the light of experience and the responses of the provinces, and has established the following:

490   2.   With regard to the number of participants in the province congregation by reason of the prior election, the norms now in force (Formula of a Province Congregation [FCP], 15, par. 1, 2°) are to be maintained.

491   3.   The provincial, with the deliberative vote of the *Cœtus prævius*, can designate up to five members in those provinces which have at least 0.5 percent of the total membership of the Society, and three in the other provinces.

492   4.   The participants in the province congregation must be

       1°   Professed of four vows: at least 50 percent

       2°   Formed members: at least 80 percent

493   5.   Of the elected and *ex officio* participants in the province congregation, there must be at least

       1°   One formed brother

       2°   Two approved members, of whom at least one is not ordained

494   6.   The socius of the provincial is to participate *ex officio* in the province congregation.

495   7.   With regard to active and passive voice in the election prior to the province congregation, the norm currently in force is to be maintained: five years in the Society for active voice (FCP 18, 1°) and eight years in the Society for passive voice (FCP 18, 2°).

496   8.   At the beginning of the congregation, the provincial will propose some questions on the state of the province, so that the congregation is able to have a consultation on the situation of the province, under the leadership of the provincial.

497   9.   For a postulate to be proposed to the general congregation or to the Superior General in the name of the province congregation, it must be approved by more than half the votes of those present, nn. 44 and 45 notwithstanding.

498   10. The Formula for a Province Congregation is to be revised in accord with the present decree.

499   11. Moreover, the general congregation mandates Father General to study and, insofar as is necessary, authorizes him to modify, with the deliberative vote of the Fathers of the Curia who have the right *ex officio* to attend a general congregation, the following points of the Formula of a Province Congregation:

1° Drawing by lot the letter of the alphabet which will come first in the list for the prior election (FCP n. 20)

2° Simplification of the process of handling the ballots in the prior election (FCP nn. 22, 23, 24, 25)

3° Modification of the norm for translating into Latin the documents of the province congregation (FCP n. 90, 3, 2°)

4° Passive voice of the superiors of common houses: possibly retaining this right in one's own province (FCP n. 17, 1, 3°)

5° Passive voice of the "applied" to other provinces: retaining and using this right in one's own province, with the prior agreement of the provincials involved (FCP n. 10, 1)

6° Incompatibility of the office of Procurator, Relator, or Substitute with that of the provincial-designate, whatever the time when he is to enter into office (before or after the congregation in question) (FCP nn. 61, 3, 4; 62; 93, 2, 3)

E. FATHER GENERAL'S ASSISTANTS AND COUNSELORS

500   In response to Father General's invitation, GC 34 has considered various questions having to do with the central government of the Society, especially with regard to the assistants and counselors of the Superior General. It has established the following norms, which modify some norms in Decree 44 of GC 31 and Decree 15 of GC 32.

I. FATHER GENERAL'S COUNCIL

501   1.   Father General shall have a council composed of about twelve members.

502   2.   The four assistants *ad providentiam* shall be general counselors.

503   3.   All regional assistants shall be general counselors.

504   4.   Thus, the general council will be composed of the four assistants *ad providentiam*, the regional assistants, and those general counselors charged with looking after important aspects of the life of the universal Society. One person can combine different functions. The secretary of the Society, as secretary, shall take part in the meetings but will not be a general counselor.

505   5.   The other major officials and the sectoral secretaries will participate in meetings of the general council whenever their particular competence would be helpful and in enlarged meetings which will be called periodically.

506   6.   If Father General constitutes a reduced group within the council to deal with administrative matters and current questions which do not require that his entire council meet together in consultation, it is recommended that

507 • the four assistants *ad providentiam* be part of this reduced group

508 • the members should have a certain stability, which means they should not be changed too often, nor should different members be changed at the same time

II. ELECTION OF THE ASSISTANTS *AD PROVIDENTIAM* AND APPOINTMENT OF THE GENERAL COUNSELORS DURING THE GENERAL CONGREGATION

509 1. Each general congregation will proceed to elect the four assistants *ad providentiam*, and Father General will renew his council according to the following procedure. This procedure is to be reviewed by the next general congregation.

510 1° The electors of each assistancy will propose to Father General by secret ballot the names of three candidates, normally from their own assistancy, who would be suitable to become general counselors and to be appointed as regional assistant.

511 2° From these names, Father General will appoint a sufficient number of general counselors, at least to cover the need for regional assistants.

512 3° The congregation will elect the four assistants *ad providentiam* according to the Formula of a General Congregation, nn. 130-37, choosing them from four different assistancies and taking account of the names of those appointed by Father General as general counselors (while retaining the freedom also to elect other persons).

513 4° Former assistants *ad providentiam* may be reelected by the general congregation, and former general counselors may be reappointed by Father General.

514   5° In addition to those appointed in the process described above, Father General retains the right to appoint other general counselors for the care of important sectors of the Society's life. These appointments are to be made after hearing the opinions of the other general counselors, and with the deliberative vote of the four assistants *ad providentiam.*

III. REPLACEMENT OF THE FOUR ASSISTANTS *AD PROVIDENTIAM* AND OF THE GENERAL COUNSELORS OUTSIDE A GENERAL CONGREGATION

515   1. The four assistants *ad providentiam* normally remain in office until the next general congregation. For their replacement outside a general congregation, the norms presently in force are confirmed.[5]

516   2. It is recommended that the general counselors who are not assistants *ad providentiam* remain in office for six to eight years, and that they not all be replaced at the same time.

517   3. When there is to be a change of a general counselor who is not an assistant *ad providentiam* but who will have to perform the task of regional assistant, Father General will ask the provincials of the assistancy concerned to propose to him three names of possible candidates, from among whom he will name the new general counselor.

518   4. For the replacement of a general counselor who is not an assistant *ad providentiam* and who will not have the task of a regional assistant, Father General will name the new general counselor after hearing the opinion of the other general counselors and with the deliberative vote of the assistants *ad providentiam.*

---

[5] Cf. *Collectio Decretorum,* n. 269, §§1–6; *Normæ Complementariæ* n. 376, §§1–6.

IV. FINAL PROVISIONS

519   1.   Once approved by the general congregation, this decree will come into force immediately after the three days allowed for intercessions (FCG 128, §1) have ended.

520   2.   This decree abrogates contrary dispositions in Decree 44 of GC 31 and Decree 15 of GC 32.

• *DECREE TWENTY-FOUR* •

THE ONGOING FORMATION
OF SUPERIORS
(RECOMMENDATION TO FATHER GENERAL)

521   In order to assist in the ongoing formation of superiors, General Congregation 34 recommends that Father General publish updated versions of the following documents: *Guidelines for Provincials, Guidelines for Local Superiors, Guidelines for the Distinction and Relations between the Director of a Work and the Religious Superior.*

DECREE TWENTY-FIVE

POWERS GRANTED AND MANDATES ENTRUSTED BY THE GENERAL CONGREGATION TO FATHER GENERAL

522   1. General Congregation 34 grants to Father General the power and responsibility to establish the authoritative and definitive version of the congregation's decrees and recommendations. This work will include the following:

523   1, 1. To make whatever corrections are clearly needed, including the correction of discriminatory language

524   1, 2. To edit the decrees and recommendations with regard to style, and to reconcile contradictions if any are detected

525   1, 3. Thus to establish the authoritative text, based on the original language(s) in which each decree or recommendation was written

526   1, 4. To have the decrees and recommendations translated accurately into the three official languages of the congregation

527   2. This work will be accomplished by members of the General Curia assisted, if necessary, by Jesuits from elsewhere; it will be finally approved by Father General with the deliberative vote of those Fathers of the General Curia who have a right *ex officio* to attend a general congregation.

528 3. GC 34 grants Father General the power to abrogate or modify decrees of past general congregations that are not in accord with the decrees of this present general congregation, after obtaining the deliberative vote of those Fathers of the General Curia who have a right *ex officio* to attend a general congregation, and without prejudice to the powers given him in other decrees.

529 4. GC 34 entrusts to Father General the power and responsibility to complete the work on the *Complementary Norms* and the *Notes to the Constitutions* according to the mind of the general congregation, with the deliberative vote of four delegates elected by the general congregation:

530 4, 1. To complete the definitive choice of texts from the decrees of GC 34 to be incorporated into the *Complementary Norms*, based on but not limited to the list drawn up by the commissions and collated by Commission 4 towards the end of the congregation

531 4, 2. To assure that discriminatory language, inconsistencies, and unnecessary repetitions are corrected

532 4, 3. To establish the final authoritative Latin text of the *Notes* and *Complementary Norms* and to authorize their accurate translation into the three official languages

533 4, 4. Thus to declare the *Constitutions*, *Notes*, and *Complementary Norms* ready for publication in one volume

534 5. GC 34 grants Father General the power to approve the minutes which could not be communicated to the delegates of the congregation, in accordance with the norms of the Formula of the General Congregation, n. 142, §4, 1[a].

CONCLUSION: CHARACTERISTICS OF OUR WAY OF PROCEEDING

535   1.   Certain attitudes, values, and patterns of behavior join together to become what has been called the Jesuit way of proceeding. The characteristics of our way of proceeding were born in the life of St. Ignatius and shared by his first companions. Jerome Nadal writes that "the form of the Society is in the life of Ignatius."[1] "God set him up as a living example of our way of proceeding."[2]

536   2.   General Congregation 34 considered which of these characteristics we need especially to draw upon today and the form they must take in the new situations and changing ministries in which we labor. We suggest that the following be included among them.

1. Deep Personal Love for Jesus Christ

537   3.   *Here it will be to ask for an intimate knowledge of our Lord, who has become human for me, that I may love him more and follow him more closely.*[3]

---

[1] Nadal, MHSI, vol. 90, *Commentarii de Instituto Societatis Iesu*, bk. 5, [§II] (p. 268) and [52*a] (p. 287).

[2] Nadal, MHSI, ibid.., [33] (p. 262).

[3] *SpEx* [104].

538   4. In remorse, gratitude, and astonishment—but above all with passionate love—first Ignatius, and then every Jesuit after him, has turned prayerfully to "Christ our Lord hanging on the Cross before me" and has asked of himself, "What have I done for Christ? What am I doing for Christ? What must I do for Christ?"[4] The questions well up from a heart moved with profound gratitude and love. This is the foundational grace that binds Jesuits to Jesus and to one another. "What is it to be a Jesuit today? It is to know that one is a sinner yet called to be a companion of Jesus as Ignatius was."[5] The mission of the reconciled sinner is the mission of reconciliation: the work of faith doing justice. A Jesuit freely gives what he has freely received: the gift of Christ's redeeming love.

539   5. Today we bring this countercultural gift of Christ to a world beguiled by self-centered human fulfillment, extravagance, and soft living, a world that prizes prestige, power, and self-sufficiency. In such a world, to preach Christ poor and humble with fidelity and courage is to expect humiliation, persecution, and even death. We have seen this happen to our brothers in recent years. Yet we move forward resolutely out of our "desire to resemble and imitate in some manner our Creator and Lord Jesus Christ . . . since he is the way which leads men to life."[6] Today, as always, it is deep, personal devotion to Jesus, himself the Way, that principally characterizes the Jesuit way of proceeding.

2. Contemplative in Action

540   6. *I shall not fail to recall that grace which he had in all circumstances, while at*

---

[4] *SpEx* [53].

[5] GC 32, D 2, n. 1.

[6] *Examen* [101].

> *work or in conversation, of feeling the*
> *presence of God and of tasting spiritual*
> *things, of being contemplative even in*
> *the midst of action; he used to interpret*
> *this as seeking God in all things.*[7]

541   7.   The God of Ignatius is the God who is at work in all things: laboring for the salvation of all as in the Contemplation to Attain Love; working immediately and directly with the exercitant as in Annotations 15 and 16; laboring as Christ the King for the liberation of the world; beginning, preserving, directing, and advancing the Society of Jesus as at the beginning and end of the Constitutions.

542   8.   For a Jesuit, therefore, not just any response to the needs of the men and women of today will do. The initiative must come from the Lord laboring in events and people here and now. God invites us to join with him in his labors, on his terms, and in his way. To discover and join the Lord, laboring to bring everything to its fullness, is central to the Jesuit way of proceeding. It is the Ignatian method of prayerful discernment, which can be described as "a constant interplay between experience, reflection, decision, and action, in line with the Jesuit ideal of being 'contemplative in action.'"[8] Through individual and communal apostolic discernment, lived in obedience, Jesuits take responsibility for their apostolic choices in today's world. Such discernment reaches out, at the same time, to embrace the larger community of all those with whom we labor in mission.

---

[7] Nadal, MHSI, vol. 47, *Epistolæ P. Hieronimi Nadal, 1546–1577,* bk. 4, p. 651.

[8] GC 32, D 4, n. 73.

3. An Apostolic Body in the Church

543 9. *Finally we decided in the affirmative;
namely, that . . . we should not break
this divinely constituted oneness and
fellowship, but rather strengthen and
consolidate it ever more, forming ourselves into one body.*[9]

544 10. Following the example of Jesus, the first Jesuits
would be sent, as far as possible, in groups of at least
two.[10] Even when dispersed, a bond of unity—with
superiors and among themselves—remained strong
through the constant communication and writing of
letters that Ignatius insisted on, and especially through
the account of conscience. Xavier, laboring far from
Rome in the Indies, put it simply: "[T]he Society is
love."[11]

545 11. Jesuits today join together because each of us
has heard the call of Christ the King. From this union
with Christ flows, of necessity, a love for one another.
We are not merely fellow workers; we are friends in the
Lord. The community to which we belong is the entire
body of the Society itself, however dispersed over the
face of the earth. Though we come from many nations
and cultures and speak many languages, our union is
enriched, not threatened, by diversity. In shared prayer,
in conversation, and in the celebration of the Eucharist,
each of us finds the spiritual resources needed for an
apostolic community. And in our service of the Lord and
his spouse, the Church, the People of God, we are
especially united to the Roman Pontiff in order to be

---

[9] First conclusion of the Deliberations of the First Fathers in
1539, MHSI, Vol. 63, p. 3.

[10] Cf. *Const.* [624].

[11] To Father Ignatius of Loyola, Cochín, 1 December 1549, p. 5.

sent on the missions he may entrust to us.[12] As men of
the Church, we cannot but think with the Church, guided by the Spirit of the Risen Lord.[13]

4. In Solidarity with Those Most in Need

546   12. *And what they should especially seek to
accomplish for God's greater glory is to
preach, hear confessions, lecture, instruct
children, give good example, visit
the poor in the hospitals, exhort the
neighbor according to the amount of
talent which each is conscious of pos-
sessing, so as to move as many as possible to prayer and devotion.*[14]

547   13. Ignatius and his followers began their preaching
in poverty. They worked with the powerful and the
powerless, with princes, kings, and bishops, but also
with the women of the street and with the victims of the
plague. They linked their ministry to the powerful with
the needs of the powerless.

548   14. Today, whatever our ministry, we Jesuits enter
into solidarity with the poor, the marginalized, and the
voiceless, in order to enable their participation in the
processes that shape the society in which we all live
and work. They, in their turn, teach us about our own
poverty as no document can. They help us to understand the meaning of the gratuity of our ministries,
giving freely what we have freely received, giving our
very lives. They show us the way to inculturate gospel

---

[12] Cf. *Formula* [1].

[13] *SpEx* [365].

[14] Instruction of Ignatius to the Fathers at the Council of
Trent, 1546.

values in situations where God is forgotten. Through such solidarity we become "agents of inculturation."[15]

5. Partnership with Others

549   15. *For that same reason too, preference ought to be shown to the aid which is given to the great nations, such as the Indies, or to important cities, or to universities, which are generally attended by numerous persons who by being aided themselves can become laborers for the help of others.*[16]

550   16. Partnership and cooperation with others in ministry is not a pragmatic strategy resulting from diminished manpower; it is an essential dimension of the contemporary Jesuit way of proceeding, rooted in the realization that to prepare our complex and divided world for the coming of the Kingdom requires a plurality of gifts, perspectives, and experiences, both international and multicultural.

551   17. Jesuits, therefore, cooperate with lay women and men in the Church, with religious, priests, and bishops of the local church in which they serve, with members of other religions, and with all men and women of goodwill. To the extent that we develop a wide-ranging web of respectful and productive relationships, we fulfil Christ's priestly prayer "that they may all be one" (John 17:21).

---

[15] Pedro Arrupe, Letter and Document on Inculturation, *AR* 17 (1978): p. 236.

[16] *Const.* [622].

6. Called to Learned Ministry

552   18. *After the pilgrim realized that it was not God's will that he remain in Jerusalem, he continually pondered within himself what he ought to do. At last he inclined more to study for some time so he would be able to help souls, and he decided to go to Barcelona.*[17]

553   19. Ignatius very quickly saw the need for learning in the service of the faith and the ministry of the Word. In the Formula of the Institute we read, "[T]his Institute requires men who are thoroughly humble and prudent in Christ as well as conspicuous in the integrity of Christian life and learning."[18] Therefore it is characteristic of a Jesuit that he embodies in creative tension this Ignatian requirement to use all human means, science, art, learning, natural virtue, with a total reliance on divine grace.

554   20. In our ministry today we respect and appreciate the good in contemporary culture and critically propose alternatives to the negative aspects of that same culture. In the context of the complex challenges and opportunities of our contemporary world, this ministry requires all the learning and intelligence, imagination and ingenuity, solid studies and rigorous analysis that we can muster. To overcome ignorance and prejudice through learning and teaching, to make the Gospel truly "Good News" in a confused and troubled world through theological reflection, is a characteristic of our Jesuit way of proceeding.

---

[17] *Autobiography* [50].

[18] *Formula* [5].

7. Men Sent, Always Available for New Missions

555   21. *If they were not given permission to remain in Jerusalem, they would return to Rome and present themselves to the Vicar of Christ, so that he could make use of them wherever he thought it would be to the greater glory of God and the service of souls.*[19]

556   22. Nadal, in promulgating the *Constitutions*, asked: Why are there Jesuits? There are diocesan priests and bishops. He answers simply that our charism, indeed our reason for existence, is that we might go where needs are not being met. Our way of proceeding encourages this mobility.[20]

557   23. A Jesuit is essentially a man on a mission, a mission he receives from the Holy Father and from his own religious superior, but ultimately from Jesus Christ himself, the one sent by the Father. Jesuits remain "ready at any hour to go to some or other parts of the world where they may be sent by the Sovereign Pontiff or their own superiors."[21]

558   24. Therefore, it is characteristic of our way of proceeding that we live with an operative freedom: open, adaptable, even eager for any mission that may be given us. Indeed, the ideal is an unconditional consecration to mission, free of any worldly interest, and free to serve all men and women. Our mission extends to the creation of this same spirit of mission in others.

---

[19] *Autobiography* [85].

[20] Nadal, MHSI, vol. 90a, *Orationes Observationes*, [281] (p. 113).

[21] *Const.* [588].

8. Ever Searching for the *Magis*

559 25. *Those who wish to give greater proof of their love, and to distinguish themselves in whatever concerns the service of the Eternal King and the Lord of all, will not only offer themselves entirely for the work . . . but make offerings of greater value and of more importance.*[22]

560 26. The *magis* is not simply one among others in a list of Jesuit characteristics. It permeates them all. The entire life of Ignatius was a pilgrim search for the *magis,* the ever greater glory of God, the ever fuller service of our neighbor, the more universal good, the more effective apostolic means. "[M]ediocrity has no place in Ignatius's worldview."[23]

561 27. Jesuits are never content with the *status quo,* the known, the tried, the already existing. We are constantly driven to discover, redefine, and reach out for the *magis*. For us, frontiers and boundaries are not obstacles or ends, but new challenges to be faced, new opportunities to be welcomed. Indeed, ours is a holy boldness, "a certain apostolic aggressivity," typical of our way of proceeding.[24]

Conclusion

562 28. Our way of proceeding is a way of challenge. But "this way of proceeding is the reason why every son of the Society will always act and react in a consistently

---

[22] *SpEx* [97].

[23] Peter-Hans Kolvenbach, To the Friends and Colleagues of the Society of Jesus, *AR* 20 (1991): p. 606.

[24] Pedro Arrupe, Our Way of Proceeding, n. 12, *AR* 17 (1979): p 697.

Jesuit and Ignatian way, even in the most unforeseen circumstances."[25]

563   29. May we ever live more faithfully this way of Christ modeled for us by St. Ignatius. For this we pray in a prayer of Father Pedro Arrupe:

> Lord, meditating on "our way of proceeding," I have discovered that the ideal of *our* way of acting is *your* way of acting.

> Give me that *sensus Christi* that I may feel with your feelings, with the sentiments of your heart, which basically are love for your Father and love for all men and women.

> Teach me how to be compassionate to the suffering, to the poor, the blind, the lame, and the lepers.

> Teach us your way so that it becomes our way today, so that we may come closer to the great ideal of St. Ignatius: to be companions of Jesus, collaborators in the work of redemption.[26]

---

[25] Ibid., n. 55, *AR* 17 (1979): p. 719.

[26] Ibid., n. 56, *AR* 17 (1979): pp. 719–22.

APPENDICES

ALLOCUTION OF POPE JOHN PAUL II

5 January 1995

Dearly beloved Delegates of the Society of Jesus,

1.   With the celebration of the Eucharist, in the course of which you invoked the Holy Spirit, you began your general congregation this morning. Your work will extend over the coming weeks.

At the very beginning you also desired to meet with the Pope, in order to underline the singular charism of fidelity to the Successor of Peter which, according to St. Ignatius, should characterize the Society of Jesus. You expect to receive "missions" from the Pope, as the Constitutions of your Institute say, "that in everything God our Lord and the Apostolic See may be better served."[1] Following in the footsteps of your Founder and his first companions, with this gesture of loyalty to the ministry of the Roman Pontiff you declare that the Society is totally and without reservation of the Church, in the Church, and for the Church.

I greet you with great joy, beloved Religious, addressing my remarks first and foremost to your superior general, Father Peter-Hans Kolvenbach, thanking him for the sentiments he has just expressed in the name of all. Along with him, I greet the general council and the 223 delegates who, representing Jesuits from all over the world, give witness to the vitality and fruitful-

---

[1] *Const.* [612].

ness of the Society of Jesus, in the midst of all the various situations and problems it faces.

2.   Your general congregation certainly understands the particular importance of this present historical moment, since it is essentially dedicated to discerning the specific contribution your Institute is called to make to the *new evangelization, on the brink of the third Christian millennium*, as well as to updating the internal organization and legislation of the Society of Jesus so that it can render ever more faithful and effective service to the Church.

So that you may better undertake the task before you, I would like to propose for your reflection a few points of reference which are surely not new to you. I am certain that these will help you in defining more carefully your contribution to the evangelizing mission of the Church in our contemporary world, especially in view of the "Great Jubilee" of the year 2000, in which a "new springtime of Christian life" will be revealed, thanks to the openness of believers to the action of the Holy Spirit.[2]

3.   First of all, the Society of Jesus is called to reaffirm unequivocally and without any hesitation its specific *way to God*, which St. Ignatius sketched out in the Formula of the Institute: *loving fidelity to your charism* will be the certain source of renewed effectiveness. The Servant of God Paul VI reminded the participants of General Congregation 32 of this: "You have a spirituality strongly traced out, an unequivocal identity, and a centuries-old confirmation which was based on the validity of methods, which, having passed through the crucible of history, still bears the imprint of the strong spirit of St. Ignatius. Hence there is absolutely no need to doubt the fact that a more profound commitment to the way followed up until now—to the special charism—will be the renewed source of spiritual and apostolic fruitfulness." The late Holy Father added: "All of us must be vigilant so that the necessary adaptation will not be accomplished to the detriment of the fundamental identity or

---

[2] Cf. John Paul II, Apostolic constitution *Tertio Millennio Adveniente*, n. 18.

essential character of the role of the Jesuit as described in the Formula of the Institute as history and the particular spirituality of the order propose it, and as authentic interpretation of the very needs of the times seem still to require it. This image must not be altered; it must not be disfigured."[3]

Do not be afraid, then, to be ever more authentic sons of St. Ignatius, living fully your original inspiration and your charism in these last days of the century, deepening your full commitment to the Society of Jesus. Your charism calls you to be witnesses to the primacy of God and of his will. "Ad maiorem Dei gloriam": the religious life, the apostolate, commitment to the world of culture, to social work, and to care of the poor must always have as their single end the greater glory of the Lord. All this points clearly to the primacy of spirituality and of prayer: neglecting them would mean betraying the gift that you are called to be for the Church and for the world.

4.   Your commitment to the new evangelization in the light of the third millennium is based on this demanding spiritual and ascetic foundation which ought to be the basis for every apostolic activity. It requires first and foremost a *renewed dedication to the actualization of the command the Lord entrusted to the Church*: "Go into all the world and proclaim the Gospel to every creature" (Mark 16:15). This command of Christ is an essential aspect of the Church's mission.

"Founded chiefly for this purpose: to strive especially for the defense and propagation of the faith,"[4] the Society of Jesus, following the example of St. Ignatius and his beloved companion St. Francis Xavier, has offered in every moment of its existence a significant contribution, including the blood of its martyrs, to the realization of the Church's missionary task throughout many parts of the world.

I am certain that this general congregation will not fail to pay appropriate attention to such a fundamental aspect of your apostolate. Today, as you well know, new nationalisms,

---

[3] *Insegnamenti di Paolo VI*, 12 (1974), pp. 1181f.

[4] *Formula* [1].

radical ideologies, religious syncretism, certain theological interpretations of the mystery of Christ and his saving work, the difficulty of finding a balance between the need for the inculturation of the Gospel and the unity of the message contained in it, as well as other political, sociological, and religious circumstances, threaten to compromise the very foundations of your presence and evangelical activity in many countries. Despite these difficulties, I encourage the whole Society to persevere in its mission to proclaim the Gospel within the perspective of the Kingdom of God.

5.   The task of evangelization also requires a *more generous self-sacrifice in order to promote the full communion of all Christians*. In my recent apostolic letter *Tertio Millennio Adveniente*, I pointed out the supreme importance of the unity of all Christians: "As the new millennium approaches, among the most ardent petitions of this special moment, the Church asks the Lord that unity among all Christians of every denomination might increase, leading to the achievement of full communion."[5] In this great struggle the whole Church ought to find the Society in the vanguard. Resisting every temptation toward individualism, independence, or parallelism, the Society is called to give a stirring testimony to fraternal concord and ecclesial harmony.

The energies that the Society devotes to collaborating in every part of the Church's life are well known. In this regard, I encourage you to keep alive this fundamental note of your charism of *serving the universal Church*, overcoming every temptation of provincialism, regionalism, or isolationism that could endanger the very existence of certain international and interprovincial works of great importance for the universal Church and for the local churches. On this occasion, I want to thank the Society for the work of the Pontifical Gregorian University, the Pontifical Biblical Institute, the Pontifical Oriental Institute, and Vatican Radio. On the other hand, however, in those places where you exercise your ministries, you must respectfully coop-

---

[5] Apostolic letter *Tertio Millennio Adveniente*, n. 16.

erate with the pastoral planning of the bishops in their teaching and in their care for the local communities entrusted to them.

A similar interior attitude should inspire theological research which Jesuits, animated by the spirit of faith, undertake in humble fidelity to the teachings of the Magisterium. What is there to say about teaching that forms the younger generation? This teaching must strive to provide students with a clear, solid, and organic knowledge of Catholic doctrine, focused on knowing how to distinguish those affirmations that must be upheld from those open to free discussion and those that cannot be accepted.

6. With these points as your bases, what emerged in the preparation of the general congregation is an insistent priority for the Third Millennium: *missionary outreach and the promotion of a dynamic of ecclesial communion* that extends into ecumenism, directs interreligious dialogue, and inspires the service of human rights and peace as foundations of a civilization of love.

It is clear that no one can hope to heal the wounds and the divisions of the world without a total commitment of self to the service of communion in the Church. We must be very attentive, therefore, lest the faithful be confused by questionable teachings, by publications or speeches clearly at variance with the Church's teachings on faith and morals, or by any attitudes that offend communion in the Spirit. In this context I want to thank the Lord for the good that the Jesuits accomplish throughout the world spreading the Gospel of salvation through the witness of your words and your lives. I encourage you to continue on this path, dear brothers, surmounting every difficulty and relying constantly on the help of God, as well as the support of the Apostolic See, which expects much from you in this period of human history, troubled, yes, but through God's providence also rich in apostolic and missionary possibilities.

7. This is the moment of new evangelization, which demands of the Society an apostolic commitment renewed and

ever more concrete "in its devotion, its methods, and its expressions."[6]

Such a commitment must be rooted first of all in faith in the Lord who can fully sustain the Society even in difficult moments like our own, so that it may never cease to work generously for the increase of the Kingdom "by means of public preaching, lectures, and any other ministry whatsoever of the Word of God, and further by means of the Spiritual Exercises, the education of children and unlettered persons in Christianity, and the spiritual consolation of Christ's faithful through hearing confessions and administering the other sacraments."[7] Indeed, this Society is of the Lord Jesus, and his is the good that it daily accomplishes in its service to culture, especially in the university world, in the formation of youth, and in the spiritual support of so many priests, religious men and women, and lay people. The fruits of divine grace are found no less in the apostolates of the parishes, in social centers, in the area of mass-media work, and in many centers for alleviating human suffering.

All this richness is part of the dynamism of the new evangelization, relying not on human calculation or refined strategies, but on a humble and confident relationship with him who is the first evangelizer, Christ: "The apostolic energy of the new evangelization springs from a radical communion with Christ, the first evangelizer."[8]

To achieve authentic forms for inculturation of the faith and to promote the values of justice, peace, and solidarity so needed in nations around the world as fruits of Christian life, we must focus every apostolic effort on the *proclamation of Christ, the Redeemer of humanity*.

It is certainly true that the Society is deeply committed to social work and to the service of the least of humanity. How could this not be so? How could one strive for the "greater glory of God" in all things, while forgetting that, as St. Irenaeus wrote,

---

[6] *Insegnamenti di Giovanni Paolo II,* 6/1 (1983), p. 698.

[7] *Formula* [1].

[8] Final Document of the 1992 CELAM Conference, Santo Domingo, n. 28.

"the glory of God is the human person fully alive?" But such a mission should never be removed from the global service of the evangelizing mission of the Church, which is responsible for the salvation of every person and of the entire person, because of our supernatural destiny.

Dear brothers, the discernment that you are called to undertake during this general congregation must define ever more precisely your apostolate as a mission of utterly transparent evangelization, characterized by a powerful sense of God's presence, of love for the Church and for each individual as the "way of the Church," by a recognition of the gift of your vocation, and by the joy that comes from fidelity to God's mercy.

8.   Forming future apostles for such ascetic and pastoral directions is a fundamental need. You should always insist on a solid and lengthy formation for the professed of the Society. Your founder explicitly insisted that no one should be admitted to profession without thorough formation.[9] Pope Paul VI recognized that "[w]herever in the Church, even in the most difficult and extreme fields, in the crossroads of ideologies, in the front line between the deepest human desires and the perennial message of the Gospel, there have been, and there are, Jesuits."[10] Because this continues to be true, you must "not accede to the easy temptation of softening this formation, which invests such importance in each of its aspects: human, spiritual, doctrinal, disciplinary, and pastoral."[11]

I am fully aware of the great effort that has been expended to respond to such expectations. In this regard, I also want to express my appreciation for how much the Society of Jesus has done to improve the formation of the brothers, who are irreplaceable members of your order's life and apostolate.

9. My dear Jesuits, the recent synod of bishops dedicated to the consecrated life and to its mission in the Church and in the world has addressed to all religious an urgent appeal that *they*

---

[9] Cf. *Formula* [5].

[10] *Insegnamenti di Paolo VI*, 12 (1974), p. 1181.

[11] *Insegnamenti di Giovanni Paolo II*, 5/1 (1982), p. 715.

perform their prophetic mission at the service of the new evangelization, giving visible and clear witness in their style of life, in their work and prayer, in radical imitation of our chaste, poor, and obedient Lord. May this appeal inform and accompany the labors you are about to undertake, and guide the choices you are called upon to make. Be well assured that the Church needs your able contribution to proclaim the Gospel of Christ more effectively to the people of our time.

May Holy Mary, who sustained and illumined your Founder, help you to "keep always before your eyes God and then the nature of this Institute."[12] May she guide you with maternal love.

In support of all your generous plans, I ask God for abundant heavenly gifts for each of you, and from my heart I impart on you and on all the members of the Society of Jesus a special Apostolic Blessing.

---

[12] *Formula* [1].

INTRODUCTORY DISCOURSES
OF FATHER GENERAL

1: ON THE CALL OR VOCATION
OF THIS CONGREGATION

5 January 1995

In the Constitutions, which will have an important place in this General Congregation 34, St. Ignatius creatively characterizes how the ordinary government must serve the whole Society. To justify the absence of a regular general congregation or of a general chapter at set periods—"for example, every three or six years, more or less" [678]—Ignatius observes that "it does not seem good in our Lord that such a congregation should be held at definite intervals or very often; for the Superior General through the communication which he has with the whole Society and through the help he gets from those near him, can spare the Society as a whole from that work and distraction as far as possible" [677].

This introduction fits into the concern to spare the members of GC 34 the effort of meticulously studying Part Eight of the *Constitutions* and of losing time on an in-depth examination. Its sole purpose is to remind us of what a general congregation meant for Master Ignatius, what he expected from it, and what the Society today, in our concrete situation at the end of the second millennium, can personally and communally expect from it.

At the beginning of the congregation, it is good to recall "in the Lord" that, despite its administrative and juridical appearances, this assembly has its source and origins in the spiritual experience of Ignatius and his first companions. Before it acquired its present structure and became the plan now outlined in the Constitutions, the general congregation was a lived event whose thrust was to prolong the deliberations and the encounter of the first Fathers as friends in the Lord. The general congregation is of course the supreme authority, the highest level of power in the Society; but for Master Ignatius the congregation was above all a "personal union" [677], an encounter of persons. Here is how he approaches the chapter in question: "Now let us come to the union of persons which takes place in congregations of the Society" [677]. If in the depths of his vocation and mission, the Jesuit is a man who is sent and if, because he is sent, he belongs to an apostolic body scattered more or less all over the world, then for Ignatius there are only two ways that a Jesuit can feel a part of the Society: (1) by the union of hearts and minds, maintained by a wide exchange of information—correspondence—and by reciprocal visits; and (2) by means of the visible and tangible union of the companions in a general congregation. A congregation is always a spiritual union in the Spirit, and sometimes a "corporal union" [677], as one secretary expressed it. It is no surprise then to see Ignatius slowly abandon the term "chapter" for his preferred term, "congregation," not only to avoid any monastic tendency in the Society but also to proclaim in the very word itself that the general congregation is the whole Society. One only has to study the text of the *Constitutions* to see that for the first Jesuits there was no difference or distinction between the Society as an apostolic body and the general congregation. When the congregation meets, then "conveniet Societas," and to convoke a general congregation is to "Societatem . . . congregare."

Thus, as Ignatius himself conceived it, the general congregation is the Society itself, responsible for its whole apostolic body. While it is the supreme authority, it is not so as a body above the Society or even within the Society, but instead because it is the Society itself in the personal encounter of the companions of Jesus. In its beginnings the Society could be identified with the founding Jesuits, or a bit later with the small number of professed who made up the "Societas professa." But it is striking that Ignatius maintained, at least in principle, his perspective on the general congregation as a gathering of the whole Society which could help "toward uniting the distant members with their head and among themselves" (before [655], title of Part VIII).

As usual, apostolic work prevails in Ignatius's thought. If for the sake of mission general congregations must not be multiplied without reason, so also for the sake of the same mission those sent to Rome should be only "those who can come conveniently. Thus it is clear that those who are physically ill are not included, nor are those who are in places very distant, for example, in the Indies, nor those who have in their hands some undertakings of grave importance which cannot be omitted without great inconvenience" [682]. In four hundred and fifty years the Society has called only thirty-four general congregations, and only seven of those without an election. Thus the Society has remained faithful to Ignatius's apostolic concern.

Seeing you here today in this *aula* and knowing what most of you are involved in, I realize very well that those of you who were easily able to come are few, and those who have come from far away are many, interrupting apostolic work of great importance. This is only one more reason to ensure that, as St. Ignatius insisted, the business at hand be dealt with as soon as possible [711]. The absence of 90 percent of the Society does not matter, for Ignatius's perspective has remained unchanged: it is the entire Society which is here; and, before being delegates, participants, elected or convoked, all are first and foremost members of one and the same body of the Society. Gathered together in a general congregation, in the spirit of Ignatius we are none other than members of the universal Society, which is not a federation of provinces and regions and not a conglomeration of assistancies, but one single apostolic body. It would go against Ignatius's idea of a meeting of friends in the Lord for one to see himself as delegated or elected to defend or promote some ideology or a particular opinion of a province or region.

Furthermore, this assembly does not operate like a parliamentary system. While respecting the interaction of majority and minority votes, Ignatius introduces a non-parliamentary factor when he invites us to be more charismatic than democratic. He invites us to discover that to some of us God our Lord has given more abundant gifts to feel and express what would be conducive to God's service [686]. Thus while ensuring each participant's freedom and rights, Ignatius reminds us that a congregation is an event which goes beyond a well-run and well-managed meeting. It is a privileged moment for us as the Society of Jesus to experience intensely the responsibility of each and all of us for our common work of serving the greater glory of God.

Nevertheless the participants in a general congregation are by no means anonymous Jesuits, standardized gears of a well-oiled machine. Ignatius's goal for a general congregation is to gain the best-possible information for a discernment solidly based on experience and on reading the signs of the times, thus bringing us to the best decision in order to adjust and strengthen our missionary service [683]. The participants will be all the more valuable for this process of communal discernment the more they reflect some aspect of the mission, life, work, prayer, and cooperation of the Society in their own culture and traditions, according to their formation and experience and their theological perspectives. "For to a great extent the congregation is an aid toward settling something wisely, either through the greater information which it possesses or through some more distinguished persons who express their opinion" [679].

In this congregation as well, the Society has paid more attention to qualitative than to quantitative representation. This has been precisely to gain as universal a view as possible, without skimming over the real problems of the Society, the Church, and the world at the end of the second millennium, and without confining ourselves to the detailed and the personal, the particular and the ephemeral. Thus in this general congregation, assistancies with many Jesuits are less represented than those with fewer, precisely to permit the greatest presence of all the aspects and dimensions of the Society's life and work in the world. We must call upon the entire accumulated experience of the members of the general congregation. Chapter 7 of Part VIII of the *Constitutions* deals with how to decide in matters other than the election of a superior; in many numbers of this chapter, Ignatius describes with his usual meticulousness how all are called to give the best of themselves in their participation and sharing to arrive at the best-possible decision. With no better material means than table and paper, copies and books, Ignatius demonstrates his concern that each participant place all his personal qualities as so many gifts of God at the disposal of all. All their presentations must be submitted in writing—*verba volant, scripta manent*—and are deposited on a table placed in the midst of the general congregation. Copies are made so that nothing may be lost of someone's personal contribution made in the service of all. Even once a decision has been taken, Ignatius leaves open the possibility of returning to it [711ff. and 716], convinced that the Spirit might speak through precisely a late intervention. For Ignatius such respect for everyone's sharing and participating on the basis of his own experiences and convictions is a condition for deciding "in a manner conducive to the greater glory of God our Lord" [711], even if in the end "the side to which the majority inclines will prevail and the whole congregation will accept it as from the hand of God our Lord" [715].

By putting together each one's qualities and by a genuine exchange of gifts, the general congregation is called to a true communal discernment on questions of importance that involve the future [680], or even on some very difficult questions which concern the entire Society or its manner of proceeding, for the greater service of God our Lord [680]. Ignatius, who is always very sensitive to the tension between apostolic work and common life, hopes on the one hand that the general congregation will work on these questions expeditiously to avoid long absences from apostolic work [711]. On the other hand, proceeding expeditiously should not prevent seeking unanimity, if possible, precisely because of the need for clear and unified missionary action. Thus discernment in common is undertaken less to gain a majority vote than to work toward the consent of all to a union of action which is for the glory of God and the good of the Society.

Since the days of St. Ignatius and his first companions, one single mission has always united the Society: to serve Christ, our Lord and Savior, by continuing his work throughout the world. But this mission must be realized in very diverse ecclesial conditions, in extremely varied life contexts and work situations, and in response to very different needs. Our personal temperaments and preferences, our talents and tastes, our desires and dreams are so pronounced, especially today, that individualism seems a lesser evil: allowing a semblance of peaceful coexistence which seems, realistically speaking, to be the most one can expect for union among us.

Nevertheless, Ignatius expected that when friends in the Lord deliberate and discern in common, they would all decide along the same lines. These lines would not lead to uniformity; they would extinguish neither the rich diversity of personal and cultural gifts nor the disconcerting variety of conditions in which we must act. Rather, "along the same lines" would lead to a union of minds and hearts which would underlie and sustain any action of the apostolic body of the Society.

For a communal discernment to result in this union, it must be led by the same Spirit, as the first Jesuits often put it. Ignatius expressed it slightly differently:

> [S]ince the light to perceive what can best be decided upon must come down from the First and Supreme Wisdom, Masses and prayers will be offered in the place where the congregation is held as well as in the other regions of the Society. This should be done throughout the time the congregation lasts and the matters which should be settled within that time

are being discussed, to obtain the grace to conclude them in a manner conducive to greater glory to God our Lord. [711]

In elaborating a whole program of conscientization and discernment in common, GC 32 in Decree 4 (73ff.) describes this way of proceeding as a constant interrelation between "experience, reflection, decision, action" according to the Jesuit ideal, "in actione contemplativus." According to Decree 4, the result will be a transformation of our habitual ways of thinking, a conversion of spirits as well as of hearts, and this transformation will produce apostolic decisions.

We can still turn to the first companions to learn what is a true deliberation, reflection, and discussion that leaves room for the Spirit to intervene. Thus we will be able to speak of contemplative prayer during an authentic interplay between these elements—not only before and after—an interplay in which the Spirit can break through; and we will let ourselves be seized by that same Spirit. The Spirit's intervention keeps us from hardening our opinions, from stiffening our expressions and even from absolutizing our most intimate convictions and our most valuable experiences. Would we not deprive the Spirit of all freedom to intervene if we desired to reach a decision at all costs and in feverish haste, setting by ourselves the conditions of God's response? On the contrary, does not the interrelation of "contemplation and action" in discernment mean that we do not want to enclose the Society within the false certitude of a watertight project that covers everything? Does it not mean rather that we want to leave some uncertainty that would allow the Spirit, through events and inspirations, to overturn our projects and call our plans into question?

This margin of uncertainty will not paralyze the Society's work: rather it will affirm that even a general congregation of the Society of Jesus exercises no lordship over the Lord's vine. It will free us from the paralyzing obsession of wanting to be masters of a field which we of course have to plant and water, but to which only God gives life. Moreover, if some who did not know Ignatius's life in the Spirit were to read the chapter on a general congregation called to deal with business, they would find a sober and meticulous exposition to assure good order and an effective and efficient dispatching of business, in an atmosphere which respects each one's freedom of expression, and which is clearly oriented toward taking decisions. For Ignatius, a general congregation is first of all a meeting with a particular organization and administration, with procedures and votes, which means a labor based on serious evaluation and laborious discussion, and hours of demanding work, not to mention the moments when we despair of ever reaching any decisions at all. The general congregation will never be the expression of a disincarnate spirituality.

And yet, Ignatius does not hesitate to attribute to this highly complex mechanism the most specific and the best of what the Spirit taught him so that "all may turn out as is expedient for his greater service, praise, and glory" [693]. Above all, the general congregation fits into the dynamism which pushes the Society toward its end—Glory—that is inscribed as much in the Spirit's call as in the human response to that call. While service, praise, and glory are proposed to us as the purpose of the general congregation, we are nevertheless referred back to our historical condition, to our experience and our know-how, to our enthusiasm and our patience in the concrete work which is a general congregation.

Ignatius likes to link "spirit" and "way of doing things," the famous "way of proceeding" which we will have to update in this very general congregation. Thus we are totally removed from a spirituality which is restricted to the religious domain, but also from a socioeconomic seminar to analyze the problems of our day. To be fully a general congregation in the spirit of Ignatius, the Spirit must be able to work in a certain kind of practice which we call discernment in common. It is well known that what makes the difference, what transforms this meeting into a congregation of the Society of Jesus, is finally our intention. But our intention must not remain on the abstract level of desire: to be authentic, it must be translated into our attitude here; it must be incarnated in our involvement in this meeting of the whole Society. Concretely this means taking the congregation to heart, even if none of you has sent himself to Rome: if you are here, it is because of someone else's will expressed in a nomination, a vote, or a call.

Even so, discernment in common is much more than friendly and congenial participation: it calls on our entire person to bring our contribution with all that we are as bearers of the Spirit, and it also calls on us to renounce ourselves by recognizing the Spirit speaking to us through the other. As early as their first deliberations in Rome, our companions already knew that a discernment in common could not succeed without the freedom gained by going beyond self-love, by letting go of one's particular views. Accepting this renunciation made in the Spirit in no way means bowing resignedly before the predominant majority opinion; rather, it calls one's personal certitudes into question in the conviction that by so doing the Spirit can lead us to a more intensely clear convergence and, concretely, to a more valuable service.

During this general congregation there will also be moments when we will simply have to question the Spirit together and, in the light of the Spirit, put our points of view together in order to sense bit by bit the common inclination by which the same Spirit is leading our discernment. According to the words of Decree 4 of GC 32, such an attitude will require a transformation of our entire person, of our customary schemes of thought, and a conversion of spirits as well as of hearts, from which our apostolic decisions will result (73). In their reactions to the tabloids, some Jesuits commented that the gaze on the surface of the earth, covered with people, as suggested by St. Ignatius in the contemplation on the Incarnation, can only be a valid starting point for a vision of current reality if this gaze allows itself to be illuminated by a vision of faith and an act of hope rooted in the same love of Christ (cf. GC 32, D 4, n. 15). This condition makes the difference in personal attitude between a panoramic consideration of our world in order to develop a sociopolitical, cultural, or economic policy, and a contemplation of this same reality for the purposes of a discernment which would lead to apostolic choices and decisions. Along the same lines, these reactions to the tabloids also insisted on the need to personalize this kind of analysis. Ignatius in the First Week of the Exercises tries to make us become aware of our connivance with a death-dealing history and our solidarity with perverted human society. In the same way, we must not list the miseries and pains of our age without bravely discerning our personal and communal complicity, so that the discernment might consequently lead us in the same Spirit to apostolic decisions and choices which will engage us personally and communally to proclaim the Gospel of the Lord in the years to come. Without this total availability to service, proof of the praise and glory of God, a communal discernment would not deserve the name, and neither would a general congregation of the Society of Jesus.

Master Ignatius knew that this was a question of life and death for the Society. Consequently, he did not hesitate to list all the obstacles to the gift of self in a discernment. Among them he draws attention to a "lack of judgment or a notable obstinacy in one's personal opinions" [184]. Those who have set themselves up as all-knowing can also sometimes be problematic [656ff.], or Jesuits of high prestige who are used to the favor of the great of this world [656]. But according to Ignatius the most significant obstacle to the union so necessary in Christ our Lord for the proper functioning of the Society is too great a number of insufficiently mortified Jesuits [657].

The fragility of our person comes on top of the difficulty, with which Ignatius was very familiar, of assuring union of hearts among so many Jesuits scattered among the faithful and among unbelievers in various parts of the world [655]. Here once again we feel the Spirit breaking through. In admitting that humanly speaking it is an impossible mission to get so many and such different companions to come to a decision along the same lines, Ignatius recognizes that discernment in common is less a task to be accomplished than a gift of God to be received. It is precisely because it is a gift to be received that Ignatius counts on the prayerful accompaniment of the whole Society [693 and 711]. This is the same link which joins us in the general congregation to Jesuits spread out all over the world, whom we are called to represent as a whole.

In this way, gathered together in a general congregation which is the Society of Jesus, we engage in a discernment in common which is a constant interrelation of apostolic contemplation and action under the influence of the Spirit; according to the great resources which the Lord has entrusted to us, we take on those problems of our day which the Lord wants to entrust to us here on the threshold of the third millennium:

- by taking on the joys and pains of the men and women who the Lord places on our path for us to help

- in solidarity with all those who suffer from destitution and sickness, from injustice and violence, to whom the Lord wants to send us

- in communion with the Lord's Church which must be able to count on us as men of the Church in its universal solicitudes and its pastoral concerns

- and by speaking and acting in the name of our brother Jesuits scattered throughout the earth but united with our gathering from which they hope for both old and new in order to move forward in their mission with greater clarity and stronger courage

May this mission, our mission, be constantly before us in this congregation as we contemplate the mysteries of the One who is sent, the Lord. In this way may our choices and decisions to renew our apostolic action be stamped by what the Spirit will teach us to lead us to his Truth.

2: ON THE MISSION AND BODY OF THE SOCIETY

6 January 1995

Our confrère Pierre Teilhard de Chardin on several occasions expressed the desire to change the name of today's solemnity, or at least to change the prefix. To emphasize that we are celebrating the day on which our Lord revealed himself with full clarity as the foundation of all and of everything, beginning and end, alpha and omega, we should speak of a "dia-phany" and not of an "epi-phany." For it is less a question of a sudden bursting into history of him who is its creator and savior than of a mysterious and silent "dia-phany" by which Christ sheds light on the true foundation of all beings, by acting in them and by them to lead all towards their fulfillment, God becoming all in all. Teilhard, in his own words, did not read the story of the Magi as if it were photographic truth but a truth that provides enlightenment about him who fills the universe with his dynamic presence, about him who alone gives meaning to our history, about him who, in all and for all, is forever the all-high God.

It is this "dia-phany," this revelation of God in "all created things," which dazzled and deeply moved Ignatius. In today's mystery, the search for God takes place by means of the book and the star; likewise, when he states a "principle and foundation" for the adventure of the Spirit to which he invites us, Ignatius proclaims that for a man or woman there is no authentic search for God without insertion into the created world, and that, on the other hand, no solidarity with men and women and no engagement with the created world can ever be authentic without a discovery of God. In keeping with this vision, his Constitutions are based on this mystique of God's presence to his work, on this "dia-phanous" or quite simply "theo-phanous" design of a creation which again has to be made just and beautiful, true and peaceful, united and reconciled with God, as on the first day.

Out of this perspective the Society of Jesus was born, in the conviction that to serve God who reveals himself as God-with-us is *ayudar a las almas* (to help souls), is to help men and women disengage themselves from the tarnished and confused image that they have of themselves, in order to discover themselves, in God's light, as in complete likeness with him. It is with a similar viewpoint that Ignatius in the *Constitutions* [814] recalls that the best way to glorify God our Lord, who wishes to be glorified with what he gives as Creator (that is, nature) and with what he gives as author of grace (namely, the supernatural), is to cultivate carefully the natural means—

with, however, one condition: that we are not to put our confidence in them, but that we make use of them to cooperate with divine grace.

That is "the path of divine service on which we have entered" [134]. But Ignatius would not be Ignatius if he did not consider "this road towards God" as a path which God himself in Christ, who is the "way," had revealed to him by giving the grace to "start" (*Autobiography* [11]).

But let us return to the Gospel to contemplate the Magi on their journey. Magi from the Orient! This is something quite shattering—at least unexpected. Did Matthew forget Leviticus's advice: "Do not turn to mediums, or wizards; do not seek them out, to be defiled by them: I am the Lord your God" (19:31)? Or did Matthew have the modern mentality which believes that there is nothing new to discover in the West, while a bewitching and exotic light comes from the Orient? At all events, these quite unusual Magi, great searchers of the heavens, lived with the same question which will cause the first apostles to ask, "Rabbi, where are you staying?" (John 1:38).

What leads them to ask this question is a star which acts not only as a means, but as an item of sharing, in Teilhard's expression, or an instrument of union, in the spirit of Ignatius. In today's Gospel we discover that the word of God is not only entrusted to Scripture and its exegetes, but it manifests itself also in the open book of the night, which sings the glory of God while it responds to the watchman's expectation through the light of a dawn which announces the new day (Ps. 130:6).

"We have seen his star in the East, and have come to worship the Lord." These are the Magi, prototypes of a Church which is the offspring of paganism; they force the chosen people to open their books, to discover in them that fundamentally they reveal the Christ as clearly as did the heavens, which guided those travelers by means of the star. The opening of the sacred books "that I too may come and worship him" makes clear even to the heart of the usurper the hidden desire of a kingdom of justice and truth. The Magi were able to help Herod encounter the king awaited by his people, even though the recognition implied the renunciation of his own royalty. As did the Magi, he should have taken a different route. This refusal of a different route is also the fate of the scribes who, in their pitiful blindness, did not see in the Scriptures him who came not to destroy them but rather to give them the fullness of their divine meaning.

And there is the infant with his mother. It is not the Virgin with the Infant; it is the Infant with the Virgin, acknowledging that his only glory on earth is to be fully human, by means of his mother. When Ignatius proposes this mystery of Christ's life for our contemplation, he repeats four times "to adore": to come to adore (*SpEx* [267]) before returning by a different route. This adoration is concretely expressed by the gifts: gold for the king, incense for God, myrrh for the mortal in expectation of immortality. But if the Magi gave only gifts, they would have given nothing. In adoration they gave themselves and thus made "offerings of greater value and of more importance" (*SpEx* [97]). These Magi whose profession it was to search, to discern, to see, saw only a small infant, but they recognized what went infinitely beyond their perceptions: there appeared—diaphanously—in the weakness of this infant the glory "of the eternal King and Lord of all" (*SpEx* [97]).

A star, a book, a new-born infant . . . a king, tempted by riches, as very often happens (*SpEx* [142]) under the standard of Lucifer, the mortal enemy of our human nature (*SpEx* [136]); some scribes who in their obsession to save their acquired truth do not decide to deny themselves in order to go to God, and thus remain in the second "class" of Ignatius (*SpEx* [154]); and the Magi who, by turning, chose this other road which Ignatius calls in the Constitutions "the path of Christ our Lord" [582] on which the traveling companion "accepts and desires with all possible energy whatever Christ our Lord has loved and embraced" [101].

It is the alternative road, the one among all the others that leads to God, which should guide this general congregation if it wishes to be a congregation of the Society of Jesus. Are we on this road in so obvious a way that it is clear to all? Are we dragging our feet along this road, or are we seen "to go forward in the path of the divine service" [260] and even "to run in the path of Christ our Lord" [582]? Or have we, rather, lost our way and no longer know where we are going? As in the case of the scribes of Jerusalem, the intellectual capacity and the verbal ability of the Society are such that in the general congregation words will not be lacking to express "the path of Ignatius, the pilgrim" in decrees and words, in laws and messages; but following the Magi is a question of setting out to make choices and refusing to go astray; it is a question of getting personally involved in concrete deeds (*SpEx* [230]).

The Magi were aware that the path leading to where the infant remained went against the current. For the infant was scarcely born and already a hostile world was weaving around him, silently but effectively, a full network of alliances and plots, of accusations and enmities. The overall picture, reported by the press, sufficiently shows that our path towards God, as that of Christ, while it will certainly not be determined, will still be strongly affected by the machinations of the prince of this world and his Herods. If the path under Christ's standard, emblazoned with poverty, humiliation, and injustice (*SpEx* [147]), collides with the triad of "riches, honor, pride," it is not because there is no other solution, but because the companions of Jesus, his servants and his friends [146], are setting out to "help all" ([146]), not in a dream world or an unreal world, but in our world as it is and as it will, if left to itself, go to destruction. As a result Ignatius wished that "in the vineyard of Christ our Lord which is so extensive," the Society would be able to choose the part "which has the greater need; because of the lack of other workers or because of the misery and weakness of one's fellow men and women in it and the danger of their eternal condemnation" (*Const.* [622]). "Similarly, the Society ought to labor more intensely in those places where the enemy of Christ our Lord has sown cockle, and especially where he has spread bad opinion about the Society or stirred up ill will against it so as to impede the fruit which the Society could produce" [622].

Therefore, in a world where production and consumption, market and profit are more and more evident as an unavoidable aspect of ownership, should not our path towards God be that of the poor, as we commit ourselves with them and for them to recall to all that the human person does not live by bread alone but by this word of Christ, who demands for each one without exception the integrity of humanity and the destruction of every dehumanizing structure? In a world where religious and cultural differences so often lead to violence and war to maintain and strengthen themselves, should not our path towards God witness to a union of hearts and of spirits in which diversity is understood as mutual enrichment? In a world which is desperately seeking happiness and pleasure derived from the desire for possessions, seduction, and power while scorning the rights of others, cannot our path towards God open up others to the meaning of the beatitudes? There is no doubt that words which speak of the good have filled venerable books for centuries, but the announcement of the good news takes place not by the repetition of words, but rather by the testimony of life, by witnesses of flesh and blood who, by prophetically living Christ's Gospel, make the path towards God incarnate. If we look into ourselves and our communities, can we say, in keeping with the directives given by GC 32, that we are companions of Jesus, that we are committed under the standard of the cross, that we are taking part in the decisive struggle of our age, namely, the struggle for the faith and the struggle for the justice which that faith implies (GC 32, D 2, n. 2)? Let us go further: are we where we are expected to be in order to be living witnesses of the good news?

It will be a great grace if we leave this general congregation with a clear personal and communal answer to these questions which are fundamental to the fecundity of the tremendous work which the Society produces.

On returning to their homeland, did the Magi announce the good news? The gospel account says nothing about this. Ignatius observed: "Though this is not mentioned in the Scripture it must be considered as stated. . . . For Scripture supposes that we have understanding" (*SpEx* [299]). As a matter of fact, he knew from experience that when we meet God and have a passion for him, we can only desire this grace for others. Once we are enriched with this intimacy with the Lord, we ask only to become impoverished in order to enrich others with this abundance. This is something that the Christian Orient has grasped; and in the well-known "Akathistos Hymn," it sings of the Magi that, "having become bearers of God, they return, fulfilling your prophecy; while proclaiming you before all as the Christ, they leave Herod like a fool incapable of singing Alleluia." The meeting with the Lord changed them. God truly reveals himself only by turning our hearts inside out. In the Epiphany it is not a message that is communicated or information that is exchanged. There is a meeting of the new-born with the Magi, and this reciprocal recognition makes the Magi living witnesses of the good news. By their transformed being they become the good news and thus proclaim in this dialogue of life the Light of the nations. If it should happen that when examining our identity as Jesuits, we sense that we are no longer these living witnesses to the Gospel, the primary cause is a lack of the personal experience of God, whatever form it may take.

Four years ago Pope John Paul II, while speaking to the religious of Latin America, remarked that "it can sometimes happen that the People of God do not always encounter the hoped-for support among consecrated souls because perhaps they do not reflect in their way of living a sufficiently strong sense of the God that they should communicate." It is true that everything connected with evangelization—to continue the epiphany which has been entrusted to us as our responsibility—is in transition or crisis. The demand for evangelization now extends to every part of the globe; but its urgency is no longer felt as it was at the time of the first Jesuits. Today's Gospel proves that no one can be forced to embrace the faith against his will; and in the encounter with the Magi from a religion outside the covenant, Matthew proclaims the Epiphany to all of humanity and to each individual—without denying that this recognition should come first of all from the chosen people.

Faced with this reality, which is both old and new, our terminology has lost its certitude; and a theology which takes into account God's will to manifest himself as Savior of all, transcending the unique vocation of the irreplaceable Church and Gospel, stammers as it searches for an identity. This hesitation, or even confusion, concerning evangelization has not only left a feeling of insecurity in this whole area of the Lord's manifestation to the world; it has weakened and even stifled the missionary spirit which has always characterized the Society. Because the apostolic body of the Society has no other purpose than to be involved "especially in the concerns of the missions" (found here and there in the Constitutions), to permit this spirit to be extinguished would at the same time mean to deprive each of us of his vocation and of his mission. While making available the greatest possible diversity in way and means, the Constitutions, however, remain very clear about what concerns the end of the missions: "to help people meet Christ, God's epiphany." Even today we have to assure ourselves, concerning a candidate for the Society, that he is desirous and "zealous for the salvation of souls. For that reason he should also have an affection toward our Institute, which is directly ordered to help and dispose souls to gain their ultimate end from the hand of God our Creator and Lord" [156]. Our mission, which is our consecration to Christ, is that of aiding "our neighbors to attain the ultimate end for which they were created [307] or, more clearly yet, "to attain to beatitude" [163].

Have not these words, which at first seem antiquated, found a new urgency? Through the postulates the Society has given new scope to the mission of coming to the aid of others and to this rejection of conquest. There is a rejection of stridency and publicity, of proselytism and of counting numbers of converts, and a thrust towards encounter and interreligious dialogue, towards broad collaboration with all men and women of goodwill, towards the promotion of justice and the defense of peace, of human rights and of the environment, by means of the dialogue of life and by common seeking for the truth, by insertion in difficult surroundings, and by the submerging that makes of our life a simple question, by the testimony also of him who inspires all these aspects of his mission among humanity and the celebration of Christian vitality. We are given a whole new range for the full living of this ideal which Father Arrupe summed up in these few words: "men and women for others," thus translating the Constitutions' "ayudar a las almas." Pope John Paul, as he calls us to a new evangelization, asks us to make serious efforts to discover and put into practice a new language, a new approach, a new way to respond to the new challenges and to the new stakes for humanity, which needs to be helped to become in the reality of our time in the image and likeness of God, as he manifested himself on the day of the Epiphany.

Father Arrupe dared to express this in a mystical manner when he stated: "[M]an, the first word of the Spiritual Exercises, is the point of departure of the spiritual experience which Ignatius lived and taught, and is also—when taken to its completion by way of excellence and development—the be-all and end-all of life when conceived as contemplation" (EE 430). This view only echoes the conviction of John Paul II, which has been frequently repeated: "The human person is the way of the Church, the necessary way for the Church . . . and this is . . . because the human person—every man or woman without exception—has been redeemed by Christ, because Christ has in some way united himself to humanity" (*Redemptor Hominis,* 14).

Have not the words of the Constitutions, when thus viewed, found a new vitality that calls out to us? It is fortunate that we are looking for a new terminology for our mission and for new theological motivation, but this depends on a revival of our missionary thrust; for from a weakening of this spirit, we can expect only the death of the Society. In the Society from its beginnings, this spirit was expressed on the practical order in a universal availability. We willingly identify ourselves as messengers, but the account of the Epiphany, as well as the stories of the other biblical figures, teaches us that a messenger should set out for the place that the mission calls him. He should, therefore, be able to leave what is familiar to him in every sense of the word and give up his certitudes and habits to become truly immersed in situations which are painful for human living, especially the situation of the poor to whom the Gospel was announced before all others.

This universal availability doubtless takes for granted an involvement and gift of self, but today even more—and this is an aspect of the new evangelization—requires the courage to be accepting, to let oneself be transformed with complete freedom, so that the good news may and can become clear. Without this universal availability, which is concretely lived out in mobility and the choice of priorities, the Society is no longer capable of helping others go forward on the road which is theirs to the Lord. "The Society of Jesus in its history has always been distinguished, through the many and different forms of its apostolic ministry, by mobility and the dynamism with which its founder infused it and which has made it capable of grasping the signs of the times and, as a result, of being in the vanguard of the renewal which the Church wishes" (John Paul II, Address to the Provincials, n. 6). It is understandable that this task will thrust us into painful situations, into the temptation of being content to provide others only with mortal bread and of abandoning the need to give them the bread of life as well, in efforts to open new fields of apostolic activity and to close what no longer corresponds to our present-day mission, in places where the decrease in the number and quality of our capabilities in manpower and resources runs the risk of exhausting energies which are already indispensable for mere survival. We can pretend to be giving up a position of strength and security, and there is hardly any doubt that the Society has today reasons to be proud of its surprising activity in almost all the world. It is an undeniable fact, but it only makes sense if all this activity is an expression of the purpose for which it was founded.

The general congregation will have to measure the Society's spiritual vitality, its life in the spirit; for, as Ignatius reminds us in the Constitutions,

[f]or the preservation and development not only of the body or exterior of the Society but also of the spirit, and for the attainment of the objective it seeks, which is to aid souls to reach their ultimate and supernatural end, the means which unite the human instrument with God . . . are more effective than those which equip it in relation to men and women. Such means are, for example, goodness and virtue, and especially charity, and a pure intention of the divine service, and familiarity with God our Lord in spiritual exercises of devotion, and sincere zeal for souls for the sake of glory to him who created and redeemed them and not for any other benefit. [813]

In the Spiritual Exercises Ignatius rightly focuses the entire mystery of the Epiphany on the adoration of the Magi: they see just a poor infant and fall on their knees or, rather, before an Oriental they fall prostrate. The poor infant has remained the poor of God while being the resurrected Lord. And then the question is put to all of us: "But who do you say that I am?" (Matt 16:15). This general congregation has the responsibility not to give a ready-made response, presented in one of its decrees, but it should put itself in the presence of this infant and make a colloquy with Ignatius: How is it that, though he is the Creator, he has stooped to become human (*SpEx* [53]), being able again to say who he is, that is to say, what we are inasmuch as we are companions of Jesus for the life of the world? As a participant in this general congregation, on the brink of the third millennium, I ask myself, Who am I? and "[a]ccording to the light that I have received, I will beg for grace to follow and imitate more closely our Lord, who has just become man for me" (*SpEx* [109]).

3: ON OUR LAW AND OUR LIFE

7 January 1995

We want for a few moments to recall how Ignatius and his first companions entrusted the *Constitutions* to us. It is well known that we are dealing with an original work, of such originality that a specialist from the Gregorian was led to assert, "This law is not a law, this code is not a code." While remaining true to himself as a pilgrim on the road to the absolute of God, Ignatius outlines the reality of the road to travel even in the legislation of the Society of Jesus. There is no need to repeat here the original development of the different parts of the *Constitutions*, which were proposed as stages of a long journey to be made, from admission to the apostolic body of the Society up to the definitive incorporation, by which a personal commitment was bit by bit transformed into a union of hearts and spirits with those who wished to be made into one body, "nos reducere ad unum corpus." As Ignatius marked out the way to God for us, he took the seeming risk of ceaselessly repeating himself and in this way, according to the opinion of Nicholas Bobadilla, of creating "a labyrinth of great confusion."

Ignatius, however, does not repeat himself for the joy of repetition; he was very aware of the distinctiveness of each stage on this long journey. The obedience of a novice cannot be that of a formed Jesuit. The sense of belonging to an apostolic body cannot be the same for one who is sent alone on a mission and for one who fulfills this mission in the framework of a community. We can expect maturation, growth from life in the Spirit. In the Constitutions Ignatius wishes each to be able to advance towards God according to the particular demands of each stage, of each mission entrusted to him. In our sometimes exaggerated concern for equality for all, have we not neglected or ignored differences in experiences and individuals instead of appreciating their importance and letting this mature? Ignatius was not familiar with our temptation immediately and almost automatically to see all differences in terms of master and slave, or of striker and stricken. As a result, he was not afraid to have confidence in those "who will be men who are spiritual and sufficiently advanced to run in the path of Christ our Lord to the extent that their bodily strength and exterior occupations allow" in everything that concerns the life in the Spirit [582], with the assurance that those who are not yet sufficiently advanced will be able to discover in the Constitutions advice and instruction for making progress on the way.

The companion as Ignatius would like him to be and become is not an outlaw, but one who wishes to find in the Constitutions a help for progress and for thus giving greater service. Precisely because it is a matter of someone wishing to be helped in his desire, Ignatius refuses to give any orders and remains satisfied with making challenges along with their motivation: what it is good to do [280], what it is essential to do [284], what could be helpful [282]. Nothing is imposed from without, and even less under pain of sin [602]; everything is founded on the desire, or at least the desire for the desire [102], of going forward freely and generously on the way which Ignatius proposes. Should anyone wish not to go forward on this way, he is completely free to go away. For life in the Society is just one way among many others. It is this liberty that transforms itself into a gift of life for service to the missions that are entrusted; it draws from this interior law of charity and love what the Holy Spirit writes and imprints on hearts. For it is this law which should help and inspire more that any external constitution [134].

Always a realist, St. Ignatius acknowledges in the Constitutions that there will always be in the Society members who cannot fully live according to these views of liberty and responsibility; he limits himself to remarking that there should not be too many who are Jesuits in name only and remain such because of the advantages of belonging [657]. For too large a number would paralyze the proper functioning of the Society.

For those who are able to carry the burden of this vocation (*Formula* [4]), the Constitutions should open the way, thanks to the experience which is accumulated in them and which they hand on, while avoiding at the same time an extreme rigor and an excessive laxity, a demagogic permissiveness and a militaristic discipline [822]. They in no way negate the fact that every companion will live in a permanent election, in a constant discernment which will lead him to be placed with Christ, in order to be made by the Spirit capable of making in everyday life the decisions which Christ made, of making them here and now, today in our mission.

The Constitutions and the interpretations subsequently given them in general congregations should facilitate this discernment by pointing out the obstacles after many unfortunate experiences; by indicating, when necessary, the paths which experience shows lead nowhere; by establishing, for the extreme but always possible cases, limits by which one can be assured of taking the good way; but also by shedding light on the way by discernment of the signs of the times and by formulating responses to new challenges and involvements; and by preparing by precise and concrete decisions the apostolic body of the Society, and especially those involved in initial and permanent formation, for the new tasks to be accomplished on our way towards God. Without this book of challenges and reminders, our desire to go forward remains without perspectives and without energy. The legislative work which particularly awaits this general congregation will help the Society go forward with more clarity and greater unity.

It is important to learn from Ignatius's experience how to confront the eternal problem which brings the letter into conflict with the Spirit, the institution into conflict with the charism. St. Paul sums up the difficulty in a few words: "Without the Spirit, the letter kills . . . but without the letter that Spirit has no voice" (2 Cor. 3:6). All one has to do is to open up the book of the *Spiritual Exercises* and to leaf through the book of the *Constitutions* to come face to face with Ignatius and his great inspirations, his wide horizons, his worldwide measures; and also with an Ignatius who goes into the least detail and particulars of conduct and process. We do not have a double personality here, or two parallel records of activity. Ignatius allows himself to be taken over by the logic of the Incarnate Word in whom true infinity and actual finiteness are joined together. Ignatius make no choice between right and love, between vision and management, between letter and Spirit. As he contemplates the mysteries of the life of the Incarnate One, Ignatius sinks his gaze into all the density of the world and neither scorns nor neglects anything that lives or dies, but discovers and proclaims it in Christ, the beginning and end, dead and risen.

Should we be surprised, then, that the *Constitutions* were composed precisely after many Eucharists, in which the Infinite freely enclosed himself in the finiteness of this bread that is broken and this wine that is poured out for the life of the world? It is in this faith that Ignatius searched for confirmation of his discernment, the presence of the Spirit in this text of the *Constitutions*. For him, it is a question of life and death. For if the Society was not established by human means, it could consequently be neither maintained nor developed by them, but only by the all-powerful hand of Christ, our God and Lord [812]. Because the Society should be a body which serves God and which God can use for his work for the world (*SpEx* [236]: "God works and labors"), Ignatius desires the text of the *Constitutions* to be at the service of what the Spirit says to the Church, and that the Spirit may be able to use this text of the *Constitutions* to lead the people of God to all Truth.

Ignatius never wished to consider this work definitively ended. He did not wish to leave us a cut-and-dried system, a spirituality that was closed in on itself. Father Diego Laínez stated that Ignatius never published the *Constitutions* and that they were never brought to completion by him as if there were nothing more to be added to them. In every sense, since he conceived the *Constitutions* as a way toward God, Ignatius was unable to consider them as forever set and determined. On the other hand, since he wished to have the Constitutions share in the *magis*, in the greater service, Ignatius did not wish to limit their thrust, which was inspired by a loving wholeheartedness for the following of Christ. Father Laínez saw in this unfinished work of Ignatius a summons to a creative fidelity, to the Society's responsibility, when gathered in general congregation, to renew, enrich, and clarify, with new apostolic experiences, demands, and urgencies, the way pointed out to us by the pilgrim Ignatius.

May the Spirit guide us in our work on legislation, so that by the intercession of our Lady of the Way and of Ignatius the pilgrim, the interpretation that we are going to give the Constitutions may be in all and for all our Ignatian way towards God.

•   *APPENDIX THREE*   •

Introduction of Father General to the Final Voting on the Society's Law

24 February 1995

Today we begin the voting on what is called our proper law. Inspired by the Second Vatican Council, an earlier general congregation called for its revision so that a return to our sources would renew our apostolic way of proceeding in light of the challenges of the new evangelization on this threshold of the third millennium. After passing through so many competent and expert hands, after being shaped by our experiences and hopes, the revision is now presented to this general congregation for the approval of the whole Society. May the Lord bless all who have given their very best to this revision and all who have contributed to it from near and far.

This revision could have been done in a totally different manner; it could have adopted other procedures or formulations. But it could not have had a different purpose. The confirmation of its creative fidelity is the fortunate concurrence between the goal of our revision and that formulated in the deliberations of our first companions here in Rome in 1539. After heated and laborious debate, those first companions established once and for always a threefold orientation for the Constitutions and for every subsequent revision:

- first, to be able better and more appropriately to accomplish their original desire that in every action they might fulfill God's will which placed them with the Son to continue his work and his mission, in the world and for the life of the world

- next, to preserve the Society more surely as a ready instrument that the Spirit gathers into one apostolic body, so that the same Spirit can then scatter its members throughout the world to serve the missions received from the Vicar of Christ

- and finally, to guarantee that each of the companions has what he needs spiritually and temporally in order to accomplish the mission he is sent to perform

It is precisely this orientation which determined the results of the first companions' deliberations. It motivated Master Ignatius as he drew up the Constitutions; and—under the inspiration and guidance of the Constitutions and all previous general congregations—it ought also to be the basis for our revision as we add and delete, complement and clarify, reorganize and rephrase in contemporary language what it means to be a companion of Jesus in his company, both for today and for tomorrow.

In this work or revision some amount of the arbitrary and incomplete can never be avoided, no matter how many precautions have been taken. It was Master Ignatius's express desire that there always be an element of the open-ended, of an indispensable apostolic freedom, so that "God our Lord may be more served and glorified in all things" (*Const.* [824]).

Thus between openness and procedure, between faith and law, in writing the *Constitutions* Master Ignatius dared to run the risk of designing "a pathway to God" which would be neither a disincarnate spirituality nor a spirituality trapped in activity. Ignatius the pilgrim wants us to be constantly alert and in an attitude of faithful discernment and creativity with respect to the will of God. The risks of our Constitutions come from this balance—the risk of always aiming for greater service, of making ourselves available to the gratuity and unpredictability of God's fidelity, the risk of living in the contradictory tension of being contemplative in action, of being universally available in a work which is inculturated; and today the risk of having to discern and make decisions in the midst of today's confusion and among the many unknowns of our future. In our Lord and in his service we will have to accept all these risks; they are part of our vocation and mission.

At the end of February exactly 450 years ago, Ignatius was finishing that part of his spiritual diary which reflected his struggle with the very real risks contained in the sections of the *Constitutions* which deal with our apostolic poverty. This is why he sought confirmation from the Blessed Trinity. While we search, through our reflection and voting, to express our creative fidelity to the gift which Ignatius received for the Lord's Church, let us pray with him:

> Eternal Father, confirm us; eternal Son, confirm us; eternal Spirit, confirm us; Blessed Trinity, confirm us; our one and only God, confirm us.

APPENDIX FOUR

HOMILY OF FATHER GENERAL AT THE CLOSING MASS

22 March 1995

Almost three months have passed since our communal discernment began in the Church of the Holy Spirit. This unremitting labor of renewal of our way of being and of our always becoming better companions of Jesus comes to a close tonight in this act of thanksgiving.

The general congregation concludes before the image of our Lady of the Way who incarnates so well a spirituality which, as a way to God, passes through the street, through the joys and the sorrows, the anguish and the hopes of humanity.

It concludes also before the altar of St. Ignatius the pilgrim, who has constantly accompanied us in our deliberations and voting for the renewal of the Constitutions in creative fidelity.

It concludes, finally, before the altar of St. Francis Xavier, as we acknowledge that in the present state of the Society we have ever greater need of his missionary passion to announce with greater zeal and vigor the Gospel of the Lord, the entire Gospel, and nothing but the Gospel, as servants of Christ's mission.

To this undertaking this evening's Word of God brings full meaning. It is the Lord who comes to fulfill the law and the prophets. Jesus confronts what had been spoken to the men and women of old and what he speaks to us now. But this new law, this law of Christ, does not sweep away the words of Moses and the words of the prophets. Not a letter nor a stroke of the pen will be suppressed of what God our Father has revealed as law for his people. Jesus does not replace it with a better or superior system. If he comes to fulfill this law, it is to assume it personally as a new commandment of love which knows no limits or calculations; it is to live it fully in the paschal mystery, loving his own who are in the world until the end.

In the spirit of this evening's Gospel, nothing of the laws and *Constitutions*, of the decrees and declarations, of the *Complementary Norms* and *Notes,* in the measure that they are grafted on to this law of the love of Christ, nothing is negligible and all merits to be assumed personally in the Lord by each companion.

Everything the general congregation has tried so hard to elaborate needs to pass though our hearts, so that for today and for tomorrow in the service of our brothers and sisters we more effectively resemble the Lord Jesus, often by becoming in the eyes of our contemporaries fools and madmen for him who first became such for us (*SpEx* [167]) and who nevertheless labors only for life, the true life of the world.

It is by the side of the Son that the intense work of General Congregation 34 will really be accomplished. In fact the abundance of words and the multiplicity of texts conceal as under a bushel the lamp of a great basic desire for conversion. Through all the encouragement of or cooperation with the laity and others, through all the urgency of ecumenism and interreligious dialogue, the clarifications of the vows for our day, the renewal of our commitment to justice in the name of the Lord, through all the insistence on authentic "thinking with the Church" in the delicate context of our times—to mention only these examples—the general congregation is calling for a change of mentality, a greater transparency in our mission and a conversion of heart for "an offering of greater value" (*SpEx* [97]). Why try to delude ourselves? It is conversion or the absence of conversion which is the deciding factor for the living-out of this congregation, for the future of all that this general congregation has elaborated, clarified, and decided. That the general congregation was able to appeal to this conversion of heart by means of its decrees and its norms is testimony that the grace of holiness has not been abandoned, even if our examen has revealed that we carry this grace in very fragile vessels of clay.

We thank the Lord that he gives us this opportunity to begin anew to live the words and gestures, to bring to reality the choices and desires of Christ that our labors of three months have tried to recognize. And by the intercession of our Lady of the Way, let us ask in the words of St. Ignatius the grace that we may always know the most holy will of the Lord and that we may accomplish it perfectly.

REPLY OF THE HOLY FATHER
AT THE END OF THE CONGREGATION

Vatican City
Secretariat of State
8 April 1995

Very Reverend Father Peter-Hans Kolvenbach, S.J.
Superior General of the Society of Jesus
Rome

Very Reverend Father General,

The Holy Father was very pleased with the message which you sent in the name of your fellow religious at the end of General Congregation 34 of the Society of Jesus.

His Holiness expresses through me his keen appreciation for the work that has been done. He exhorts you to persevere in the Ignatian ideal of service to the Church, and he asks you with confidence to continue the many initiatives of evangelization to which the Society has always dedicated itself. He reminds you that primary among these is the proclamation of the Gospel to those who do not yet know Christ. He recommends in particular the spread of Ignatian spirituality through the preaching of the Spiritual Exercises, which has brought so much good to souls.

The Holy Father sends his best wishes to all members of the Society, and asks the numerous saints and martyrs of the

Society of Jesus to watch over you. He imparts to you and to your fellow religious his Apostolic Blessing.

I take the opportunity to extend to you my own personal best regards.

Sincerely yours in our Lord,
Giovanni Battista Re

REPLY OF THE HOLY FATHER ON POINTS WHICH TOUCH PONTIFICAL LAW

Vatican City
Secretariat of State
10 June 1995

Very Reverend Father Peter-Hans Kolvenbach, S.J.
Superior General of the Society of Jesus
Rome

Very Reverend Father General,

In your letter of 6 May, you presented for the approval of the Holy Father the modifications, decided upon by General Congregation 34, of some points which touch on the pontifical law for the Constitutions of the Society.

I wish to inform you that His Holiness, on 8 June 1995, has approved the following proposed modifications:

1.   The simple vow not to seek positions of honor is restricted to the episcopate and to the positions of Vicar General and of Episcopal Vicar.

2.   To the superior general is granted the faculty of suppressing any house whatsoever of the Society that he deems appropriate, after hearing his council.

3.   To formed coadjutors is granted the right to participate with active, but not passive, voice in general congregations (including those in which the superior general is elected) by

means of an appropriate representation which is not to surpass in its totality, counting both spiritual coadjutors and temporal coadjutors, 10 percent of the members of the general congregation.

The Holy Father wishes to stress that such changes ought not in any way be interpreted as a weakening of the structure of grades and of the need for them; this would contradict what St. Ignatius wanted for his Society, which is based on two essential elements: the priesthood and the vow of obedience of the professed to the Supreme Pontiff.

His Holiness is happy with the good work accomplished by GC 34 in a serene climate of charity, of fraternal collaboration, and of devoted respect for the directives of the Apostolic See. Wishing you blessings from heaven, he willingly imparts to you and to all members of the Society an Apostolic Blessing.

I take the opportunity to confirm my own best wishes and regard for you.

Yours in the Lord,
Giovanni Battista Re

REPLY OF THE HOLY FATHER ON RECEIVING THE DECREES OF THE CONGREGATION

To Very Reverend Father Peter-Hans Kolvenbach, S.J.
Superior General of the Society of Jesus

You have very thoughtfully sent to me the official edition both of the decrees of General Congregation 34 and of the "Complementary Norms" to the *Constitutions of the Society of Jesus,* also the fruit of the recent general congregation.

I thank you sincerely for this renewed expression of devotion and ecclesial union; at the same time, I assure you that I am joined in spirit with you and with the entire Society of Jesus at this significant moment in the life of the Institute. I am certain that the general congregation which is now completed will provide every Jesuit with an important occasion for reflection and for a deepening of spirit in the face of today's challenges, enabling you to carry out with fresh energy your esteemed apostolic work in the Church and in the world.

At the audience for the delegates on 5 January, I recalled that "your general congregation certainly understands the particular importance of this present historical moment, since it is essentially dedicated to discerning the specific contribution your Institute is called to make to the new evangelization on the brink of the third Christian millennium, as well as to updating the internal organization and legislation of the Society of Jesus so that it can render ever more faithful and effective service to the Church" (*L'Osservatore Romano,* 6 January 1995, p. 5).

I wanted then to recall some points of reference, already well rooted in your spirit, to you who were desirous to receive from the Successor of Peter his "missions" and directives, "in order that God our Lord and the Apostolic See may be better served (*Const.* [612])."

Now that the documents produced by General Congregation 34 have been published, I offer to the Almighty Lord, Giver of every good gift, a joyful prayer of thanksgiving for the enormous work accomplished and for the generous response given by the general congregation to the expectations placed upon it. Truly, Holy Mary, who sustained and enlightened your founder and whom I invoked with confidence at the beginning of your important meeting, has given you a mother's guidance and has helped you to keep before your eyes God, above every other thing, and then the nature of the Society of Jesus (*Formula Instituti* [1]).

My dear brothers, always be faithful to the genuine charism of Ignatius! What has been decided in this Thirty-fourth General Congregation of the Society must be implemented in fidelity to the spirit and original intention of the founder. The congregation's action can, therefore, in no way be interpreted as a weakening of the structure of grades and of the need for them, since that would be contrary to what St. Ignatius wanted for the Society, a sacerdotal order, which has an essential and characteristic element the fourth vow of obedience to the Supreme Pontiff.

Therefore, my hope is that all the members of the Society of Jesus may welcome with religious spirit the documents issued by General Congregation 34 and that they may implement them with faithful generosity, striving to be ever more authentic sons of St. Ignatius, living your original inspiration and charism to the fullest and without hesitation in these final years of the century.

With these wishes and invoking the protection of the Blessed Virgin and St. Ignatius on the entire Society of Jesus, I impart to you and your fellow religious a heartfelt special Apostolic Blessing.

From the Vatican

27 September 1995, the 455th anniversary
    of the approval of the Society of Jesus

John Paul II

LIST OF DELEGATES

(in alphabetical order)

Kolvenbach Peter-Hans

Agúndez Melecio (CAS)
Aizpún José Javier (GUJ)
Aloysius Irudayam A. (MDU)
Alvarez Bolado Alfonso (CAS)
Amaladoss Michael (MDU)
Amalanathan V. Anthony M.
(AND)
Arroyo Edward B. (NOR)
Assandri Andrés (URU)
Audras Jean-Noël (GAL)
Azevedo Marcello de C. (BRC)
Azzopardi Cecil (DUM)

Baiker Alois (HEL)
Baptista Javier (BOL)
Barla Henry (RAN)
Barredo Fernando (ECU)
Bélanger Pierre (GLC)
Belchior José Carlos (POR)
Bellefeuille Jean (GLC)
Bernas Joaquin G. (PHI)
Besanceney Paul (AOR)
Blanco Benito (ANT)
Bosco A. X. J. (AND)
Boulad Henri (PRO)

Bratina Lojze (SVN)
Brieskorn Norbert (GSU)
Buckley Michael J. (CFN)
Busto Sáiz José Ramón (CAS)

Cacho Ignacio (LOY)
Cardó Carlos (PER)
Carrión Jorge (ECU)
Carroll Peter (ZAM)
Caruana Charles (MAL)
Case Francis E. (ORE)
Cavassa Ernesto (PER)
Chang Ch'un-shen Aloysius B.
(CHN)
Changanacherry Jose (GUJ)
Charlier Jean (BME)
Chemplany Mathew (PAT)
Cobo González Sergio (MEX)
Coleman John A. (CFN)
Colomer Casanova Julio (ARA)
Connor James L. (MAR)
Cornado João Pedro (BAH)
Coumau Bernard (GAL)
Crampsey James (BRI)
Cribb Ian (ASL)
Čupr Josef (BOH)
Czerny Michael (CSU)

Da Costa Ralph (KAR)
Danuwinata Franciscus Xaverius
    (IDO)
Daoust Joseph P. (DET)
De la Marche Marc (BSE)
Decloux Simon (BME)
Dideberg Daniel (BME)
Dijon Xavier (BME)
Doan Joseph (VIE)
Donahue John R. (MAR)
D'Souza Lisbert (BOM)

Earle George (BRI)
Egaña Francisco Javier (LOY)
Eguíluz Jesús María (LOY)
Ekwa Bis Isal Martin (ACE)

Fagin Gerald (NOR)
Falla Sánchez Ricardo (CAM)
Farias Terence (KAR)
Fernandes Julian (KAR)
Fernández Franco Fernando
    (GUJ)
Fernández-Martos José María
    (TOL)
Ferreira Pedro Vicente (BRS)
Fonseca Conrad (BOM)
Franke Bernd (GSU)

Galli Agide (AOC)
García Diaz Mariano (PAR)
García-Mata Ignacio (ARG)
Gellard Jacques (GAL)
Gerhartz Johannes Günter (GSE)
Ghirlanda Gianfranco (ITA)
Glynn L. Edward (MAR)
Gomes Aelred (CCU)
González José Adolfo (COL)
Gonzalez Buelta Benjamin (ANT)
González Modroño Isidro (CAS)
Goñi Alejandro (VEN)

Gray Howard J. (DET)
Grinten Steven van der (NER)
Guillemot Jean-Jacques (GAL)
Hampson Joseph (ZIM)
Harnett Philip (HIB)
Hidaka Ronald (ZAM)
Howell Patrick (ORE)

Ibáñez Manuel (BET)
Ilboudo Jean (AOC)
Ivern Francisco (BRC)

Jackson Charles (CFN)
Jerome Rosario D. (MDU)
Jeyaraj Donatus (MDU)
Junges José Roque (BRM)

Kalathil Joseph (JAM)
Kerketta John (RAN)
Kestler Theodore (ORE-ASK)
Kim Jung-Taek Andrew (KOR)
Kinerk E. Edward (MIS)
King Geoffrey (ASL)
Klink Peter J. (WIS)
Komma Gerwin (ASR)
Koso Toshiaki (JPN)
Köster Wendelin (GSE)
Kożuch Mieczysław (PME)
Krapka Emil (SVK)
Kubik Władysław (PME)
Kujur Angelus (DUM)
Kunnunkal Thomas (PAT-DEL)
Kurukula Aratchi Peter (SRI)

Lafontaine James F. (NEN)
Lakra Christopher (RAN)
Laschenski Sigmund (IDO-TAI)
Leeuwen Hans van (NER)
Lo William (CHN-MHK)
Locke John (PAT-NEP)
Loisy Edouard de (AOC)

Lombardi Federico (ITA)
López Rivera Francisco (MEX)
Lucey Gregory F. (WIS)
Mac Dowell João (BRC)
Machín Díaz Jorge (CUB)
Maclean Eric R. (CSU)
Madelin Henri (GAL)
Marshall Guillermo (CHL)
Matungulu Otene Marcel (ACE)
McDade John (BRI)
Menéndez Valentín (CAM)
Merz Eugene F. (WIS)
Metena M'Nteba (ACE)
Meures Franz (GSE)
Minj Patras (MAP)
Miralles Massanés Josep (TAR)
Misquitta Kenneth (PUN)
Mollá Llácer Darío E. (ARA)
Morales Orozco José (MEX)
Morujão Manuel (POR)
Mudavassery Edward (HAZ)
Murickan Joseph (KER)
Murphy Laurence (HIB)

Naik Gregory (GOA)
Ndolo Muwawa (ACE)
Nemeshegyi Péter (HUN)
Nemesszeghy Ervin (HUN)
Nicolás Adolfo (JPN)

O'Callaghan John (CHG)
Ochagavía Juan (CHL)
O'Hanlon Gerard (HIB)
O'Keefe Vincent T. (NYK)
Opiela Stanisław (RUS)
Oraá Jaime (LOY)
Orgebin Jacques (GAL)
Orsy Ladislas (NYK)

Padberg John W. (MIS)
Padiyara Cherian (CCU)

Painadath Sebastian (KER)
Pandolfo Salvatore (ITA)
Parkes Joseph P. (NYK)
Pełka Florian (PMA)
Perekkatt Varkey (PAT-DEL)
Perz Zygmunt (PMA)
Picó Fernando A. (PRI)
Pietras Henryk (PME)
Pittau Giuseppe (JPN)
Pozaić Valentin (CRO)
Privett John A. (CFN)
Pšeničnjak Franjo (CRO)
Puni Emil (ROM)
Putranta Carolus B. (IDO)

R.C. Chacko (HAZ)
Randrianasolo Jean-Baptiste (MDG)
Rasolo Louis (MDG)
Recolons Marcos (BOL)
Régent Bruno (GAL)
Remolina Gerardo (COL)
Restrepo Alvaro (COL)
Rhoden João Claudio (BRM)
Riedlsperger Alois (ASR)
Roberts Anthony P. (JAM)
Rdz-Izquierdo G. Guillermo (BET)
Rossi de Gasperis Francesco (ITA)
Rotelli Gian Giacomo (ITA)
Rotsaert Mark (BSE)
Royón Lara Elías (TOL)

Saldanha Julian (BOM)
Salvini Gian Paolo (ITA)
Sánchez del Río Luis Tomás (TOL)
Sarkis Paul (PRO)
Saulaitis Antanas (LIT)
Scannone Juan Carlos (ARG)
Schaeffer Bradley M. (CHG)

Schineller J. Peter (NYK-NIG)
Seremak Jerzy (PMA)
Shirima Valerian (AOR)
Sosa Arturo (VEN)
Steczek Bogusław (PME)
Sundborg Stephen V. (ORE)

Tabora Joel E. (PHI)
Taborda Francisco de Assis
　(BRM)
Taft Robert F. (NEN)
Tan Chee Ing Paul (IDO-MAS)
Tejera Arroyo Manuel (BET)
Tetlow Joseph A. (MIS)
Thelen Albert R. (WIS)
Tigga Satyaprakash (MAP)
Tojeira José María (CAM)
Tuñí Josep-Oriol (TAR)

Uren William (ASL)

Valero Urbano (CAS)
Váni Emil (SVK)
Vásquez Noel D. (PHI)
Villanueva Alfredo (CHN)
Vitório Jaldemir (BAH)
Von Nidda Roland (ZIM)

Walsh Maurice B. (NEN)
Werner Götz (GSE)
Wild Robert A. (CHG)
Wobeto Affonso (BRM)

Zuloaga Ismael (CHN)
Zwiefelhofer Hans (GSU)

INDEX

OF PERSONS NOTED
IN HISTORICAL PREFACE

(prepared by the Institute of Jesuit Sources)

Note: Numbers printed in italics refer to the page of this volume.

INDEX OF TOPICS

(prepared by the Institute of Jesuit Sources)

Note: Numbers printed in italics refer to pages of this volume; ordinary numbers indicate marginal numbers in the text.

Jesuit priestly mission, 163–66,
183–84
with relation to diocesan bishops,
160
with relation to Jesuit brothers,
162
proclamation of Gospel
affects structure of cultures, 43
requires dialogue with other religions, 45, 49
procuratores ad negotia, 3
province congregation, new regulations, 489–99
purity of the angels, 233
relationes prævise, 4–5, 10
religions
fourfold dialogue among, 131–32
need for dialogue among, 120,
130, 133, 154
variety of, 128
renewal of Society, bases of
confident relationship with Christ,
252
faith in the Lord, *252*
proclamation of Christ, *252*
reports, procedure followed in preparing, *11–13*
search for God, requires insertion
into created world, *266*
service of faith and promotion of justice, 24, 32–33, 36, 39–40, 47–
49, 50–52, 54–55, 85, 172, 210,
388, 410–15, 425
service, of Jesuits in Church, 298–301
Society of Jesus, special responsibility
dedication to mission of the
Church, *249*
missionary outreach, *250*
new evangelization, *248*
promotion of full communion of
all Christians, *250*
serving the universal Church, *250*
Society of Jesus, a sacerdotal order,
289–90

Society of Jesus, future course
cultivate clear missionary spirit,
272
practice new evangelism, *272–75*
reflect strongly the God to be
communicated, *271*
superiors, formation of, 521
suppression of houses, power granted to Father General, *287*
temporal coadjutor, term abolished,
216
topics for discussion in GC 34, selection of
final, *13–14*
preliminary, *10–11*
triduum of prayer, *7–8*
universities
importance of, in Jesuit ministry,
404–6
Jesuit response, 408–15
structural challenges, 407
university, and faith and justice, 410–
15
vocation, Jesuit
diversity of vocations, 202
grades in Society, 202
unity of, 201–5
vocations
need for, 292
prayer for, 295
promotion of, 293, 96
way of proceeding, and ideals of St.
Ignatius, 535–63
Jesuits available for new missions,
555–58
Jesuits called to learned ministry,
552–54
Jesuits searching for the *magis,*
559–61
Jesuits form a partnership with
others, 549–51
Jesuits form an apostolic body in
the Church, 543–45
Jesuits stand in solidarity with
those in need, 546–48